Fitting In

Written by Nancy A. Jaekle

Cover Concept: Brenda J Appleman
Copy: Laura Kruger
Photo of me by Daniel Karnadi
Editor: Whitney Porter
Foreword: Rev. Dr. David Weyrick

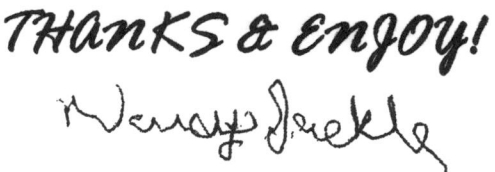

Copyright © 2019 Nancy Jaekle

All rights reserved.

ISBN: 9781089199342

DEDICATION

To all the people who helped raise me, and especially, thank you to my late parents, Walter R. and Gwen W. Jaekle; to my brother Richard G. Jaekle; to my teachers who showed me the way; and, to all the mentors that I had throughout the course of my life, thank you.

The people above and many others took me under their wings and gave me the guidance and support I needed to succeed.

This book was made possible through the gift of one of my late professors and mentors Paul Otis Evans who passed away in 2018.

FOREWORD

Courage.

Patience.

Determination.

Realism.

Faith.

These are just a few of the characteristics displayed by Nancy Jaekle throughout her amazing life.

I have had the privilege of knowing Nancy for many years and was honored and humbled when she asked me to write the introduction to her captivating autobiography. Honored, because I was her pastor for many of those years and have gotten to know her well. Humbled, because those characteristics are sometimes lacking in my own life and I speculate in the lives of others as well.

Nancy is a person of great courage. From her experience as a kid on a spooky theme park ride, to starting college, to dealing with her declining physical limitations, she has always, as she put it, "craved the thrill of adventure as long as I felt reasonably certain that I would still be in one piece." Yet, she also faced sorrows with that same courage, "Saying goodbye to my mother was the hardest thing I ever had to do. My father and mother died within 11 months of each other."

If patience is indeed a virtue, then Nancy is virtuous. From dealing with those who did not understand her, to public transportation, to her mother's stroke, and her journalism career, Nancy has maintained a calmness of spirit that has allowed her to deal with her life with a peace that passes all understanding.

Nancy and I are the same age; both Baby Boomers who were born when Dwight Eisenhower was the President. He once wrote, "Pull the string, and it will follow wherever you wish. Push it, and it will go nowhere at all."

Nancy has always been a string puller. By that I mean she has a determination about her that allows her to keep moving forward. Her determination in writing health related articles is a great example as well as her ability to work at home when maneuvering became more difficult. She wrote, "As time went on, I began to discipline myself and to get on a better schedule. Some of the doctors that I interviewed preferred to have conversations in the evening . . . So sometimes as late as 9:30 at night, I would be conducting an interview."

It seems to me most people really don't have a clue when it comes to cerebral palsy. There are many myths and misconceptions, as Nancy well knows. And because of her extensive medical writing, she also knows the facts and has been upfront and honest about the facts. That's her characteristic of realism.

She wrote, "Too much stress causes my CP to go haywire. For several nights, I had some insomnia. However, it was more than that because I could not seem to get my arms calm enough to allow me to sleep." And during another difficult time she displayed realism when she wrote, "Perhaps my body was just tired from all the stress of moving, my parents' deaths, and adjusting to a new life alone. I was not the only one who noticed these subtle changes in my balance."

Finally, Nancy's faith is an inspiration to me and others who have seen her live it. She served as a Presbyterian Deacon and performed, "many tasks for individuals in the congregation including visiting the sick and shut-in, helping the food banks, and ministering to the lonely." She is a Stephen Minister. "I'd studied nine months to finally become ordained. Since becoming a Stephen Minister, I have counseled people and hopefully helped them to understand and to support them in times of need. Many people simply need someone to listen and pray with, during hard times."

And let me tell you, she can sing and sing well! I always enjoyed hearing her voice rise above the congregation when singing the great hymns of the church.

In her book, Nancy asks, "'Where do I fit in?'" That was the million dollar question." I'll tell you. She fits into the hearts and lives of all of us who know her and love her.

Reverend Dr. David Weyrick

1

My parents were only married eleven months when I entered the world on a bright, sunny Thursday in mid-March. In the mid-fifty's, it was only proper that a couple be married a year before starting a family. In fact, my maternal grandmother was somewhat distraught by my early arrival and wondered what kinds of gossip would circulate. Since my mother was well into her thirties, she was advised to start a family as soon as possible. In those days, women usually planned to start a family in their early 20's, as was the custom back then.

My mother, Gwendolyn, came from an upper middle class family who resided on Riverside Drive in New York City. Her father, George Lester Williamson, owned a tailoring business that outfitted students at private boarding schools in and around the tri-state area. He was the youngest of nine children. My grandmother, Alice Davis Williamson, worked as a bookkeeper and a general manager. Both of my grandparents were extremely hardworking people who never indulged themselves with a holiday or any other leisurely enjoyment.

According to my grandmother, her pattern of being extremely thrifty in life was to ensure that when she grew and her body systems began to breakdown, she would be able to afford around the clock nursing care at home. A diabetic and prone to ulcer sores on her feet and ankles, she hated doctors and despised hospitals even more.

Living on Riverside Drive denoted a certain prestige and class. Being an only child, my mother was doted on by her maiden aunts. In fact, she had an entirely different wardrobe especially set-aside for when she went out with them. As a little girl, Christmas was her favorite time of year. The tree always remained outside on the fire escape until Christmas Eve when her Auntie Georgie donned a Santa suit and came prancing in with a sack full of gifts and all the trimmings for a beautiful tree.

Back in the 1930s, it was not unusual for a bright child to skip a grade or two. Since my mother skipped twice in grammar school, she graduated from secondary school at the tender age of sixteen, but still almost the tallest girl in her class. Career options were limited for women in those days. Essentially, they could become a teacher or a nurse. When my mother graduated high school, jobs were even more limited because of the Depression, and many young women, even those with college degrees worked behind the counters of Macy's department stores in New York.

Becoming a teacher really appealed to my mother, and I truly believe that she would have been a wonderful one. She was bright, compassionate, encouraging, and supportive. She had all the right qualities for motivating students to reach their potential. Unfortunately, due to the reality of life for most degree-holding women in this era, her parents could not understand her reasoning for wanting to further her education when so many college graduates ended up in such meager jobs.

Despite my mother's charms, obtaining employment was difficult for a sixteen-year-old fresh out of high school. Several weeks and unsuccessful interviews into her job search, my mother decided to stretch the truth a bit and tell potential employers that she was eighteen. Not long afterwards, she was hired.

Because she knew typing and shorthand, one of her first jobs was in a secretarial pool with a woman for a boss who favored each one of her employees in a different way. Being young and buxom, my mother was self-conscious and she would normally attempt to hide how top-heavy she was by slouching at her desk. Noticing this, her boss demanded that she sit up straight and walk with her head held high. "If you have it, flaunt it," her boss told her.

Embarrassed and upset, my mother relayed the incident to her mother who was livid with rage.

"How dare that woman! I'm going to go down there and give her a piece of my mind." Aghast at the prospect of a scene and fearful of losing her job, my mother pleaded, "Please, don't go down there! She's my boss, for heaven's sake!"

Tempted as my grandmother was to go down to the office, she respected her daughter's wishes.

In addition to her secretarial job, my mother had a thirst for knowledge. She often took courses at Columbia University at night. Between studying and maintaining an active social life, she also helped her parents at their business on the weekends. A few years later, she landed a job at McCall's in the sales department filing geographically. She always amazed us by knowing all the tiny towns across the nation many of which most people had never heard of. In addition to her filing skills, she trained potential salesmen about their territories. She was very happy in her position until they day she discovered that her male trainees were making more than she was. Demanding an explanation, she was told that because she was a single woman still living at home, she did not need a larger salary. After all, these men had families to support. Discrimination existed for my mother in the workplace as it still does for many today. Despite the good fight, we have yet to win.

My father, Walter R. Jaekle, also entered adult life during the Depression and faced challenges of his own. He came from a middle class family who resided for a short time in Bayonne before moving to Cranford, New Jersey. They lived on Spruce Street in an old-fashioned yellow Colonial with three bedrooms, a spacious kitchen, and a sun porch. The house stands as beautiful today as it stood thirty-eight years ago when my grandparents sold it to retire in Florida.

My paternal grandfather Charles Anthony Jaekle was the youngest and only son of five children. My paternal grandmother, Martha Roth Jaekle, was the youngest and only daughter of two children. Unfortunately, both died in their mid-thirties of tuberculosis. Consequently, my father's widowed paternal grandmother; my great-great-grandmother, pitched-in and singlehandedly raised her two orphaned grandchildren.

Both of German descent, Charles and Martha had three children of which my father was their second son and middle child. The name Walter was not of his parents' choosing, but of my grandfather's eldest sister Betty. It seems that Betty had a way of intimidating the females of the clan including my grandmother who reluctantly gave in even though she herself did not like the name. To her dying day, she always referred to her second son as Dick.

Contrary to his older brother Charles, my father was a quiet and more sedate child. He often described his childhood as being very wholesome. He hung around with the kids on the block, went ice skating and sledding in the winter, and participated in neighborhood games of baseball or football in the summer. As most growing boys do, he often raided the refrigerator and could be seen walking down the block chomping on pig's feet or knuckles. Delicious.

During the Depression, times were hard and money was tight. In the Jaekle household, one particular Christmas was very sparse. Being in business for himself did have its disadvantages, and my grandfather was last to be paid, that is if there was any money left after paying all of his employees. However, many times, he barely brought enough home for food and essentials. That Christmas, each stocking contained an apple and an orange. There were no other presents to be had. My grandmother was in tears, but at least they had a roof over their heads and food in their bellies. Overwhelmed by some of the elaborate Christmases people have but really cannot afford, my father always recalled this one Christmas when they did not have much except for each other.

In his school days, my father was an average student who liked to complete his assignments as quickly as possible. His teachers always wrote on his report card, "If only Dick would slow down…" His handwriting was also very poor and oftentimes we would kid him by proclaiming that he should have become a doctor. My father often enjoyed the company of his peers, but other times he was a loner who shut himself off from the world to either read or sleep. Childhood depression was unheard of in those days, but it existed nevertheless. Since there was no chance for medical intervention, one merely learned to crawl his way out of it. I know my grandmother also suffered a few depressive episodes and always managed to eventually work her way out of it.

Upon graduating from high school, my father entered the Air Force. Several months later, he returned home to marry his high school sweetheart, Roberta (Bobbi) Willis. They were young and in love. Despite strong objections from both sides of the family, they eloped. Their brief union produced a daughter named Cindy with whom my father eventually lost contact. After several battles, the couple divorced.

Slowly picking up the pieces of his life, my father continued to help his father in the laundry business; he had a regular truck route where he picked up and delivered for customers. At night, he attended Union College, a small school that met in Orange Avenue School in the evenings. Unfortunately, he never completed his Associate's Degree.

My father's brother, Charles Roth Jaekle, the first-born son, was a very bright, outgoing child with an eye for mischief and adventure. Nicknamed Sonny, he was always into something, even raising pigeons. Unlike most boys, Charles had no desire to participate in athletics of any kind, not even during gym class. One day, my grandmother received a note from his gym teacher requesting a conference. Charles was failing gym. "How could any kid fail gym?" she thought to herself. Finally, the appointed hour came and she confronted his teacher to ask what the problem was. "Whenever I ask my students to do pushups, they all cooperate except Charles." His teacher asked, "Do you know what he does? Well, Charles places both of his hands on his shoulders and then moves both of his index fingers up and down and claims that those are his pushups. Mrs. Jaekle, your son is mocking me in front of the entire class." Trying to suppress her laughter as she relayed the incident to my grandfather, they decided that athletics were definitely not in their son's future, but he still had to be punished for knowingly embarrassing his teacher. After a severe scolding, Charles had to apologize to his teacher and was grounded for one week.

At the age of 17, my uncle Charles ran away from home and enlisted in the service. With his unlimited zest for life, he also attended several universities including Notre Dame before settling down. While he was stationed in Virginia, he met Ann Holt Murden, a southern gal, who came from an upper middle-class family and who was studying to be a teacher. They were married in November 1945.

Eventually, to everyone's surprise, this adventurous, yet serious, young man announced that he was headed for the ministry. He had heard the "calling." Intending to follow in the faith he was raised, Charles was ordained as a Lutheran minister. Shortly thereafter, he decided that the Lutheran ministry was not exactly what he wanted and he entered the priesthood of the Episcopal Church.

With a growing interest in pastoral care and counseling, Charles became one of the founders of the Pastoral Care and Counseling Center of Greater Washington, D.C. opening with a mere handful of pastoral counselors.

My father's sister, my aunt Carolyn Jaekle's arrival on February 26, 1934, came with mixed emotions from her two older brothers. "A baby sister, huh! One might not be so bad especially if she was a little redhead like the girl down the street." And, lo and behold, Carolyn did not disappoint her siblings and entered this world as a carrot top. In many respects, however, she was an only child. Younger by twelve and eight years respectively, by the time she was in the seventh grade both brothers had already left the nest.

Ever since I can remember, Carolyn has taken pride in her beautiful teeth. On one particular occasion when her mother took her to the dentist, he thought she needed braces. Not only were braces uncomfortable and even painful, but they were also an expense that the family could not afford unless absolutely necessary. A few weeks later, Carolyn's parents asked for a second opinion. Another dentist was consulted who thought Carolyn had the beginnings of wonderful teeth and suggested that they let nature take its course. Today, she has a perfect set of teeth that most of us would envy.

Upon high school graduation, she decided to pursue a career in nursing. Contrary to her Aunt Marie's wishes, she enrolled in Muhlenberg School of Nursing in Plainfield.

"Are you going to let her scrub bedpans for a living?" Aunt Marie demanded of her mother.

"If that's what she wants to do I am not going to stand in her way," replied her mother.

Unfortunately, Carolyn finished in the bottom half of her class and received her Associate's Degree. In those days, this was the qualification required to be the equivalent of a Registered Nurse. After graduation, she and three other friends spent the summer touring the country and picked up work in their field along the way.

In Arizona, she met Joseph Mattaino, a serviceman with aspirations of becoming an engineer. Within weeks, they fell in love and he asked her to marry him. She agreed, but said that first he must come to New Jersey to meet her family and start courting her properly. He did just as she wished and they were married that following July in Trinity Lutheran Church in Cranford, New Jersey followed by a small reception at home.

During the summer of 1953, my parents were each vacationing separately at a resort in the Poconos when, after a dip in the pool, my father came to ask my mother if she could spare a cigarette.

Always ready to help a fellow smoker in need, she flippantly said to him, "I suppose you're a Fuller Brush man."

Somewhat startled by her remark, he replied, "Yes, I am but how did you know?"

I do not know whether it was sheer luck or mere coincidence, but that statement led to a relationship that endured over fifty years.

The commute between my father's home in Cranford and my mother's in Manhattan was significant. Happy and in love, neither of them minded the trek. Several months later, it was time to meet the prospective families. One afternoon, my father brought his bride-to-be to his parents' home for lunch. As always, Mrs. Jaekle set an attractive table filled with hot, delicious food. Indeed, she was a wonderful cook. Everyone was a bit nervous, and conversation was strained at first, but then, as the meal progressed, the tension lessened and everyone became more relaxed. When the last remnants of dessert were removed from the table, my dad politely excused himself. Thinking that he probably only went to the bathroom, my mother resumed helping with the dishes. One hour passed and no Dick. When another hour slipped by, my mother inquired as to his whereabouts. "Oh, Dick went to lie down. He does that every afternoon." Even after fifty years, he still napped every afternoon. I do not think he needed the rest as much as he needed an emotional break during the day.

On April 24, 1954, my parents were married in St. Mark Episcopal Church in Manhattan. A small, but elegant reception followed. Two months later, my mother discovered she was pregnant. It was time to search for an obstetrician. Wanting the best for herself and her unborn child, she chose a Park Avenue specialist. Only one of the top-notch physicians would preside at my birth.

By the doctor's careful calculations, I was due to arrive in February of 1955. Somehow, however, I was not informed of the scheduled arrival and made my grand appearance three weeks later on Thursday, March 12th, 1955. On that particular day, our physician had more than his share of problems. After a long and complicated labor, he was forced to perform a caesarean birth for another patient. Meanwhile, he learned that his wife had been brought into the emergency room with a broken foot. To make matters worse, my mother was having a difficult labor and needed his professional expertise, which he had neither the time nor the energy to provide.

Because of the circumstances for the doctor, he sedated my mother so much that she could not recall anything about the actual birth itself. Evidently, sometime during the birthing process, the umbilical cord became wrapped around my neck and cut off my oxygen supply. Seeing that I was being strangulated, the doctor had to resort to a low forceps delivery. When I was finally pulled from the womb, I was blue and gasping for breath. Immediately, I was suctioned and given oxygen.

Even though I weighed exactly seven pounds, a relatively healthy birth weight, I was placed in an incubator where I

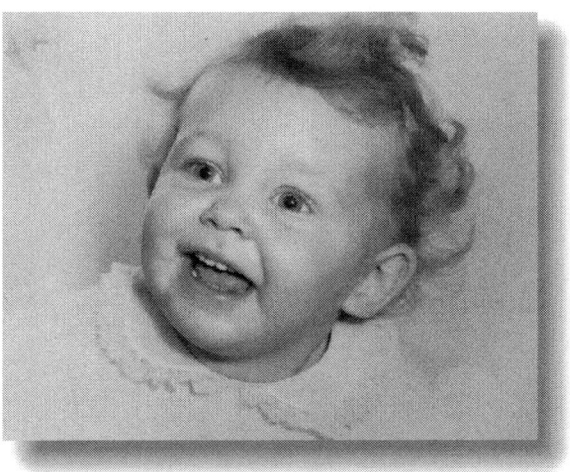

received oxygen for ten days. Meanwhile, my mother was sent home to recuperate from the strenuous ordeal and I remained at Doctor's Hospital under the vigilant care of the nursery staff.

One of the night nurses took a special interest in me and brought a rocking chair from home so that she could rock me whenever she had the time. Even back then, medical professionals knew the value of touch and how vital it was to the newborn's survival.

During those first few days, my grandfather Williamson visited me daily and brought news of my progress to my extremely anxious and concerned folks. As the first and only daughter and granddaughter, I was their little treasure. After a two-week hospitalization, my parents brought me home. Wrapped in layers of bunting, I came home to awaiting grandparents laden with gifts for me. So eager and happy to have her precious baby home at last, my mother nicknamed me her "little fighter."

Since I was born in windy March, I remained indoors for the next two months. Because my lungs were in a weakened state, physicians thought it best not to take any chances so that I would not catch a cold or pneumonia.

During the next few months, I basked in the attention of my devoted parents. My eyes focused properly, I smiled and cooed and sat up with help. However, my pediatrician noticed that I had some head lag. When I was brought into a sitting position, my head would fall backwards. Evidently, my neck and back muscles were underdeveloped and therefore, I had poor control of my head. Even though my pediatrician thought I might overcome this within a few months, it was a symptom of possible neurological damage not to be overlooked.

My parents lived in a three-room apartment on Oliver Street in Brooklyn. Within a few weeks after my arrival, they had an early nighttime routine established. While my mother cleaned up the kitchen after dinner, my father would sit on the sofa with me cradled in his arms as he fed me my bedtime bottle. Just as I was about to drift off, our downstairs neighbor, Camille Cozzolino, would come tapping on the door ever so softly, but loudly enough to arouse me from my sweet slumber. It was party time.

Camille and her husband, John, a policeman, had a little daughter, Mari, who was only three months older than I. In time, both families became the best of friends and would often take turns babysitting for one another. During the day, both mothers would push their baby carriages and walk miles simply window-shopping. Sometimes, on the way back home from these walks, we would stop by the local butcher shop. Upon seeing us, the butcher would give me a slice of bologna, which was my favorite cold cut. Every time we passed the shop, I would inquire about my "bowbow."

With only a three-month age difference, Mari and I were compatible chums. Because we were such close friends, our parents were too. However, even with the slight age difference, my parents began noticing that I failed to achieve the usual developmental milestones. For instance, when held in an upright position, my legs and feet would turn inward. I also had trouble with my arms, particularly my right one. Every time someone would offer me an object, I would grab it with the left hand. Every so often, my parents would try to pry my right hand open to place an object in it and I would pout and cry crocodile tears. The action did not hurt, it was just uncomfortable and it was easier to use my left hand instead.

When the time came to return to the pediatrician, he was concerned and suggested to my parents that they have me evaluated at the prestigious Rusk Institute of Physical Medicine and Rehabilitation in New York. The doctors thought my condition might be cerebral palsy.

Concerned more about the obvious lack of coordination in my arms, my parents were astounded when doctors prescribed braces for my legs. At the age of nine months, they were more concerned that I strengthen my leg muscles and establish the proper walking pattern than they were about my uncoordinated arms.

In our living room, we had a round coffee table that I liked to use to pull myself up. Eventually and ever so slowly, I started to walk around the table. While I had my share of falls, I always managed to pull myself up again and walk around and around the table. Seeing how eager I was to walk and despite my heavy, clumsy braces, my mother decided to help me. Like most furniture arrangements, our coffee table was placed in front of the sofa and I enjoyed wedging myself between these two objects. Since I demonstrated all the signs of wanting to walk, my mother decided to boost my confidence by pulling the coffee table inch by inch away from the sofa, always widening the space between the two pieces of furniture. This way I was practicing my walking in familiar surroundings, and, at the same time, I had the advantage of the carpet underneath me to pad me from those many tumbles I took. Eventually, I left those boundaries and ventured elsewhere as my curiosity got the better of me. The philosophy of helping the child become mobile first and foremost still remains true today. A child who is able to get around via his own means will be happier, more communicative, and more independent than one who remains stationary.

Even as I got older and became engrossed in more advanced toys requiring finer motor coordination, I still kept my right hand clutched in a tight fist, and if anyone attempted to pry it open, I drew back and pouted. Upset by my reaction, my Grandma Williamson had a brainstorm.

I was intrigued by cosmetics as most little girls are, and my grandmother decided to paint my fingernails with bright red nail polish. Not only did the bright color capture my attention, but also I was so proud to partake in such a ladylike endeavor I could not imagine anything quite as grand. So, every time I encountered one of my elders, I simply could not resist showing off my beautiful nails. Of course, to show off these beauties, I had to open my hands – both of them. Ha-ha, a little psychology and imagination paid off. Each time I opened my fist to admire those nails, I was exercising those tight hand muscles.

By this time, my father was transferred back to New Jersey and we were living in a four room garden apartment in Elizabeth. We missed the Cozzolino's terribly and I longed for my friend, Mari. We had become great chums by then and even though I could not do as much as Mari physically, I enjoyed her companionship. I guess because we were practically raised together, Mari seldom questioned my inability to do the things she did. She seemed to accept me limitations and all. However, as we grew older, the differences in our physical abilities were even more apparent, but it still did not hinder our friendship.

Prior to our move, my parents were talking about the possibility of having another baby. Despite the complications surrounding my birth, my mother desperately wanted a second child. Being an only child herself, she knew the minuses far outweighed the pluses. Knowing for certain that she did not want to have anything more to do with the obstetrician who delivered me, and since we were now living in New Jersey, she contacted the Union County Medical Association for some possible referrals. Unable to obtain any of her records from the doctor who delivered me, she knew that finding a competent physician would be that much more difficult. Finally, she chose Dr. Richard Bataglia who served as acting head of Obstetrics and Gynecology at Elizabeth General Medical Center. Because of his acumen and fastidiousness, he was known around the hospital as "King Richard."

    Before Dr. Bataglia consented to my mother getting pregnant again, he wanted to examine the forceps marks around my neck to determine the position of the instrument. Since I had been a low-forceps delivery and the complications resulted from the prior physician's negligence, this obstetrician decided in favor of a second pregnancy.

    Within months, my mother was happily pregnant again and coincidently so was her friend, Camille. Becoming rounder and rounder each day, lifting me was becoming quite a chore especially with my braces on. Those awkward and bulky braces made it hard even for the most agile person to move me around. On one particularly trying day, my mother was having a tough time situating me in the front section of the shopping cart. Beads of perspiration were dotting her brow as she attempted and reattempted to position me in the seat. Finally, a good-natured woman who happened to witness the predicament offered to lend a hand. After a little discussion and reshuffling, they did get me into that cart and there I sat quite content.

As my mother grew in size, I sensed that some kind of change was about to take place within my family. She told me that she had a baby in her tummy and that when it was born I would either have a brother or a sister. Being only three years old, I had little idea of what having a sibling would mean and the kinds of changes that would take place within the family structure.

When the time came for the blessed event, I was taken to my grandparents' apartment in New York City where I would remain until the next week or so. Knowing that my father would be coming every night, I had accepted this temporary arrangement rather well.

When they dropped me off at my grandparents, my parents assumed they would have plenty of time to get back across the river to the hospital. Unfortunately, they did not anticipate running out of gas on the New Jersey Turnpike. Not wanting to disrupt his schedule, Dad always had the bad habit of waiting until the last minute to refuel. Even though it read empty, he always thought by some miracle that he could get another forty miles or so.

Annoyed with himself for causing this unnecessary dilemma, Dad really had no choice but to run through the six lanes of traffic to reach the nearest gas station, which happened to be on the other side of the turnpike. Seeing my father leap over several lanes of commuter traffic, it's a wonder my mother did not have the baby then and there.

Despite their untimely delay, they managed to reach the hospital in ample time. Like most expectant fathers, mine assumed that he would be sent to the waiting room to pace the floors and puff on his cigarettes as he anxiously awaited the blessed event. Little did he know King Richard had something quite different in mind for him.

Because of the complications with my birth, King Richard was determined to take every precaution to ensure a normal delivery and insisted that Dad help Mom to literally "walk the baby out." Since walking stimulates oxygen supply, strolling up and down the halls was exactly what they did. By the time Mom reached the final stages of labor, they knew every nook and cranny of that corridor as well as every floor tile, ceiling crack, etc. They simply walked and walked and walked. Finally, her water broke and they knew it would not be much longer.

At 5:27 in the afternoon, Richard George Jaekle entered the world. In fact, he arrived just in time for supper, and believe me, he has not missed a meal yet. Weighing seven pounds, eleven ounces, he was a beautiful, healthy, bouncing boy. I think just about everyone shed a tear of welcome relief to know that both mother and son survived the trauma of birth. My mother was so overwhelmed with joy that she could not stop crying. To the dismay and the surprise of the nursing staff, Mom flatly refused to hold her baby. Alarmed by such a negative reaction, the nurse finally consulted her chart and called her physician who surmised that his patient was having a reaction to the anesthetic. Sure enough, he was right and the next day Rick received all the lovin' he could want.

Meanwhile, his "big sister" was basking in the attention of her doting grandparents. Since the Williamsons owned their own outfitting business, they brought me to work with them every day. My grandfather fixed up a little office for me complete with an old typewriter, plenty of paper and, of course, crayons. Naturally, as most 3-1/2 year olds, I became bored very quickly and frequent trips to the ladies' room became an adventure rather than a necessity.

A week later, it was time for everyone to come home. I longed to see my mother and, with some trepidation, I wanted to become acquainted with my new baby brother. Who knew what really lurked in the mind of a 3-1/2 year old? But one look at this tiny bundle brought a quiver to my lips and a tear to my eye, which, in a matter of seconds, lead to a crying jag unlike no other. Who knows what came over me? I had looked forward to seeing "my baby," and now that he was here, I could not hold back the tears. Watching me cry caused my grandmother to whimper, which then lead to Mother shedding a tear or two that woke up the wee one. Then the flood gates really let loose.

During the next few days, as we began to establish a routine, slowly but surely, we somehow managed to make the necessary adjustments to accommodate this new family member. Our cabinets were filled with bottles, diapers and formula. Rattles, bassinettes, and toys dominated the scene. Especially

since we were still living in a two bedroom apartment, it was clutter galore.

Besides attending to the needs of a "special" child, my mother now had an infant to care for while tending to herself as she recuperated from childbirth. Since my father was in sales and needed to return to work as soon as possible, they decided to hire a homemaker's aide through the Visiting Nurses Association.

Shortly thereafter, Louise, a pleasant, dark haired woman in her mid-forties came to rescue an exhausted mother from her two young children. Aside from performing light housekeeping duties, preparing dinner, and doing the laundry, Louise was also supposed to make the baby's formula.

Besides sterilizing the bottles and nipples, making formula was a rather simple task. Yet, for some unexplained reason, this chore frightened her so much so that she made a bargain with Mother that she would do the ironing if Mother did the formula. Considering it was an even exchange, the new arrangement worked out rather well.

Having Louise with us gave my mother time to get back on her feet and introduced an extra playmate for me. Of course, I did my small part too. Every time my brother needed either changing or burping, I would be the one to fetch the diapers. I loved being a big sister. Oh, there were times when I was a bit jealous or overwhelmed by the attention and especially the presents that seemed to accompany our friends as they came to welcome my baby brother. Most people, however, were kind and brought me a small token so I would not feel left out.

Since we moved to the suburbs, I had been quite lonely for I still missed my friend Mari. Little did I know, she too, was adjusting to a new sibling, John Jr., who was born a month earlier. My life had become so sheltered and structured that my parents thought that perhaps it was time for me to explore the world beyond our apartment and to enter nursery school.

The idea of nursery school struck a positive chord with grandma Jaekle, especially, who recognized my need for new playmates and to develop independence from my mother. Dr. Levy in Brooklyn, our former pediatrician, wholeheartedly approved of the idea when my mother conferred with him.

As fond as we were of our former pediatrician, distance made it unwise for us to retain him as my primary care physician. So we searched for a local pediatrician. Fortunately, we did not need to look very far because my mother remembered the physician who examined my brother when he was born at Elizabeth General Hospital, Dr. Herbert E. Poch.

A well-recognized pediatrician with a growing practice in Elizabeth, Dr. Poch was delighted to have me as one of his new patients. As his first patient with cerebral palsy, he was extremely circumspect with my care. I remember when I was about six, my mother took me to a pediadontist to have my first dental checkup. Thinking that I needed the care of a specialist, we went to Dr. Walter Schwartz, DDS, who had a practice in Roselle Park. He catered to the needs of children, and he had Disney characters featured on the walls of his office, songs playing, and prizes with each visit.

He identified six cavities when examining me. Because of

my athetoid type movements, he thought it best to hospitalize me, knock me out, and do the fillings all in one sitting. When Dr. Poch heard of his approach, he was adamantly opposed because he felt the risk was too great. He felt I should have one filling done at a time like everyone else.

Dr. Poch thought nursery school was a wonderful idea and recommended one in Elizabeth for children with special needs. Unlike conventional classrooms, this one had standing tables for the more involved youngsters so that as they learned some simple cognitive functions, they would be strengthening their legs at the same time. Otherwise, it had the usual array of equipment found in most early childhood classrooms. However, the one characteristic that set this nursery school apart from the rest is that it offered therapy - physical, occupational, and speech to its students.

Housed in a renovated old mansion, the classroom was large and stocked with a variety of toys, puzzles, beads to string, easels for painting, and even a baby grand piano for our sing-a-longs. Aside from it being a brightly lit room, its walls were covered with letters of the alphabet, numbers and different shapes of all kinds and colors. A small kitchen adjacent to the classroom provided the usual goodies at snack time and a birthday cake whenever the occasion arose.

While the school held plenty of appeal and I was

intrigued with all of the activities, especially the arts and crafts, the thought of leaving mother behind brought uncontrollable, heart-wrenching sobs that captured everyone's attention. These were episodes of separation anxiety at its best. Faced with mixed emotions, my parents began to wonder if they were doing the right thing by sending me to nursery school.

Fortunately, Grandma Jaekle stepped into the picture with her words of experience and said, "Give her time, it will happen!" Since she was not working then, she kindly volunteered to stay with Ricky while Mom slowly cut the apron strings and eased me into the classroom. Believe me, this was not an easy task. In fact, Mom sat outside of the classroom for six long weeks until I finally relented. Peer pressure did the trick. At last, the light dawned on my young mind that if all of these other youngsters could forgo their mothers for the time being, then so could I. One day, I announced to my mother that she could go home now and I would see her later.

Even though I was timid and shy at first, I think that for the most part I enjoyed nursery school. Just being with the other children and acquiring social skills afforded me an advantage that some others did not have. While I was there, I met a little boy, Emanuel, who had a milder form of cerebral palsy, but he was educable mentally retarded. Some of the activities proved difficult for Emanuel, but still he persevered. I remember this dark haired little boy with big, brown eyes seemed to always enjoy music the best. Perhaps, music was the one activity he could participate in without feeling either self-conscious or inept.

When it came time to go home, we would all anxiously await the arrival of Uncle Al, our faithful and dependable driver. A short, stocky man in his mid-forties, the kids loved Uncle Al and he loved them. A kind, even tempered individual, who was adept at manipulating braces, balancing crutches, and maneuvering wheelchairs, he possessed all the necessary skills for his job to drive everyone to and from school. As much as he loved his occupation, I think the true highlight of his year was playing Santa and handing out presents to the kids.

Upon my arrival home each day, I was anxious to see my mother and play with my brother. Usually, I was very content just to amuse Ricky with his toys and watch some television until my father came home from work. Then, we would sup together. By this time, I sat on two phone books to reach the table and Ricky sat in the highchair. He was never content for too long and eventually made his way into my father's lap. We soon realized that it wasn't so much Dad he wanted, but rather Dad's mashed potatoes. He loved sticking his little, fat fingers into that white, mushy stuff and playing with it. I guess Dad did not really mind this small intrusion especially since it seemed the only way to get through dinner semi-peaceably.

After dinner I would sometimes find myself across the

hall at the apartment of our neighbor Lisa scrubbing the kitchen sink. While this seemed a rather unusual chore for a little girl, it did have some practical purposes. A newlywed, with high hopes of having a family someday, Lisa was a nurse who had taken a special interest in me. We would often enjoy doing little projects together. Since her husband frequently worked the nightshift, she would call and invite me over and we would scrub the sink.

Pulling the chair over to the kitchen counter, we made sure we had everything before we started: cleanser, sponge, and Brillo pad for those tough stains. Kneeling on the chair with Lisa holding me securely in place, we would scour the sink. Pouring the cleanser and scrubbing with the sponge was fun, but the rubbing action also helped to strengthen my fingers so they would fan out on their own instead of remaining in a tight little fist. Meanwhile, we would have a chat and I would recall the highlights of my day in nursery school.

While I was socializing with Lisa, my parents were busy getting my brother settled for the night so that when I returned, they were ready to start my nighttime ritual, which included reading my favorite Little Golden Book, Daddies. If Dad read that book once, he read it 500 times. Sometimes, to see how alert I was or just to tease me, he would skip a page. His trick never worked on me because I always caught him. In fact, I listened to that book being read so much that I could recite it verbatim.

I enjoyed other bedtime stories too. Some of the more traditional ones were: The Three Bears, The Five Little Kittens, and as I grew into somewhat more sophisticated reading, I loved the book, All About Coins. I had a piggy bank that was given to me by my godfather, John Rankie, and I liked to jingle it and listen to the coins clatter around inside. Even though I was a bit young to realize the value of money, I was fascinated by the different sizes of the coins. In this particular book, there were four round holes cut out of its cover and each one held a nickel, penny, quarter or dime. Even though I was a mere 4-1/2, I loved to sit with my father and try to insert each coin into the right circle.

Time marched on. Between nursery school and Romper Room, I was becoming a real whiz kid. I was already able to recite the Pledge of Allegiance, and I knew my colors, the alphabet, and most of my numbers. In fact, I was even learning how to print my name. Holding a pencil, even a big, fat one was a challenge, but with some encouragement and a bigger hand over mine, I could print my letters. Since most of the other kids were able to print with a little assistance, why couldn't I? I remember sitting at the dining room table with my parents, tracing those letters over and over again. With practice and persistence, I was able to print my full name and a few numbers by the time I entered kindergarten.

By this time, my parents had saved enough for a down payment on a single-family house. Let's face it, by now we were bursting at the seams. There was just not enough room to raise two growing children in a two-bedroom garden apartment. With a playpen and a baby carriage as permanent fixtures in our living room, there was not much room for anything else. It was time to move.

Knowing that we wanted to remain in the area, and since Dad had been permanently transferred, our first consideration for the location of our new home was the schools in the area for me. Prior to my graduation from nursery school, a conference held between the school administrator and the psychologist indicated that I was a candidate to be mainstreamed in the public education system. Because I had mastered the goals set forth in the Individualized Education Plan (IEP) (i.e. independence with bathroom and eating habits), the team concluded that it was within my reach to be successfully integrated into a traditional classroom setting.

Even though my parents knew that I had the intellectual ability to compete in a regular classroom, they were apprehensive as to whether or not I would be accepted by the other "normal" children. Would I be the subject of teasing, belittling, and/or criticism? Since we were without a crystal ball, we were unable to predict the future. While kids have a tendency to be cruel, especially when the scope of the situation is beyond their understanding, the same is true of adults. Despite their fears and concerns for me, my parents simply chose to focus on the positive.

My parents set out to explore the educational systems in Union county. Even though Westfield and Scotch Plains schools were considered to be among the best, both towns featured busing to and from the building. At that time, my mother was adamant that we move to a town where busing would not be an issue. She strongly felt that a completely new environment was enough for me to cope with.

Simultaneously, my paternal grandparents who were living in Cranford had decided to retire and head south. Seeing that we were in the market for a new home, they offered us first dibs on their house for a mere fraction of the price. While a handsome colonial standing on a lovely manicured street proved extremely tempting, the final analysis gave my parents reason to decline. Ideally, the location would have been perfect – right around the corner from the high school. While there were plenty of redeeming features, the one lacking was the one I needed the most – an accessible elementary school. My parents continued their search for several more weeks, and our realtor suggested that we try Roselle. There a new development of fifty-three houses had been constructed, and there was a grammar school just around the corner.

A small, suburban town, Roselle is rich with history. Over a century ago, the town was dotted with large stately homes owned by the affluent upper class who hired servants to help keep their households running smoothly. Years later, as the population began to change and servants were no longer needed. Many of them decided to stay on, but to live in smaller, more modest homes of their own. Roselle also is the site of the First Presbyterian Church where Thomas Alva Edison chose to test his famous electrolier making this church the first one in the world to be lighted with electricity.

Tired and frustrated, we decided to leave no stone unturned, as they say. We climbed into our station wagon and drove over to Roselle to investigate. As we drove through the quiet tree-lined streets of the town, we could not help but to be impressed by its charm. We passed several homes with lush, green yards, and saw barefoot children running around playing in a safe, carefree environment. Finally, we approached the development our realtor had mentioned, which consisted mostly of split-levels with a few ranch-style homes mixed in. Having

been part of the Smith Woods, there were still hefty mounds of dirt to be leveled off. Neighborhood kids loved to climb these vast mounds and slide down on their bellies. What fun! With two streets interlocking in a semi-circle, most of the houses were still for sale, and the majority of them were being bought by young families with small children.

FITTING IN

After spending considerable time mulling over which style of house best suited our needs, my parents purchased a split level. In those days, these freshly built structures stood on dirt lawns with unpaved driveways. Mail routes had not even been assigned yet. On rainy days, we, as new homeowners, walked on planks of leftover wood so as to avoid the mud as we made our way to the front door.

Once inside, barren of carpeting and furniture, the house echoed with every sound. With three bedrooms, my brother and I each got our own – I had the pink one and he had the blue one. As Rick still slept in the crib surrounded by baby furniture, which had been mine, I now acquired my Aunt Carol's bedroom set that my grandparents gave us when they moved to Florida.

Living in a split level meant three floors of stairs to climb and I had little idea how to negotiate them. However, because the stairs were inside the house, I could practice until I mastered the technique before I used them in public.

Since I was receiving physical and occupational therapy at the New Jersey Orthopedic Hospital in East Orange, they suggested that double banisters be installed on both sides of the staircase. Gripping the banister and puling myself up the stairs proved little problem, but coming down those slippery steps was entirely another matter. Since we were without carpeting, I knew that if I ever missed my step and fell I would be rolling down those hard, uncushioned steps. We knew that somehow I needed to conquer that fear and the best way to do that was simply to practice mounting the stairs over and over again. Eventually, I would build up my confidence.

While I did have my share of tumbles, the physical therapist assured my parents that this was to be expected. Since I was still a novice at it, they would need to encourage me even more. We were not in our house more than two weeks before we experienced our first near catastrophe. My parents were still sorting and unpacking boxes, rearranging furniture and trying to put the household in livable order, when suddenly they realized that Ricky was gone. At twenty-two months of age, where in the world could this little toddler have gone? Fortunately, seconds later our doorbell rang and there stood one of our new neighbors holding Ricky with one hand and my old doll carriage with the other. "I think this little boy must be yours," she said to my teary-eyed mother.

Since everyone was so busy unpacking, this little tyke thought he would wander off and check out the new neighborhood. Because he loved pushing my doll carriage, he just toddled off. Fortunately, he was spotted by a handful of mothers engaged in a friendly chat who happened to notice an unfamiliar child wandering up the block. From that time on, my parents made certain that both of us children were within earshot distance at all times.

We moved into our new home Memorial Day weekend, and, a few weeks later, we needed to meet with the Child Study Team to discuss how I would be mainstreamed into one of their kindergarten classes. Back in the 1960s, mainstreaming was a new concept. Children with special needs were placed in special education classes. Whether the disability was physical, emotional, or cognitive, the child was classified and placed in a special class. Later, in some school districts, special needs students were placed in self-contained classrooms.

Having had the advantage of attending a nursery school of special needs children, my parents and physiatrist felt that I had acquired the necessary skills to cope in a mainstreamed public school environment. Even though I still wore a partial brace on my right leg, the doctor promised that this orthopedic appliance would come off by the time I entered kindergarten. And, so it did.

To be considered for placement in the public school system, I had to be evaluated by the school psychologist who was part of the Child Study Team. Being the first child with special needs in Union county to be considered for mainstreaming, I also was the first child to be tested.

A young psychologist, a novice, who never had the experience of testing a physically involved child, did not understand my unique needs. Common sense should have had them seat me at a child's size desk and chair. Disregarding her training, the psychologist insisted that I sit at an adult-sized table and chair. Not only were my feet unable to touch the floor, but I was also extremely afraid of falling over especially since it was a straight back chair without any arms to which to cling. I was not only uncomfortable, but a nervous wreck fearing I would topple over any second.

For obvious reasons, I did not test well. If it were not for my mother prying the details out of me, I probably would not have made it into public school. When I told her about sitting in the big chair and then being asked to jump up and down, hopping on one foot and such, she knew something had gone terribly amiss. After explaining the situation to the director of rehabilitation at the New Jersey Orthopedic Hospital, she too, suspected that I had not been tested fairly. We were not seeking any special favors. We were just asking to have the test structured to measure only my cognitive intelligence and not my physical capabilities.

Knowing that I was a fairly intelligent child, the director wrote a letter asking to have me retested by one of their psychologists, and, if necessary, their specialist could be present in the room. Fortunately, all parties agreed to this arrangement.

A few weeks later, I found myself sitting in a child-sized chair opposite a warm, pleasant, older, white-haired psychologist

FITTING IN

named Dr. Bice. A soft-spoken, grandfatherly type, he made the test seem like a game. We colored, fit different shapes together, read a story, and the time just flew. My parents, who were anxiously waiting, sitting on the other side of the door, could not imagine the cause of all those giggles they heard. Ninety minutes later, I appeared in the arms of my new friend, happy and relaxed, ready to meet the challenges of a regular kindergarten class.

2

As the first youngster to be mainstreamed into the Roselle Public School System, I would open doors and build a foundation for future generations of children to follow. Therefore, it was imperative that the experience proved a positive one not only for me, but for the teaching staff as well.

Prior to the first day of school, there was a staff conference between members of the Child Study Team, Principal Anna Mae Moore, kindergarten teacher Marilyn Carlyle, and my mother to familiarize everyone with my needs. This conference would also alleviate any fears and concerns about my well-being.

Anna Mae Moore, a short, petite older woman with years of experience in the education field, was most receptive to having a child with special physical needs under her domain. She said, "She is such a sweet child with a marvelous disposition and winning smile no one could resist. Even at such a young age, she is determined to succeed, and as dedicated educators, it is our duty to help her as best we can."

Standing before this group of professionals, my mother described me as a "challenge." "Think of Nancy as a challenge for you to use your skill, training, and creativity to help. She may not always be able to do a given task the exact same way as her peers, but by employing some ingenuity on your part, she just might fool you and perhaps even herself."

Since my balance was still rather unsteady, perhaps the biggest concern shared by these educators was the possibility that I might topple over or trip. Indeed, I would have my share of bumps and bruises. Knowing this, my physical therapist taught me how to fall to minimize the impact. As for my parents, their main concern was that my classmates accept and not mimic or poke fun at their daughter. Kids can be cruel. However, children are taught by example, and it is the teacher who sets the tone for the classroom.

Clad in a blue and white plaid dress with smocking across the bodice and small Peter Pan collar, I set happily off for my first day of school. Because I no longer needed to wear my leg brace, I was fitted with saddle shoes, and now I almost looked like "one of the gang." Separation anxiety long forgotten, I smiled and waved to my mother as I entered the classroom door.

Overcome by a sense of pride, I knew that I was a big girl now ready to take on the world of kindergarten.

Once inside the brightly decorated classroom, the number of kids crying and clinging to their mothers, not wanting them to escape their sight, dumbfounded me. Forgetting that I, too, had once gone through separation anxiety, I quietly stood there and stared until my new teacher escorted me to my seat and gave me a puzzle to do. At that point, I guess she envisioned me joining the chorus of tear-stained faces, and therefore she did her best to distract me.

Eventually, all the parents left, the tears were soon forgotten, and everyone scrambled to their seat and class began. Miss Marilyn Carlyle a single, tall, thin woman with bright blue eyes and short brown hair started the session by calling out everyone's name and hanging a big name tag around their neck. The tag served two purposes: to help familiarize herself with each pupil, and to help us become acquainted with the letters of our own names, as we would soon learn how to print them. As the day wore on, we soon noticed that several items had our name neatly printed on them: crayons, lunch boxes, coat hooks, and even some workbooks.

Aside from a curious glance or two, I think most of my peers accepted me. For the most part, kids learn through observation. Since Miss Carlyle spoke to me kindly and occasionally offered to lend a hand, some of my peers did the same. For example, when we undertook a craft project that seemed to require more fine motor control than I had, one of my little girlfriends would come to my rescue.

To my knowledge, none of my classmates had ever encountered someone with an awkward gait or involuntary movements and slurred speech before, so I venture to guess I was the featured subject of many dinnertime conversations. Kids have the uncanny knack for saying exactly what is on their minds; and Lord only knows how I was described. I bet some of the tales told by my peers raised more than a few eyebrows.

Aside from most of the angelic faces scattered about the classroom, there is always one devil lurking in the midst. Mine happened to be a little black boy named Reggie who loved to practice his antics on me. A little character, Reggie was the product of a broken home, and was currently living with a foster family. His hands and arms were covered with scars, many of which were self-induced. For some mysterious reason, Reggie loved to eat paste. Even though the paste was mostly made from flour and water, he consumed enough of it that I was certain his insides would stick together. In addition to his taste for paste, he would chew a piece of crayon now and then. No doubt, Reggie had an unusual diet. Unfortunately, Reggie liked me, and to show his affection he would attempt to pull the chair out from under me as I tried to sit down or tried to trip me as I walked past.

Under the vigilant eye of the teacher, he was caught most of the time and ended up sulking in the corner.

One day, the inevitable happened and I slipped off my little chair and fell backwards giving my head a good whack on the corner of the bookcase. At first, I was stunned, and then within seconds I realized what had happened and I began to cry. Aside from the physical pain, I was embarrassed. Here I was sitting on the floor slightly dazed with everyone gawking at me trying to figure out what happened. The school nurse was quickly summoned, and between both her and Miss Carlyle, they managed to calm me down and evaluate the situation. I was probably frightened more than anything else, but as a precautionary measure, the school nurse suggested to my mother that she contact our pediatrician. Still not quite myself, my mother and I managed to walk the short distance home. No sooner had we reached the front door than I vomited. Shortly afterwards, mom called Dr. Poch who thought my upset stomach was a combination of nerves and excitement, but to be on the safe side, he recommended that my head be X-rayed.

Since it was next to impossible to reach my father, our next door neighbor, Marge Law, drove us to the hospital. Meanwhile, my brother was left with our neighbor across the street, Helen Jago. All during the ride, my mother tried to explain about X-rays. She said, "Despite the fact the big machine will make a lot of noise, it will not hurt. The doctors are only taking picture of the inside of your head."

As soon as we entered the room and I saw that huge machine suspended from the ceiling, I screamed bloody murder. People standing in the hall must have thought the technicians were sticking me with needles. Of course, they weren't. By the time the pictures were over, I was soaked with perspiration and tears and my mother was a nervous wreck. After we both calmed down and I was rewarded with a lollipop, we met Marge in the lobby and drove home. Exhausted, but relieved, we collected Ricky and recounted the day's episode for my stunned father.

By Monday, I was back to myself and anxious to tell Miss Carlyle what it was like to have an X-ray taken. Even though my version was greatly embellished, I'm sure she read well between the lines. After overcoming this ordeal, I went on to pass kindergarten with flying colors and was soon bound for the first grade.

My first grade teacher Ruth Lehr, was a tall, big-boned woman in her late 50's with short curly greying hair. Kind and soft-spoken, she seldom raised her voice. Years of experience taught her more persuasive methods to maintain discipline and respect from her young students. As with Miss Carlyle, my mother went over to the school beforehand to give her the "sales pitch" that I would be a "challenge" to her teaching career.

With a big emphasis on reading and writing, first grade is

where children are taught the basic fundamentals of their education and adhere, hopefully, to the serious business of learning. As a first grader, it is important to be able to draw simple objects such as a circle, square, triangle, and a line because it is from four figures that our creative talents emerge in a variety of designs from within. Since we spent a part of everyday drawing and practicing our numbers and letters, it soon became apparent that I was having tremendous difficulty in this area. Even though I knew how to hold a pencil and a crayon, I did not know how to transfer the image of what I saw in front of me and in my mind onto the paper in front of me. I was growing more and more frustrated because I couldn't seem to draw like my classmates did.

Detecting this inability, Mrs. Lehr told my mother who mentioned it to one of my therapists at New Jersey Orthopedic Hospital in East Orange. Contrary to what my teacher thought, this was not an unusual problem. As it was explained to us, the problem was that my fine motor skills were slower to develop, and therefore, I needed a little extra help.

Under the tutelage of a special education therapist, I learned the basics of drawing. We practiced drawing circles in the sand box, in the air, using watercolors and eventually with crayons. We traced circles, squares and the rest over and over again. With her big hand gently over mine, she helped me master essential drawing skills I needed to get me through first grade and slightly beyond. Eventually, I was able to put some simple figures together to form a house consisting of a square and a triangle or a snowman of three rather round lopsided circles. Since drawing a "house" complete with windows, a door, and a chimney seemed to be my forte, it soon became like my "trademark" whenever we were asked to submit a drawing.

Despite my limited coordination, I loved crafts, especially making collages and seasonal items. Every Tuesday morning, we assembled in the art room to have a session with Mr. Friedman, the instructor. Mr. Friedman, a short, middle-aged man with wavy brown hair and a potbelly, always tried to foster our creativity through an array of mediums. One day, when the class became too rowdy, he told everyone to sit on the floor with their hands in their laps. At the request, I was beside myself with fear. I knew I was not able to get down on the floor. Not wanting to make Mr. Friedman angrier than he was, I just sat there fearing that I would be the target of another angry outburst. His face crimson, he merely lashed out in an attempt to regain order in the class.

From then on, every Tuesday morning thereafter, at home, a mysterious stomachache seemed to overcome me. Just as I was about to head out the front door the pain seemed to strike. Lasting for approximately one hour, the quivering in my belly would slowly subside, and I could easily be persuaded to go to school. The first couple of episodes, I got away with it;

however, by the third consecutive Tuesday, my parents noticed a pattern was definitely emerging and became suspicious. So, Mom decided to play detective.

A parent-teacher conference with Mrs. Lehr revealed the only difference in Tuesday mornings was that we had art class with Mr. Freidman. So, the question now arose: what was he doing to impose such fear? After consulting him and learning of the unfortunate incident, he explained that his anger was never directed at me, but that I probably misunderstood. Then, he promised to apologize and to clear up any misunderstandings. The next day he appeared at the classroom door and asked to speak with me. Hesitantly, he approached me and explained that he was not mad at me and would never ask me to do anything I could not do. Somewhat relieved, I agreed to return to his class.

By the time I reached second grade, the written workload was becoming too great for me to handle. My teacher, Eleanor Ells, a petite woman of average height with blonde hair worn in a pageboy style, was sensitive enough to realize that I did not have the fine motor dexterity to physically keep up with it. We had started to print in full sentences, which eventually lead to writing simple, short stories. This was coupled with our weekly spelling test and simple arithmetic we were learning to do. So, writing became a burdensome chore that many times left me frustrated and overwhelmed.

To remain in the mainstream-learning environment, it was imperative that I keep up with the rest of the class. I needed a solution and fast. Time was of the essence.

After we confronted my occupational therapist, Miss Swift, with this new dilemma, she came up with a rather inventive solution. I was going to learn to type. This big-boned, middle –aged woman with brown wavy hair, a turned-up nose, and dark framed glasses decided to introduce me to the typewriter. Using a Model A, IBM electric typewriter, she taught me the touch system. On one of the first models that the company ever manufactured, I learned a skill which has remained with me all of my life.

Weighing a good 80 pounds, the greyish-colored machine rested on a child-sized table in front of a full-length mirror at the rear corner of the room. Each set of keys was covered over with colored gum paper and a bold, bright chart was placed on the easel pointing out the correct letter of each key. Since I was left-handed, it was only natural that I learned to type using that hand. At that time, my right hand was plagued with involuntary movement so much so that I taught myself to sit on it so I would be able to concentrate on what I was doing. Dr. Sidney Keats, my physiatrist then, was very impressed by the fact that I had found a way to control my "trigger," as he so often referred to my right arm.

Using all four fingers, I practiced "a, s, d, f, g" over and over again. Then, moving over to the right side of the keyboard, I mastered the keys "h, j, k, l, ;." As the weeks flew by, I learned all of the letters both upper and lower case. Eventually, I was spelling simple words and then extended to sentences.

When it became apparent to everyone, especially my parents and teachers how this skill could aid me in the classroom, there was no doubt that I needed to have a typewriter of my own. Instead of waiting for the Board of Education to finance this machine, we were informed by Miss Swift that IBM donated old models to people with special needs. All that was required was a written prescription by a physician. In a matter of weeks the typewriter was in our home, ready to be delivered to my third grade classroom.

In second grade, the class was divided into reading groups – Group I was for the best readers down to Group III which was for the slower student who seemed to be having difficulty with the material itself or reading comprehension. Unfortunately, I was placed in Group III amid the slower students who were mostly the class clowns. Kids are not stupid and it did not take them long to figure out the process of the classification and the connotations of each one. Fortunately, the present education system seems to be kinder and more humane where reading groups have individual names that do not so blatantly categorize students.

While Mrs. Ells worked with one reading group, the others were left to complete workbook assignments on their own. For the most part, this arrangement worked out well – everybody was doing something productive. In Group III, with the exception of a few of us, most of these kids had ongoing discipline problems and their continued disruptive behavior prevented other students from concentrating on our reading lesson. These "clowns" were too busy sticking pencils up their noses and performing other cantankerous acts to notice the disruptive effects on those of us who truly wanted to learn. As a result, I suffered the consequences of not mastering the basics. Reflecting back on those early days, I think most of those troublemakers suffered from yet-to-be-diagnosed learning disabilities that were hindering their ability to focus on the task at hand.

Although she chose to remain childless, Mrs. Ells was a warm and motherly person. Once when my mother was hospitalized with an alleged gallbladder attack, Dad needed to step-in as primary caretaker. Like most men, he was all thumbs when it came to combing my hair the way it was supposed to be done. Sensing my anxiety over my mother's illness, coupled with the fact that my father could not seem to get a barrette to stay in place, Mrs. Ells, a kind-hearted soul, came to the rescue. I arrived to school a few minutes before class, and she re-combed my hair giving it that extra touch that only a woman can appreciate.

As much as I looked forward to the third grade, I was sorry to leave Mrs. Ells. To me, she was the epitome of what a teacher should be: intelligent, capable, and sensitive to the needs of others.

In those days, for a child of eight, I led a fairly busy life. Aside from attending school five days a week, I also received physical and occupational therapy. Prior to the days when we were a two-car family, we rode the bus back and forth from East Orange for therapy. In fact, Ricky, who was about two years old, often fell asleep on the ride home and Mom would carry him the block and a half to the house. I, too, was often tired and sleepy from a long day, and so she would drag us both home. After several months of witnessing the return of this weary threesome, our neighbor, Helen, offered to watch my brother for the afternoon during her twin daughters' nap time. This arrangement did not present much of a problem.

We spent the summer between second and third grade mourning the loss of Grandma Williamson who had recently passed away due to cardiac failure complicated by uncontrolled diabetes. She probably would have lived at least ten years longer if she had adhered to her physician's advice and followed a rigid diet; however she craved sweets, especially pastry. Even though she had round-the-clock nursing care at home, somehow she managed to sneak candy and other goodies when she thought no one was looking. Oftentimes, she refused her medicine, which meant the nurses had to sneak it into her food. Unfortunately, she never was the model patient.

Recently retired from business, my grandfather was now a widower, living in the same Riverside Drive apartment that he and his wife had occupied for some thirty years. It was a difficult adjustment, but in time, he reestablished himself and his routine. One of the decisions he made during those first months was to give up his car. Since transportation in the city was so easy to access, he decided that he no longer wanted the responsibility of a car. Since my family was in need of a second car to travel to and from my therapy sessions, he gave it to my mother.

Elated by the prospect of having a second car, Mom needed to reestablish herself behind the wheel and learn the ropes of country driving as opposed to city driving. For several dusk-filled nights thereafter, my parents would pack us into our shiny, black, two-door Ford, and we would go to the grocery store, which would give my mother a chance to practice her driving skills.

For several years our Friday night ritual consisted of going to our local grocery store to do the weekly grocery shopping. We always seemed to get the same lady at the checkout and she became a good friend of mine. She even allowed me to help her pack the grocery bags. I was delighted. Betty had enough faith in me to teach me how to do a "real job." I learned that canned goods and boxes went on the bottom and smaller, lighter items go on top. One might wonder what a checkout lady like Betty could possibly give an eight-year-old girl with cerebral palsy. Well, my job involved opening the paper bags and getting them ready for bagging the next order.

As little and as insignificant as that chore may seem, for me it was the most important job on earth. Someone had put their faith and trust in me to perform a responsible task. I was helping someone else.

Upon seeing this uncoordinated girl at the counter helping Betty, I am sure customers had mixed reactions, which probably ranged from "that poor retarded girl" to "it is good she feels so useful." Once in a while when the checkout line grew too long, Betty's boss would wink at her, and being very diplomatic, she would ask me to take a break, and I sat leaning against the glass window watching the customers stock their carriages. Feeling a bit rejected and relieved at the same time, my feelings really were not hurt. Deep down I knew it was hard on Betty to have me hanging around her counter, but I felt that if she really wanted to lose my presence she would come up with a way to do so.

As soon as I saw my mother headed for the checkout line, I knew it was almost time for that special treat. Since the drug store was only a building away, we would push the cart inside and head for the soda fountain and a heaping dish of chocolate ice cream.

We always tried to make it home by 9 o'clock to watch the Flintstones, my favorite Bedrock family. As a rule, cartoons did not appeal to me, but this particular one held me with fascination. Perhaps, it was the adult theme with the cast of characters having real problems or the creativity of the writers who had animal-like creatures as household appliances. Whatever the reason, I was a true Flintstones fan who lived not only for each weekly episode, but for the themed coloring books and crayons as well.

For the most part, Saturdays were relaxed and leisurely.

Unlike my brother, I could not have cared less about the morning's lineup of cartoons. I was not interested in watching cartoon characters being slapped around, rolled over, or otherwise abused. Even though these cartoon characters always seemed to bounce back without blemish, I disliked watching these violent acts.

Even so, Rick would spend hours sitting in front of the television immersed in his Tinker Toys, or as he grew older, his Erector Set, and he built the most elaborate bridges and towers. He always accentuated his creations with the help of his Matchbox cars and other clever inventions.

By the hour, he sat sprawled out in front of the boob tube doing his "thing." No matter how captivating the program, his hands were never idle as he always had them into something. In fact, I doubt we owned one transistor radio that he had not pulled completely apart and reassembled.

On Saturday afternoons, I usually took a nap. Somehow, I needed that extra sleep. Between keeping up with homework, therapy sessions, and the overall mayhem of a busy household, I craved those extra forty winks. Of course, if something more fascinating or exciting came up, I would happily forgo the nap. For instance, if I was invited to spend the afternoon with my neighborhood friend, Nancy Wysocki or go on some other kind of outing, I was always ready to attend.

A couple of years younger, Nancy was tall for her age with serious brown eyes and pixie haircut. As a little girl, she loved to host tea parties and serve refreshments in dainty china-like cups with matching saucers. Of course, we only pretended to have tea. We usually preferred grape juice because that purplish drink left the best mustache.

If my parents were not going out for the evening or expecting company, sometimes we would drive over to our favorite pizza parlor for supper. Actually, it was a bar with a family room in the back. It was a very warm and friendly place with a relaxing atmosphere. As delicious as pizza is, it is a tricky food to handle with all the gobs of stringy, melted mozzarella from every direction. Aside from cajoling my parents to cut it up for me, I usually found a way to eat the sloppy stuff.

Sunday meant church school and a visit from Grandpa Williamson. In an effort to combat loneliness and boredom since my grandmother's death, every Sunday he would hop on the #111 bus from New York City and come to visit us. Even at the ripe age of seventy, he was a tall, handsome man with gentle grey eyes and a neatly trimmed mustache who always looked very dapper in his navy-blue pinstriped suit. Usually he arrived on the 11:55 bus, which dropped him off in front of the Spa Diner on Westfield Avenue in Roselle Park, where he would wait for us to pick him up.

After a round of hugs and kisses, we would cram into the car and head for home. Upon arriving home, we then would squeeze into the kitchen for a light lunch. I remember grandpa seemed to favor ham and cheese while I choose peanut butter and jelly. Apparently, I was going through the PB&J phase. Sometimes, we all agreed to have grilled cheese sandwiches, which made life a lot simpler, especially for my mother, the short order cook. Later, in the afternoon, there was usually some kind of sports event on television. While my father watched, Ricky and I played with our grandfather.

We usually sat down to dinner around six o'clock which gave everyone a good two hours before grandpa had to leave. Enjoying a hearty pot roast or leg of lamb with roasted potatoes and vegetables, we devoured the main course and eagerly looked forward to a tempting dessert. We were not big dessert eaters, but on Sundays we treated ourselves. On special occasions, Grandpa brought a couple of deep-dish apple pies from the city.

After the coffee was poured and the dessert served, we received our weekly allowances. Through the school system, Ricky and I had each opened a savings account. While he was still lingering over his coffee, grandpa would slowly reach into his pocket and pull out sixty-five cents for each of us. He always had the exact change: two quarters, one dime, and one nickel. With eyes as big as saucers, we would accept the shiny coins and promise to keep them in a safe place. On Wednesday mornings, we would drop our coins into a little brown envelope, with the correct amount filled in, and deposit the money into our savings accounts. Each teacher was responsible for collecting the money and stamping each student's passbook. While sixty-five cents may not seem like much, especially by today's standards, by the time we had finished grammar school it had accumulated into a hefty sum.

After Sunday dinner, with full bellies, we would settle ourselves comfortably in the living room to watch the Ed Sullivan Show. At that time, I had a favorite little wooden rocker that I loved to sit in because it held me so well that I was able to maintain control of my constantly moving arms and really focus on whatever I was doing. A regular little busybody, I always had one ear tuned into the television and the other one picking up the last minute tidbits of conversation. I patiently rocked myself until I saw it was time for Grandpa to leave. At approximately 7:35, we affectionately bade him good-bye, never missing an opportunity to discuss our plans for the following Sunday. As much as I looked forward to our weekly visits, I also counted the hours until Monday morning and the start of a new school week.

During the summer, I had been busy practicing my typing skills on the electric typewriter that IBM had given me. It was an older model, but it worked. I remember peering out the window and watching my father remove this big, grey, awkward-looking machine from the trunk of his station wagon. He carried it in and set the typewriter on the child-size table and chair that we had moved to the corner of the dining room. My parents decided to put the typewriter where they were able to keep an eye on it and deter my brother from thinking that it was a brand new toy for him to take apart.

As with any new endeavor, practice makes perfect. The more I practiced, the faster I became. Even though, my occupational therapist, Miss Swift, insisted that I use the correct finger for each key, I soon discovered that I could type faster and more accurately if I only used one finger instead of all five. With each stroke of the keyboard, my finger became more nimble and easier to control. No longer was I simply performing typing exercises, but I was starting to form words and sentences.

The dog days of August were rapidly coming to a close and it was time to prepare for the third grade. As was customary every year, my mother and I went shopping for a new dress and shoes. Despite my new outfit, I knew this term was going to be different because I would be the only kid in the entire school with an electric typewriter! As excited as I was to have the means to help me keep the same pace as my classmates, I wondered how they would react to my typing when they were glued to their pencils. Would they resent preferential treatment? How would my teachers feel about accepting this additional responsibility in the classroom? I would soon find out.

FITTING IN

That year, our school acquired a new third grade teacher, Mrs. Virginia Trippi. A very attractive, short, thin woman with an oval-shaped face and dark hair and eyes, she was determined to help all of her pupils the best she could. With only a few years of teaching experience, she was assigned to instruct a class that would challenge the ability of even the most gifted individuals. Aside from the average twenty or so students, there were three boys with behavior problems and me, accompanied by an electric typewriter. Indeed, she had her hands full.

A few days into the semester, Mrs. Trippi decided to make some changes in the seating assignments. Since I was the "model" student so to speak, she arranged to have all three boys with behavior problems sitting around me. Arnold, Fred, and Reggie who were eager to do anything except learn surrounded me. Aside from calling out, making wisecracks, eating paste, cutting their hair, and teasing me, they were little angels. I was always missing a pencil or dodging spitballs. Even though I was able to cope with those petty annoyances, I was not about to tolerate them planting thumbtacks on my chair to watch my reaction as I got pricked.

After about a week of putting up with them and their little dirty tricks, my mother insisted that my seat be changed. The next day Dad delivered my typewriter to class and since the outlet was located in the back of the classroom, I moved my seat to be closer to the typewriter and out of reach of those little imps.

As Dad rolled the typewriter in on a special table, all eyes were agog waiting to see how this heavy, awkward machine worked. "Can I touch it?" "How does it work?" "Here, let me plug it in?" All of these were questions raised by excited, curious students who wanted an opportunity to experiment with the awesome machine themselves. Despite our constant attempts to dissuade the kids from playing with the typewriter, some small hand would always find its way to the keyboard to strike a key or two. I guess curiosity got the better of them and they could not forgo that ongoing temptation.

Even though I now had a typewriter in the classroom, I was not completely dependent on it. While I used it for taking spelling tests, writing short essays and other similar assignments, I still relied on my pencil for math and learning penmanship.

In third grade, students are taught to convert the printed word into written word. So, we now spent a part of every afternoon practicing forming our letters. Since we now had ink pens, many of us enjoyed the messy task of refilling them every so often. I think almost every kid in the class returned home with ink stains either on their hands or their clothes or sometimes both.

Since learning to use a fountain pen proved rather difficult considering that it had to be refilled and properly handled, we decided that it was best for me to work with a ballpoint pen. Actually, fountain pens were on their way out and ballpoint pens were more "user friendly." So, with a ballpoint pen grasped firmly in my left hand and the lined paper clipped neatly on my clipboard, I practiced each penmanship stroke. Oftentimes, merely watching the teacher did not help. However, when she covered my hand with her own and gently guided me through the strokes, I really caught on. In fact, she used this technique to assist many of us who were having a hard time learning the proper placement of the pen for each letter.

 Writing is similar to drawing in that each letter must connect with the other one to form a single word. With drawing, one takes a series of lines or objects and creates a picture. Despite the difficulty of forming letters, it was important that I try to master the skill as best as I could so I would have somewhat of a decent signature to carry with me through life.

 With great effort and determination, I labored over every letter. As beads of perspiration dotted my brow, I struggled to maintain the grip and to exert enough pressure on the pen to do what was asked of me. "Now, make the letter "M" which is like three small mountains." And, I would make the letter "M." In an attempt to keep up with the rest of the class, sometimes I would grip the pen so hard that my knuckles would turn white and a vague numbness would overwhelm my hand. As the tingling feeling continued to intrude, I would need to relinquish the pen and cradle my overworked hand in my lap.

Witnessing the intensity of my struggle to keep pace with my classmates, Mrs. Trippi often encouraged me to stop and rest my hand. As this most certainly was not a contest, it really did not matter whether or not I made three letters or ten letters in a given time span. The object of the lesson was that I knew how to make the specific letter.

Meanwhile, while almost everyone was absorbed in learning to correctly form each letter of the alphabet, the three little troublemakers were growing more and more restless. Unable to concentrate on the task at hand, they started to pick on one another. The intensity of their squabbling grew louder by the minute until Mrs. Trippi had no choice but to intercede and take charge. On this particular day, tempers flared and harsh words were exchanged. Maintaining order in the classroom was virtually impossible. Finally, two of the boys broke into a fistfight. Determined to break it up as quickly as possible, Mrs. Trippi physically tore them apart. Enraged with angry hostility, one boy who was only a few inches shorter than her began throwing punches at her. Startled, she tried to turn away but the more unwilling she was to respond, the angrier he became. As the rest of us sat awestruck by this outrageous display of violence, Mrs. Trippi fought him all the way down to the principal's office.

Hearing her cries echoing down the halls, other teachers tried to come to her rescue. After several attempts failed, not wanting to make the situation worse, her coworkers quickly decided that their best efforts be spent trying to calm some of her hysterical students who had witnessed the explosive scene.

I remember, Mr. Grill, one of the fifth grade teachers, hurrying in and trying to bring some order to the chaos that had occurred only minutes ago. Many of us were quite shaken and near tears as we tried to convey our interpretations of the scene. Finally, several minutes later, Mrs. Trippi returned and told us that our terror of a classmate had been expelled. Sighs of relief spread throughout the class as all of us tried to pick up the pieces of scattered articles that had been tossed about in the scuffle. Within a few days, our class resumed its normal routine and everyone, including our two other troublemakers, seemed much calmer. I think they too were traumatized by what had occurred and were trying to mentally recuperate.

Meanwhile, we continued to practice reading aloud in our designated groups. Unfortunately, I was still part of Group III and mixed in with the rest of the slow learners. Sitting in our child-size wooden chairs arranged in a semi-circle at the front corner of the room, we listened to each other sound out every word. This was a slow and tedious process for some to endure, and their eyes would roam about the room waiting patiently for their turn.

Since I became bored and listless with the current reading

group, I wanted to move ahead. Knowing that I could probably do much better if I did not have to contend with the "troublesome twosome," my parents decided to look into some private tutoring. Perhaps, with some one-on-one instruction I could advance to the next reading level and escape the "slow learners." There were also certain negative connotations associated with Groups III and IV by some of the others. Some of the more condescending adjectives used were: dummy, retard, and slowpoke. Being classified with the "slow group" did not enhance my self-esteem either because now I was pegged as the handicapped girl who also had a reading deficit.

A parent-teacher conference confirmed my parents' decision to hire a tutor for the summer to see if, with some private instruction, I could do better. So, with the help of the Board of Education, we found out the names of tutors available for summer home instruction. Because of her background in remedial reading, Mrs. Silverman came highly recommended. She was also a primary grade teacher so she knew what to expect.

Unlike some of my peers, I really loved school, and so I did not mind giving up one hour a day to practice reading. I thought of the experience as fun, and having the attention focused solely on me was a bonus I relished. With the primer and workbook in hand, I was ready for my first lesson.

FITTING IN

On a bright, sunny Tuesday, a couple of weeks after school closed for summer recess, Mrs. S. rang our front doorbell. Clad in a blue and white pantsuit with dangling earrings, she greeted us warmly and proceeded to the card table we had set up in the living room to begin our lesson. In her shopping bag, she had brought several other attractive books with brightly colored jackets. After she piled them on the table, she said, "If we work hard, by the end of the summer, you will be able to read all of these books by yourself."

Slightly overwhelmed, yet impressed by her enthusiasm, I was willing to give it a shot. For several months, my father and I had closed every evening with The Adventures of the Bobbsey Twins. He would read a couple of chapters as I lay there captivated by the predicaments of these four lively kids. Escaping some close calls, Bert, Nan, Freddie, and Flossie were always bound for excitement and intrigue.

With the help of my tutor, slowly and steadily my reading abilities seemed to improve. Distractions far removed coupled with the one-on-one attention, I was rapidly becoming a good, strong, solid reader. Within weeks, I had finished one entire reader, and more importantly, I had advanced one grade level in my skill.

Now, as I looked forward to entering the fourth grade, the social stigma of being placed in the last reading group would hopefully be removed. No longer would I be seen as a child with a possible learning disability and classified as "slow," but rather would be viewed as someone who found a way to overcome her challenges and move on.

3

Thanks to the tutoring sessions of the past summer, not only had I boosted my reading level, but I had gained significant self-confidence in my ability to relate to others as well. Entering the fourth grade, I witnessed some administrative changes in the school I had grown to love so dearly. One was the retirement of our beloved principal, Anna Mae Moore. That took its toll on everyone. An outstanding leader and educator, to who my family and I were deeply indebted, Ms. Moore created a positive and nurturing atmosphere where I found acceptance and warmth in a mainstreamed learning environment.

While my educational experience was not always a happy one, I feel that it was as normal as it could have been. There were times when I had to forgo participating in certain activities due to my physical limitations, but, fortunately, those moments were few and far between. Just like everyone else, I had to learn to accept my limitations and focus on the things I could do. This I learned from Anna Mae Moore, a woman who I truly missed but never forgot.

Upon returning to school that fall, we were pleasantly greeted by Leonard V. Moore, our newly appointed principal. By sheer coincidence he and Anna Mae shared the same last name, which gave everyone the false impression that they were related, but we preferred to imagine that they were husband and wife. Learning that this was not the case, some of us were terribly disappointed. If they were not married or related, then how could they possibly share the same last name? Believe me, our young minds worked overtime trying to figure out that one.

Once a teacher and guidance counselor at the high school, Mr. Moore, who had completed his administrative degree, was ready to plunge into new horizons. A tall man of medium build with a receding hairline, Mr. Moore was soft spoken and even-tempered. As the father of three growing daughters, he was most empathetic of my situation and tried to be as supportive as possible. He had a fourth grade teacher vacancy to fill and he knew he needed someone with special talents to instruct this particular fourth grade class.

Remembering one of his former students, Mr. Moore contacted Joy Wanat. In the mid-60s, there were more teachers than vacancies. Recent graduates were plentiful and openings were scarce. One really had to rely on their own resources just to get an interview. Mrs. Wanat was newly married, a recent graduate, and a by-product of the Roselle School System. This bright, attractive, energetic woman was looking for a place to start her career, and as it happened, Mr. Moore had an opening for her. As it just so happened, he had an opening for a primary school teacher.

With her major in speech and communication disorders, Mrs. Wanat was certified to teach K-12. She was eager to break into her chosen field, but decided to accept Mr. Moore's job offer and try to teach the wild group of fourth graders of which I was a part.

Joy Wanat faced a challenge when she walked into my fourth grade classroom. Not only did she have a youngster with cerebral palsy equipped with an electric typewriter, she also acquired the "trio of troublemakers" who demanded her attention nearly every second. Arnold, Fred and Harold were as wild and outrageous as ever. At times, when Harold became too restless he would threaten to cut the cord to my typewriter. I wonder if Mrs. Wanat had visions of Harold someday being electrocuted. Fortunately, the electrical outlet was in the front of the classroom, and her chances of catching Harold in the act were great.

Aside from taking weekly spelling tests, memorizing

multiplication tables, and writing short stories, we also had to report on current events. Every Wednesday we were each responsible for a summary of a newspaper article to be presented before the class.

On the day that I was to give my summary, despite the nervous giggles and vacant eyes of some of my peers, I proceeded with my presentation. I knew they were very uncomfortable watching me wrestle with some rather odd-shaped mouth contortions. I felt the pressure exacerbating my speech. However, I guess I needed the practice as much as they needed to be exposed to someone with a speech impediment. Standing there, I felt the butterflies turn into bats as I realized that hardly anyone understood what I was saying. With beads of perspiration dotting the bridge of my nose, I slowly began to learn how to handle my physical awkwardness in front of people.

As I matured and became more familiar with my uncoordinated body, I stumbled on a few techniques to help me cope with some of these anxiety-provoking situations. For instance, choosing to remain seated instead of assuming an erect position really helped to alleviate the excess body movements I was prone to experiencing. Placing my right hand under my tush seemed to prevent it from taking a life of its own. Of course, rehearsing what I needed to say beforehand also really boosted my confidence.

Since I was now on the second floor of the building, Mrs. Wanat assigned me a "helper" every week to lend an extra hand with my coat, packing my books in my schoolbag, escorting me to and from the restroom, and walking me to the door five minutes before recess. Being dismissed before everyone else was an attractive incentive to entice volunteers.

One of those helpers was a little lost soul named Anna Mae, who came from a broken home. She was a quiet, shy, unkempt girl, who appeared most mornings unclean and disheveled.

Impressed by the metamorphosis of Eliza Doolittle, I decided to play the role of Professor Higgins and attempt to change this bashful, introverted human being into a well-groomed, self-respecting person. So, I invited her to my home and introduced her to my parents. With a timid half smile and nervous giggle, she proceeded to follow me into the bedroom. Watching her fingering each object on my dresser: the hair ribbons, the brush and combination, small bottles of perfume, a hand mirror, and some other trinkets, I knew she longed for them to be her own.

Following me into the bathroom, Anna Mae admired the vanity and towels and then asked to wash her hands and face. As she was patting her face dry, I offered her a new comb. Hesitantly, she took the comb and carefully restyled her hair slowly removing all of the knots and tangles. Then, we tried some hair ribbons. Watching her in the mirror, I could see that she was pleased with the results. I gave her a bar of soap with a decal of a pretty little girl on it. Later, I watched her as she proudly carried her gift home, wrapped in a plastic bag with a few selected hair ribbons.

When I saw her in class the next day, Anna Mae seemed more relaxed and self-assured; she seemed to be glowing. This change in outlook and disposition was much more than any bar of soap could hope to achieve, for this unexpected new radiance was the result of having a new friend who genuinely cared.

Perhaps, my attraction to Anna Mae was that she too had a handicap to overcome. Her limitations were emotional. She had to reckon with the stereotyped image of a kid raised in a broken home, and she had little time to enjoy the pleasures of childhood. She did not have a strong male role model at home and had to assume responsibility for her younger brother at an early age. She was not able to nurture her own emotional growth.

As fourth graders, Anna Mae and I were given the opportunity to join the Girl Scouts. For various reasons, I was not completely sold on the idea. While impressed by the uniform, the handbook, and all of the badges we could earn, I was not convinced that scouting was for me. Still, I promised my parents that I would try it.

On Thursday afternoons in one of the special education

classrooms, approximately 15 girls gathered for their weekly troop meeting. It seemed strange to be in such an empty building; if you shouted someone's name, your voice echoed throughout the hallways. Yet, this was the designated room and we were assigned to meet there.

Our troop leader, Winifred Wolfe was divorced and the mother of two youngsters: Cyndi, a year older than me and already a Girl Scout, and Bryan, who was often dragged to the meetings because of a sitter problem. Bryan, a chubby little boy, was accustomed to getting his own way. When he did not, the devilish antics would begin. He liked to sit under the table and make animal-like noises, but his favorite pastime was teasing us. Oftentimes, he would get out of control and his mother would need to break away from us and try to discipline him. By the end of a meeting, we would all be at our wit's end.

Despite Bryan's disruptive behavior, as a troop we managed to do good for our community. We held bake sales and sold cookies to raise money to fund various projects. For the holidays, we filled small baskets with festive munchies to take to the residents in the nursing home. We even went on a weekend camping trip.

Even though, by this time, I was beginning to enjoy the Girl Scouts, I still was not interested in a uniform. Several times my parents offered to buy me one, but I flatly rejected the idea. I guess by wearing a uniform I felt as though I would stick out from the others when I really wanted to blend in with everyone else. I also had visions of people coming up to me and remarking, "aren't you a good little scout who's trying to help others!" Even though these people probably meant well, their statements would come across as patronizing.

Marching in the town parade was another function of the Girl Scouts. While it was an honor to be part of the pomp and ceremony of this annual event, I did not have the physical endurance to march with the troop, but standing on the sidelines watching them march past still gave me such a thrill of pride and patriotism. Even though I could not be a true participant and I had to remain a spectator, I was overjoyed when my troop gave me a special salute as they strolled by.

Since I was not able to march in the parade, I still saw no reason to own a uniform. However, not wearing one did not prevent me from selling my share of Girl Scout Cookies. Back in those days, a box of cookies was 75 cents. Wearing my little Girl Scout pin on my coat, I went from door to door around the neighborhood asking people to buy a box and help support our troop.

Because the Girls Scouts are such a respected organization, selling cookies on my street presented no problem. I insisted that I display my independence and go myself. Of course, my father, the salesman, was determined to give me some pointers about selling. On the other hand, Mom began to show her overprotectiveness and was uneasy about allowing me to wander too far from the house. Be that as it may, I ventured forth and went across the street to my first stop -- the Jago's. With twinges of butterflies, I rang their doorbell and asked if they were interested in purchasing the cookies. Indeed, they were, and I sold them three boxes. After that initial success, I felt the confidence I needed to continue. I proceeded to the next house, recited my spiel, and sold another two boxes. Within an hour, I ran out of cookies and began taking orders. Since it was virtually impossible for me to jot down their orders, I asked my customers to write them out for me. Understanding my predicament, no one seemed to mind.

When I had announced how much I had sold at our next meeting, I do not know who was more surprised, the other scouts or Mrs. Wolfe. Whether or not our neighbors really liked Girl Scout cookies or felt obligated to buy them is debatable. Probably the latter is why they were so generous. I think one would need to be extremely cold-hearted to refuse a Girl Scout, especially if she is trying to be like her peers and do her share of selling.

We were surprised to learn that as a troop we had exceeded our quota and raised enough funds for our annual camping trip. The Girl Scout house was in Watchung, New

Jersey, and every troop was allowed one weekend per year. We chose an October weekend when the fall foliage was at its peak.

I remember having mixed emotions about the trip. While I wanted to go and be a part of the gang, I was not sure about sleeping on a hard wood floor or using an outhouse. Both situations left me feeling uncertain as to how I would cope. I was nervous and apprehensive, but I still wanted to test the waters and try this new venture. Mrs. Wolfe recruited my mother as a chaperone in case this overnight experience proved to be more than I could handle. I remember my parents discussing the trip, and while they were hesitant at first, they wanted me to try it too.

Approximately a dozen girls and three women set out for the Girl Scout house. With little idea as to what kind of conditions to expect, we packed much more than we needed. In addition to cartons of food and insect repellant, we packed toilet paper, soap, and plenty of warm clothes. As a bunch of novice campers, we really came with just about everything but the kitchen sink.

Upon arrival, we were delighted to find a rather large cabin complete with a huge living area, fireplace and kitchen off to the side. On one side of the room were several naked cots, which were waiting to be dressed with the bedding that we each brought from home. Located in the back of the cabin were two much smaller bedrooms to be used by the leaders and their assistants. Of course, there was no indoor plumbing, but there was an outhouse a few feet away from the cabin. The owners kept the amenities to a bare minimum so as not to spoil the rather rustic setting.

After we got settled and unpacked our belongings, we took a short hike around the campsite to gather leaves for a project we were working on. At the same time, we collected branches and twigs for the campfire we wanted to build after nightfall. Unfortunately, I could not walk as far as the rest of the girls, so I stayed close to the cabin and involved myself in some of the more domestic endeavors such as helping to setup to finish our arts and crafts project. Since this was one of my favorite activities, I did not mind not being able to join the others.

When the girls returned, excited and happy with their findings, they took special pride in showing them to me. Even though I was unable to accompany them on the expedition, I was delighted when they brought back some extra leaves so that I could complete my project too.

As the sun set our appetites increased. All of us were assigned to kitchen detail, and each of us was responsible for one chore. My task was to set the table properly. I remember setting the long picnic table as best I could despite a few occasional mishaps with paper placemats, plates, and cups, complete with plastic utensils. My involuntary motion caused me to squeeze paper cups too hard, leaving a pronounced indentation. Luckily the cups were empty so I could easily reshape them before setting them down.

Our dinner consisted of sloppy joes, salad, and homemade cupcakes for dessert. Since it was my first experience with such a soupy sandwich, I was uncertain as to how to handle it. Eventually, I gave up trying to eat it like a sandwich and resorted to a fork and spoon. Once I was able to get enough of the stuff in my mouth, I loved it!

I had thought of asking my mother for assistance eating the sloppy joe, but I did not want to appear helpless, especially in front of my friends. I am sure that the image of my mother spoon-feeding me would have left a negative impression, perhaps staining our friendships forever. I was delighted that these girls accepted me as well as they did.

That evening as we sat around the campfire toasting marshmallows and singing songs, I was overcome with a wonderful sense of peace and contentment. Listening to the soothing sounds of crickets in the quiet outdoors, I felt the warmth of friendship seeping through my veins. Somehow, I knew I was very fortunate indeed to have an experience such as this and to have a set of parents who were not afraid of letting me explore my environment with my able-bodied peers.

Finally, we decided to call it a night and prepared for bed.

Because girls that age are in various stages of sexual development, privacy is key. Therefore, the smaller bedrooms were used as changing rooms. Since we had only an outhouse, everyone had to use the kitchen sink to wash the bare minimum – hands and face. After all, we were roughing it.

Rolling out sleeping bags and finding everyone's pillow seemed an endless process. Amid the giggles and laughter, we finally settled down to a dull roar. While our flashlights came in handy to find our way to the outhouse, we discovered another use for them – to create shadow puppets on the wall. Ghost stories were featured entertainment too. There's nothing like a darkened room filled with pre-adolescents trying to outdo each other and scare themselves silly.

At first I enjoyed the silliness and the games, but as the night wore on, it got to me. Exhausted by all the physical activity and fresh air, I just wanted to fall asleep. Eventually, weariness overcame them and everyone settled down to a quite murmur. While I did not mean to put a damper on the evening's festivities, I just craved sleep. I could feel my eyelids grow heavier and heavier with each passing moment I was finally out for the night.

While it was difficult for me to physically keep up with those in the troop, I was glad to have had a camping experience. I learned about outhouses, sloppy joes, campfires, and participating in daily chores for the benefit of others. Indeed, it was an adventure of a lifetime and one that is not often experienced by someone with such physical involvement.

Because I had such a fun-filled weekend, Monday morning seemed to roll around faster than usual. Still tired from the camping trip, getting my weary body out of bed was a real chore. How I longed to crawl back under those covers and forget the world of the fourth grade. Duty called however, but since there were several of us recuperating from the wonders of the great outdoors, Mrs. Wanat decided to go easy on us.

One of my favorite and best subjects was spelling. Every week, we were given a set of words to memorize and on Fridays we were tested on them. As each word was given, I typed out what I thought to be the correct spelling. Under pressure, sometimes my involuntary movements would force me to strike the wrong key. Knowing that I had the aptitude, but not always the coordination to hit the right key, Mrs. Wanat gave me a second chance. She would then take me aside and ask me to spell the word I missed "out loud." If I got the word, then I would get credit for it.

Mrs. Wanat was a creative teacher. Her flexibility helped me remain part of the class, and my unique needs were also addressed. When it came time for our class play, Mrs. Wanat gave me a walk-on, non-speaking role. Prior to my so-called debut, I had always been part of a large chorus and blended in with the rest of the group. This time, however, I was to play the part of an old woman who purchased bread from the baker. Supposedly, after I was properly attired for the role, I was to walk up to the baker and motion to him what I wanted.

While it sounded simple enough and I was eager to do it, the closer we got to the performance, the more butterflies turned into fluttering, unceasing bats. As it turned out, I was not the only one. Knowing that I had a walk-on part increased my parents' anxiety too. Mrs. Wanat, the director, had more than enough nervousness for all of us. Since it was her first year teaching, she wanted to make a good impression.

Why is it that when one is anxious about a situation, she always imagines the worst? In addition to possibly being overcome with stage fright, I envisioned myself either tripping or somehow otherwise losing my balance. Deep down, I feared someone would either snicker or laugh at me, but I would say that unspoken possibility crept into all of our minds.

On the afternoon of the performance, everyone was agog with excitement and anticipation. Peeking through the stage curtain, we saw our fellow schoolmates file in. Parents of cast members slowly filled into the auditorium. The stage crew helped us into our costumes and added the finishing touches. At last, everyone was ready and we were all in place. Finally, the curtain parted. I followed my cue and walked on stage amid the glaring lights and thumping heartbeats. There I stood. Slowly, I walked over to the baker who states his line, and then, I walked back off stage. At that point, I thought my heartbeat was loud enough for all to hear, but, of course, that was only my imagination running amuck.

So relieved that my thirty-second appearance was over, I surprised myself by agreeing to be the "dolly" for a play my troop was performing titled, "This Is the Dolly with the Hole In Her Stocking." My role as the "dolly" was to sit in the center of the stage while the girls held hands and danced around me as they sang their little number. Naturally, as the "dolly" I sat there with a hole in my stocking. It was fun. I remember Mr. Moore snapping our pictures and I, as usual, closed my eyes just as the flash went off.

At this tender age of ten, being in the public eye was not exactly "my thing." While it was a good experience, I think I needed to grow more comfortable with myself and develop some techniques for making others comfortable around me. Unfortunately, there were very few role models of people with disabilities for me to emulate.

With the exception of one particular telethon, I discovered most of my role models within the pages of a book. Since I had learned to enjoy reading as a pastime, I came across the book Helen Keller and quickly became enchanted with it. I marveled at the way Anne Sullivan fought her way into her student's life and demanded that she practice civilized behavior. Despite Sullivan's poor eyesight, she recognized Helen's abilities and helped her become the woman that so many of us came to love and admire. Unlike Helen Keller who was nourished by one true supporter, I had the nurturing love of many people whom I respected, and I sought their encouragement.

Mainstreamed from the onset, I did not have the opportunity to interact with other children, who, like myself, had cerebral palsy. In fact, the only adults I saw were those few I saw on the telethon. As a faithful viewer of the annual cerebral palsy telethon, I recall one early Sunday morning segment where a female Presbyterian minister was conducting a worship service before millions of viewers. Taking a second glance, I noticed that she had cerebral palsy too. I was fascinated.

Ever since I can remember I have always had a deep respect and admiration for the clergy. Serving Christ by performing true humanitarian deeds and ministering to the sick, friendless, and poor is a vocation shared only by a select view. And, now, to see a woman dressed in clerical garb preach a sermon intrigued me to no end. Before my very eyes, now stood a woman with whom I could truly identify and someday, perhaps, emulate. I now had concrete proof that despite involuntary movements and slurred speech, a determined woman could succeed in life and stand side-by-side with her able-bodied professional peers.

For years, I had watched the Celebrity Parade of Stars and witnessed hundreds of brave kids throw down their crutches and take those first few independent steps. March to the tune of "look at me, I'm walking, look at me, I'm talking, we who have never walked or talked before" … really tugged at the heartstrings and pulled those purses wide open. Watching innocent, helpless children strive for independence opened the floodgates of conscientious people and the money poured in.

To raise as much money as possible, the focus on the twenty-two hour telethon was on children – the cuter the better. In fact, I almost came to the conclusion, at one point, that somehow children outgrew this neurological condition once they entered adulthood. I was wrong. Unfortunately, this was the false impression that I as well as many others received. Over the past several years, this philosophy seems to have changed, and I feel encouraged by seeing more adults with cerebral palsy assuming more meaningful roles in the spotlight.

Being raised in a mainstreamed environment where I attended regular classes, played with a neighborhood friend or two and basked in the warmth of a happy family life, there was no time to dwell on my limitations or self-pity. One of the few occasions where I was blatantly reminded of the fact that I was disabled occurred when I went for my weekly therapy session and I saw other kids with varying degrees of involvement undergoing treatment. It was there that I was confronted with my handicaps head-on. Even so, I think I merely thought of myself as someone with different needs and challenges.

As a child, I did not know much about my condition except that there had been damage to a certain part of my brain due to a lack of oxygen when I was born. While I knew its name, I really did not verbalize my desire to know very much about my neurological condition nor do I remember discussing it with any of my therapists. I am sure if I had inquired, they would have offered more information. However, since it had always been a part of me and I never knew my body otherwise, I accepted myself as I was.

Even though I had been an object of pity by some adults and a victim of torment by some rather cruel kids, I never saw myself as unusual or crippled by any means. Yes, there were times when I fought back tears and anguish, but it was only temporary and I learned to resolve those feelings with time and focus on the positive. There were instances, however, when I had some preconceived notions about myself.

I guess I was about eight or nine when I overheard a conversation between my father and his insurance agent. My father had asked him to stop by because he wanted to make some changes on his life insurance policy. Lying in bed listening to bits and pieces of conversation about premiums and funerals, I thought he was dying. As a youngster I did not realize that there were long range plans for the care of the family in case something happened to him – the breadwinner. At the time, I was frightened.

Tears started to roll down my cheeks. Listening further and with greater intensity, I overheard my named mentioned. Now, I thought I was the one who was dying. Unable to bear it any longer, I slowly edged my way downstairs. Caught on the mid-stairway, I sat down and sobbed. Hearing my woeful cries, my father quickly got up and made his way over to me.

"What's the matter?' He asked.

"I don't want to die!" I sobbed.

Suddenly, my father realized what I had overheard caused my impressionable mind to jump to some startling conclusions.

After spending several minutes calming me, he explained that we were all going to die someday and that he had been discussing how he could best protect his family. Emphasizing the fact that we were all going to die someday, he explained that he had bought a policy for me and that it probably would not be used for a long, long time.

Several years later, I learned that because I had cerebral

palsy, I was thought to be more accident prone by insurance companies and therefore, it was wise to purchase a policy while I was still a child. Recognizing that death is an eventuality that we all must face brought about a certain maturing process that helped prepare me for the fifth grade.

Because my reading level had improved so dramatically, I was placed in the more advanced class. My contact with the "troublesome trio" was no longer. I now joined the company of some of the brightest students – the more conscientious and serious ones.

That year, Myra Trieber was our teacher. A woman in her mid-forties of short stature and dark hair, Mrs. Trieber was a no-nonsense kind of person. Although she gave the impression of being rather aloof at times, she had a compassionate side too. In keeping with the tradition of assigning me "helpers" every week, she kept a running list of volunteers taped to the lid of her index file box sitting on top of her desk.

Because of the location of the outlet in the room, I now sat in the back with my electric typewriter. Impressed by my ability to type, Mrs. Trieber expected me to do all of my written work, which included long division, on the typewriter. While I had become semi-proficient at the skill, I had yet to master the art of setting margins and making columns, etc. Therefore, even adding a column of numbers proved to be a trying task. Let's face it; numbers need to be lined up exactly in order to achieve the right answer. And, Mrs. Trieber expected me to do long division on the typewriter, a next to impossible request even for someone without poor coordination.

Fortunately, within a matter of days, my mother intervened and explained that I neither had the knowledge nor dexterity to do calculations on the typewriter. So, upon the advice of my occupational therapist, we purchased some accounting paper and drew big boxes. Then Mrs. Trieber wrote out the problems beforehand and I used my clipboard to jot down the answers myself. Even though mathematics was a difficult subject for me, it was important for me to learn how to solve problems.

Now that I was in the more advanced class, I also experienced my share of competition and heartache. I was now among the "brains" of the fifth grade class. Two of my competitors were Jeffery Myers and Evelyn Brody, both of whom came from upper-middle-class homes. Both fathers were well-respected practicing attorneys who strongly emphasized the importance of education in the home. Considering their children to be among the brightest, these parents could not comprehend the reason for a child with some special needs to suddenly appear in the same class as their precious children.

Assuming that I would require special attention or that

my mere presence would somehow deter their children's studies, these presumptuous parents demonstrated an air of cold politeness. Without a doubt, every "Back-to-School-Night" seemed to present an opportunity to make subtle comments about having me in the same class as their children. They would say things like "I hear that Nancy does well in her attempt to keep up with her classmates, you must be proud." or "I guess Nancy needs a lot of help with her schoolwork" to my parents.

At first Mom felt hurt and frustrated by these cruel and degrading remarks. Several months later, when a similar situation occurred, she realized that she could not singlehandedly change attitudes overnight and, in fact, their opinions were based only on prejudgment and not fact.

While I was not exactly in the same league with their "brilliant" youngsters, I certainly had much more to contend with. For instance, homework took a long time because by the end of the day I was tired. However, I never asked for an extension. Many a night I would sit upstairs in my room behind my electric typewriter and pound out the answers until my eyes were droopy with sleep. Sometimes, my mother would come up and prompt me so that we could spend time together. With very few exceptions, I always handed in my homework on time.

As we progressed through the school year, we quickly learned that Mrs. Trieber had a penchant for assigning projects. I remember one in particular, for which we were asked to make spice charts. We had been given a sheet with a list of all the spices that we were to have samples of on our chart. "Sample" was the key word. Because not every household uses the same spices and since I only needed a small sample of the ingredients, we decided to ask for our neighbor's help.

    We lived in a close-knit neighborhood where we all helped each other. After perusing the list, we discovered, to our dismay, that I was short one spice – a bay leaf. It was time to call on the neighbors. My mother suggested that I ask Lucy France, our Italian neighbor. Within seconds after ringing her doorbell, I was standing in her foyer explaining my predicament. Checking her spice rack, she sadly discovered that she was out of bay leaves. Not wanting to disappoint me, she proceeded to call her sister who lived some twenty miles away on Staten Island. Lo and behold, she had a bay leaf. Wondering what was going to happen next, I held my breath. A split second later, she was telephoning her husband at work and asking him if he would not mind stopping at her sister's to pick up something. Known as a kind and mellow man, I venture to guess his temperament upon discovering the real purpose of the impromptu visit.

    When I relayed, the highlights of my conversation with Lucy France to my parents, they were overcome with embarrassment. To think of asking one's husband to drive over twenty miles to pick up a bay leaf for a neighbor's daughter was incomprehensible. My mother immediately called Mrs. France to explain that she should not go to all that trouble and that we would buy a box of them. However, despite my mother's pleas, she insisted on doing this good deed. So, two hours later, there stood a six-foot tall man on our doorstep carrying a baggy containing one single bay leaf.

Whenever there is a project, the competition is not necessarily just among the students, but in many cases, there is an underlying competitiveness between parents as well. If only Mrs. Trieber knew the effort that went into the spice chart project, she would have been completely flabbergasted. With a lot of help, especially from my patient grandfather, I did have a beautiful project. In fact, judging from some of the others, they had some parental involvement too. I can recall the look of pure amazement on the face of Jeffrey Meyers when we both returned to our seats with the same grade of "A-". I think receiving the same grade made Jeff a little more humble – at least for the time being.

Meanwhile, my therapy sessions continued on a weekly basis. Even though I still participated in physical therapy, the main focus shifted to occupational therapy with emphasis on activities of daily living. Prior to this point, the primary core of my treatment was devoted to honing my typing skills so that I would be able to do the bulk of my schoolwork via the typewriter. In the course of teaching me to type, Miss Swift noticed that I had a weak left wrist in comparison to my right one. So she put me on an exercise treatment program that would strengthen the joint and its surrounding ligaments. This was a dull and repetitive process. Holding my arm extended on the table with my hand flexed upward, she would try to push downward. Hopefully, this repeated act would help my wrist to become stronger.

Unfortunately, one day, after we continued this therapeutic line week after week for several months, Miss Swift turned in her resignation, terminating her association with the center and with me. While I am extremely grateful to her for teaching me a skill that would sustain me far into my future, I think she suffered "burn out" long before anyone ever realized it. Indeed she had the skills, but she lacked the imagination to employ them creatively.

A few weeks later, we welcomed a new, more innovative therapist, Beverly Bains, on board. A short woman of average proportions, Mrs. Bains brought a fresh, stimulating approach to the department of treating the whole patient. She addressed not only physical needs, but social and emotional ones as well.

In keeping with her philosophy, Mrs. Bains tried as often as possible to pair clients off and to conduct joint therapy sessions. I was paired off with Debbie, who also had athetoid cerebral palsy and was close to my age. Tall and thin with a bubbling personality, Debbie was very eager to collaborate on our project. Once we made pizza. By kneading, rolling out and shaping the dough, we applied both our gross and fine motor movements to our pie. Grating the cheese and spreading the sauce incorporated a variety of hand maneuvers testing our manual dexterity to the limit.

As we completed each task and waited to move on to the next step, we engaged in the usual conversation pattern of adolescents. With Mrs. Bains prompting and directing the flow of the topics, we chatted about what junior high school might be like, making new friends and our common interests. We discovered that we both liked swimming. A few years later, by sheer coincidence Debbie and I were reunited at the Kessler Institute for Rehabilitation in West Orange. Somehow New Jersey Orthopedic Hospital's Cerebral Palsy Center made an agreement with Kessler for the use of their heated pool to conduct Saturday morning swimming classes.

Even as a young child, I had been a fish in the water. I loved the buoyancy of my body in the water and its effect on my muscles. So, when my parents and I heard about this six-week session, we jumped at the opportunity to have the place to swim in the mid-winter as well as to meet some other kids in similar situations.

While I was delighted by the prospect of swimming, I

was somewhat hesitant to be among so many others with varying degrees of disability. Unfortunately, in some cases, children were so severely involved that they were unable to hold their head up due to weak and underdeveloped neck muscles. Furthermore, some children were impaired intellectually and did not really appreciate or even acknowledge their surroundings. And, then, of

course there were others like me who wanted the exercises as well as the social aspect of swimming.

Entering the pool area, I was almost overcome by the strong smell of chlorine. This pungent odor combined with the high temperature of sometimes as much as ninety-eight degrees made me feel weak, but the sensation soon disappeared. As soon as I hit the water I felt invigorated.

Each of us had his own personal swimming attendant who would try to get each child to do as much as he could in the water. It is a well-documented fact that the buoyancy of the water allows persons with limited mobility the physical freedom to move about with greater ease and, in some cases, less pain. For some kids, the goal was to get them to relax, and, for others, the objective was to actually learn some of the basics of swimming.

I had always loved the water. Ever since I was a small child, I was strapped into a flotation device and given the freedom to wander within specific areas of the pool. At Kessler, trained professionals had the expertise to help me learn to swim. Therefore, floatation devices were not permitted and everyone had to rely solely on their attendant.

I remember the first time the attendant let my head go completely underwater. Seconds later, I came up frightened and gasping for air. Coughing and wiping my eyes, I could not believe she let me go. Believe me that one horrifying incident cost me my confidence for a long, long time. I never completely relaxed in the pool after that. Aside from my shattered confidence, I had nightmares of drowning in the water. Despite my fears, I continued the sessions clinging to my attendant for dear life. Realizing that I had not been ready, she apologized. Even so, my trust in her was badly bruised and never quite fully mended.

Fortunately, the incident had not damped my spirit enough to destroy my love of swimming and I continued to participate in it that following summer at the Village Motel and Swim Club in Rahway. My parents decided to join the swim club to help my brother and I fight the summer doldrums. As a kid, I had conflicting emotions about these ten-week vacations. On one hand, I looked forward to the leisurely days of hanging around the house, watching television and getting together with friends. Oh, let's face it, summer vacation is too long. Although I had Nancy Wysocki to occasionally visit back and forth, I missed the routine that school provided, not to mention the socialization.

One summer when I was about eleven and the days hung particularly heavy. I was cranky and out of sorts from boredom, and so my father decided to devise a list of productive things I could do during the day such as practice my typing, water the plants, make my bed, set the table, read a couple of chapters, etc. He compiled about eight different tasks to occupy me. I also came up with a few ideas of my own which helped make it a special summer because I learned how to be my own best friend.

Experiences of the past summer helped nurture and prepare me for the sixth grade – a turning point in my life. To accommodate our sixth grade teacher, Marie Miller, an older woman who was recuperating from a bad fall, our classroom was moved to the first floor. Since the chalkboard was located on the side-wall, the desks needed to be turned to face that direction. This arrangement allowed the typewriter with its table to be situated to the side of my desk so that I literally slid from one seat to the next depending on what I needed to do.

In Mrs. Miller's class, we had a well-stocked library that ran the length of an entire wall. Needless to say, reading was highly encouraged and if I had any spare time, I was expected to have my nose in a book. Of course, those children who really enjoyed reading chose the thicker books and others who were not as interested chose the thinner ones.

When we were assigned to write a monthly book report on any work in that library, and we were exposed to a variety of literature. This exposed our young, impressionable minds to a plethora of good reading material. The idea was to get us excited by literature in the hopes that reading would develop into a lifelong habit. I always chose to read biographies or stories that had a focus on family in their theme.

The practice of writing a monthly essay helped us to hone our writing and communication skills. At first, I found this to be a burdensome task. Even though I had grown to love reading, it was still sometimes difficult for me to pick out the main theme, especially when there were several different underlying ones. However, writing was in our family's blood. Aside from my Uncle Charles, the writer in the family, my mother had a great uncle who was a famous playwright. She definitely inherited his command of language. Often, she would help me with my homework, especially if I had a composition to do, and together we would outline all of the ideas I wanted to get across in my essay. When it came to writing a book report, one suggestion was to reread the jacket after completing the book to refresh your memory as you wrote your report. I carried this concept over to whatever I was writing, and through enough experience, I developed a few methods that later evolved into a writing style of my own.

Aside from book reports, we also learned how to write a letter. Of course, to truly write a letter, one needs to have someone with whom to correspond. Since we were in the midst of the Vietnam War, Mrs. Miller thought it might be a good thing to write to our troops overseas. The mere thought of pen-paling with someone living in a foreign land really captivated our interest. In fact, the idea had my fellow students and I begging Mrs. Miller to teach us the correct format for writing a letter.

I'm not really certain as to how she went about getting the names of those whom we were to write. It might have been through the Peace Corps or the Red Cross. In our letters, we were encouraged to ask servicemen questions about their lifestyle, what kinds of food they ate, their experiences in combat, and what it meant to them to be fighting for their country. It was always a red-letter day when we received mail from one of our men. While some men sent a brief response on a postcard, others went into much more detail about their situation and thoughts about the war. Careful not to break any rules of confidentiality, the men were as descriptive as they dared to be.

We could always tell from the tone of their letters whether they received much mail or not. Some men even wrote to us from a M.A.S.H. unit while they were recuperating from an injury of some kind. It was these men who were most happy to hear from us and to know they were not forgotten.

Our correspondence with the men lasted for several months until the school year ended. It was a wonderful experience. No longer were the battle scenes shown on the news a passing dream. Now, these war scenes held some depth and realism. One of those soldiers on TV might be our latest pen pal. Many valuable lessons came from this experience. Aside from the geography we learned and the insight gained about the lifestyle of another culture, we learned to appreciate our freedom and all that it encompasses. Even after the school term came to a close, some of us continued our relationships as many of us felt the need to do our small part to cheer our soldiers overseas.

One day in late March, Mrs. Miller made an

announcement about an essay contest specifically for sixth graders. All of us were to enter. Sponsored by a local company, there were several guidelines that were to be followed. First, the 300 word essay on a particular theme, had to be written in the child's own handwriting. The reason for this is obvious. For the best chance of winning the $50 savings bond, most children would not hesitate to enlist the help of a parent or older sibling. Of course, there is a big difference in offering to give some meaningful criticism as opposed to writing the essay for the child. However, some willful parents might argue the matter. Therefore, as a means to discourage such practices, contest officials insisted that any entry be in the child's handwriting.

While the enforcement of rules is mandatory, there are extenuating circumstances, where rules, while not made to be broken, can be slightly bent. Explaining as delicately as she could as to why I could not enter the contest, Mrs. Miller promised that she would give me extra credit if I wanted to write the essay anyway. Somehow the thought of extra credit lost its appeal, especially when I had my heart set on submitting an essay.

Hearing my tale of woe, my mother decided to arrange for a parent/teacher conference to see if this situation could be mutually resolved. Reviewing the rules of the contest with my mother, Mrs. Miller underlined the one stating that any entry must be in the child's handwriting. Agreeing that there was a definite purpose to enforcing that rule, my mother asked her to write a note to accompany my entry explaining the reason as to why I used an electric typewriter. Adamantly refusing to write such a letter, Mrs. Miller insisted that the rules of this nature could not be broken. Needless to say I did not get to enter the contest. Till this day, I do not know who was more disappointed, my mother or me.

    I think that was one of a handful of times when my disability got in the way of something I really wanted to do. While there might have been a way to work around it, someone chose to block my path. Who knows? Perhaps, this was a deliberate twist of fate to prepare me to cope with the real world and to realize that I would not always get what I wanted or deserved. Today, I am sure this situation would have been handled quite differently. With the special education law, Section 504, special needs students are permitted to enter contests of all kinds. If my past situation had occurred thirty years later, this would probably have been viewed as a violation of civil rights.

    While I was jolted a bit by this slap of reality, my life went on. In addition to all the work I was doing at school, I was also in the process of conquering a lifelong phobia – a fear of dogs. Ever since I was a small child, I was terrified of dogs. If a four-legged canine came within fifty feet of me, I froze. At the sight of these mongrels, however friendly, I would literally freak out. My small body would tense into a spasm rendering me helpless and unable to move.

As a kid, my father always had a dog. From terrier to Heinz 57, he had a four-legged friend barking at his heels. Now he had a son longing for that same experience. In the past, we tried on numerous occasions to have a family pet. We would get a puppy and give it the run of the house, and I would be climbing the wall in fear. I think the real problem was that the dogs moved too fast and I startled too easily. Within a couple of days I would be a basket case and the dog would have to be returned.

Not wanting to deprive either Rick or myself from the experience of raising a puppy, my mother found inspiration in a letter from a reader of "The Polly Pointer's" column. It appears that this woman bought a puppy to keep herself company. Fearful that it would do damage to the furniture and carpeting, she brought a used playpen and kept her pup in this self-contained environment either at night or when she was not home. My parents thought this was an ingenious idea and decided to take it a step further. Aside from the usual chewing and housebreaking issues associated with puppyhood, the playpen provided a safe haven in which to temporarily keep the pup where I would be able to play with her in small doses and eventually learn to overcome my fear.

My mother always loved Scottish Terriers. She thought that with their short little legs, this independent breed would not be able to run as fast or climb on the furniture. Wow, was she wrong!

Fortunately, we had a family friend, Mary Painter, who had, during the course of her lifetime, owned five Scotties, both males and females. After considering her opinion and doing some research on our own, my parents decided to purchase our pup from the Puppy Farm in Princeton, New Jersey.

Filled with a combination of excitement and anxiety, the four of us and my grandfather climbed into our station wagon one Sunday afternoon to buy our pup. I remember nervously walking amid all of the pens noting the many puppies waiting to be adopted. While some lay curled in tight balls sleeping, others were whimpering, yet wagging their tails to claim your attention. Each puppy was cuter than the next. I hesitantly looked into each pen secretly liking those who were asleep the best for I knew I was safe from their romping.

Finally, we came across the pen marked "Scottish Terriers." Leaning over the side of the pen, we spotted the smallest, a female who was the runt of the litter. She was one tiny ball of black fur. My father gently picked her up and handed her to Rick. When Rick looked into those big, brown, soulful eyes, it was love at first sight. After some coaxing, I gingerly reached out my hand to stroke her back. It felt great to pat her, and somehow we knew this one was for us.

Upon paying the pedigree price, the owners supplied us with a small basket filled with fresh straw to bring our pup to her new home. Still unsure of myself with the puppy, I elected to sit in the front seat with my parents, while Rick and grandfather sat in the backseat attending to our new addition.

We had the playpen setup before we left so that as soon as we came home, we could introduce Bonnie Brae (an appropriate Scottish name my mother suggested) to her new quarters. Shortly afterwards, we placed Bonnie in her playpen and noticed that her little body was able to wiggle itself between the wooden bars and out of the playpen in a matter of seconds. So, the men of the household decided to put some mesh around the pen preventing any further escapes; it worked.

Even though I was still fearful, our frisky friend mesmerized me. Every move Bonnie made, whether she was awake or asleep, impressed me. I loved to watch Rick romp with her or pick her up in his arms and hug her. I was nowhere near that stage yet, but I had made some small strides. Since we kept the playpen in the rear of our long foyer, we would periodically take her out and let her roam the place. As I was not quite ready for a playful pup on my turf, I perched myself on the top step where I was certain not to miss a trick.

As the weeks passed, I gradually grew accustomed to Bonnie and her doggy ways. When she was free to roam in the kitchen and living room I could now sit comfortably on the sofa and watch. I remember the day she unexpectedly jumped up on the couch; I am not sure who was more startled, Bonnie or my catnapping father.

Eventually, most dogs are able to adapt themselves to the personalities of each person in the household and Bonnie was no exception. Instinctively, she knew she could romp and go wild with Rick, whereas with me she took a calmer, gentler approach. Sensing that I was not able to rough house, she gladly accepted my warm lap to nuzzle in on a chilly night. Since my parents took turns feeding and caring for her, there was no question of her loyalty and devotion to them as well.

Despite her kind and affectionate ways, Bonnie was a very independent canine. A characteristic of her breed, she would remain aloof at times and preferred to wander off by herself. Usually, we would find her under the bed or strangely enough down in our basement. As she grew older, Bonnie adopted a rather laid-back approach to greeting guests at the door. Instead of sauntering over to them, she sat on the top step and happily wagged her tail at them. Unlike many dogs, Bonnie displayed no aggressiveness at the sound of a knock at the door, and, no matter who arrived, she would undoubtedly lick them to death.

Physically, Bonnie was no more than twenty pounds. However, despite her small stature, she was a tiny powerhouse, full of strength, but without any sense of direction. As much as I wanted to walk Bonnie, I simply had to forgo that chore, as her strong little legs would pull me right over. Numerous times, we tried teaching her not to pull and bought a choke chain to reinforce our wishes, but to no avail; she insisted on pulling and pulling. Every time I felt bold enough to try again, I thought that my shoulder would detach from its socket; that's how strong she was.

The attachment of animals to people and vice versa is a bond that has continued since the beginning of time. It is a well-known fact that dogs and cats have a particular sensitivity to the many moods of their owners. For instance, Bonnie was able to sense if one of us was sad, happy, lonely, depressed or that we simply had a hard day. She seemed to instinctively know and to take the appropriate course of action – for a dog, that is – when one of us needed her.

Within a matter of months, Bonnie had fully assimilated herself into the family. Each of us loved her in his own way. I remember one Valentine's Day, Rick and I bought a card to give to our parents. It did not seem right to only include our names especially when Bonnie meant so much to them too. Since a dog could not write, what other alternative came to mind? Lo and behold, my brother had a brainstorm. Borrowing an inkpad from Dad, Rick inked the dog's front paw and pressed it to the card. Presto, there was Bonnie's paw print – a one and only true symbol of a pedigree's signature.

Confronting and overcoming my fear of canines took mounds of courage and a deep and abiding faith in God. When we first adopted Bonnie, there were plenty of tense and anxious moments as we gradually learned how to deal with each other. However, I believe that Bonnie's patience and tolerance of my startled reflexes gave me the determination to overcome my phobia.

Knowing that my life would always be filled with obstacles to overcome, I knew that the only way for me to accomplish and achieve my goals was to have the knowledge that God was beside me every step of the way. Practically from the cradle, my parents brought me to church and later to Sunday school. As a baptized and soon-to-be confirmed Episcopalian, I believed in God and sought a deeper faith.

For approximately 20 years, we were members of Saint Luke's Episcopal Church in Roselle. Nicknamed the "frozen few," Episcopalians are known to be rather stuffy and standoffish. Churches are forever seeking new members. Why is it then, that when most of us see a newcomer we tend to back off and wait for someone else to be the "ice breaker?" Probably, if it were not for Dolly Beaver, a new friend of my mother's, who took us under her wing and introduced us around, we probably would not have stayed.

As it turned out, Mrs. Beaver played a larger role in our acceptance than we ever dreamt or anticipated. Because she was my first Sunday school teacher, it was up to her to set some type of example for the children to follow. My Sunday school class was one of the largest in the church, fifteen in all. We were a community church with many of the families attending from neighboring towns. Therefore, I was challenged with a new set of classmates – some less accepting than the others. One young lad in particular, by the name of Calvin Carlstrum was literally forced to accept me. If not, his mother clapped him on the back of the head and read him the riot act.

Gradually, my parents acquired a circle of friends and even though the majority of the congregation had little understanding of my condition, I received lots of support, encouragement and some meaningless chatter. For some reason, whenever someone did not quite know what to say, she complimented me on my outfit for the day. No one likes to receive a complement more than me; however, hearing the same phrase echoed each week became slightly mundane and awkward.

I loved our old brick church and I had great admiration and affection for our rector, the Reverend Walter J. Moreau. Both Father Moreau and his wife, Mary, were very solicitous of my needs. Not having had a daughter of their own, they more or less "adopted" me. In the summer, we occasionally went to band concerts together as their son, Bill, played the drums.

But now I have a confession to make – I did not particularly like Sunday school. Up until the sixth grade we were studying our religion and questioning our faith, as we were deeply committed to preparing to receive the sacrament of Confirmation. In this important year of our religious training, our Sunday school teacher, Norma Tucker, a rather strong but good-natured woman, took her role very seriously. I remember memorizing the books of the Bible, both the Old and New Testaments, the Apostles' Creed, and several other teachings of Christ.

In addition to Sunday school, that year Father Moreau instituted a two-hour training session to be held Saturday mornings and taught by him. Evidently, he did not feel that we received adequate teaching in Sunday school and so he wanted to somehow supplement the curriculum with his own agenda. Even though some of the parents objected, mainly because they did not want to ruin their one day of leisurely activities to drive their child to church, Father Moreau took a firm stand. After all, most, if not all, families were able to forgo their Saturday morning routine for a football game or some other event of special significance.

With Father Moreau, we studied the Lord's Prayer and memorized it word-by-word, punctuation mark for punctuation mark; he was a stickler for detail. Every misspelled word or missing punctuation mark cost five points. Of course, we also discussed in depth the meaning of the Lord's Prayer and how and why it originated. Aside from memorizing the seven Holy sacraments, we acted them out. I supplied the doll that was to be christened for Holy Baptism. We had other classmates play the role of parents, godparents, and minister. When we studied Holy Matrimony, two classmates pretended they were getting married.

As the months flew by and this intense preparation continued, other matters needed our attention such as picking out a confirmation dress and veil. On an appointed day chosen by my mother, godmother, and Aunt Char, the three of us went shopping. After looking through a rack of appropriate dresses, we finally decided on one with a smocked bodice and full skirt. It was beautiful. We chose a veil and selected appropriate shoes careful that the heel was neither too high nor too narrow. We even remembered to ask Dad to scuff up the shoes so that I would not go sliding into a nonexistent base.

On the morning of my Confirmation, April 23, 1968, our household was a flutter of excitement. Having taken the bus out from New York City the day before, my grandfather was glowing with pride. Frantically, running around checking on every last detail, my mother accidentally slipped coming up the steps as she was carrying my newly pressed dress to my room. Outside of a bad scare and some frayed nerves, no major damage was done.

At Father Moreau's suggestion, my father walked me up the church aisle and helped me to kneel down in front of the Bishop to receive the laying of hands. This was an excellent idea. Because of all of the excitement and anticipation, my coordination was not at its best so I appreciated every helping hand that was offered to me. Suddenly, I felt my heart pounding as I gingerly walked up that aisle, my father gently guiding me, to make my Holy Confirmation and to become an adult in Christ's church. Kneeling down before the Bishop and feeling his hands resting on my head, I knew that I was blessed forever.

7th GRADE

4

After a hectic school year of essays, examinations and term projects, I luxuriated in the blissful, leisurely days of summer where schedules were forgotten and we were footloose and fancy free. While I was supposedly taking advantage of the relaxed nature of the season, I was somewhat preoccupied with entering the seventh grade. Knowing that this was my last year of elementary school, I was filled with excitement as well as trepidation. As much as I was eager to be in the "big league" and to become the envy of those still in the lower grades, I was not yet ready to leave the innocence of childhood behind.

Seventh grade. This was the first time I had to cope with changing classes, emerging hormones, my first boy/girl dance, and imagining the chaos of high school the following year. What an agenda to digest!

Yet, despite my anxieties over the upcoming term, I had a

wonderful summer. In keeping with tradition, the Cozzolino's had come to spend a few precious days with us. Even though they were now living in Staten Island as opposed to Brooklyn, we seldom saw each other due to their father's changing shifts as a policeman on harbor patrol. Arriving with suitcases and ready for fun, Aunt Camille had a gleam of mischief in her eye as she helped us decide what we were going to do over the next three days. With her daughter, Mari, who had been my closest friend practically since birth, and now John Jr., who was a month older than Rick, we had an adventurous group.

A visit from this dizzy, noisy, excitable bunch was the highlight of my summer. For almost three days, I had a friend to giggle with and confide in, and I had someone with whom to explore new places. I was in heaven. Between the swim club, the zoo, the amusement park, the movies and whatever else beckoned our interests, we had a blast!

Back in the 60s, a parent and a couple of kids could spend an entire day in a theme park for a few dollars. Nowadays, the cost is downright prohibitive for most families. The six of us would wander around hop on a few rides and explore every nook and cranny before calling it a day.

Mari and I loved to go on the Whip, the roller coaster and the merry-go-round. Despite my lack of coordination, as long as I was strapped in tight and had someone to conveniently squeeze over the bumpy spots, I was in my glory. I craved the thrill of adventure as long as I felt reasonably certain that I would still be in one piece at the end of it. For a thrill of a different variety, we decided to try the haunted house. While I was not completely sold on the idea, I agreed to give it a shot. With some reservation, I slowly climbed into the cart followed by Mari, who I would undoubtedly cling to for dear life as we rode farther and farther into this pitch-black, spooky place filled with a myriad of bats, ghosts, and skeletons all waiting to leap out as our carts slowly rolled past. Even though nothing physically touched anyone, the sound effects gave the sensation that chaos was about to erupt at any moment.

    Finally, after several minutes of almost total darkness, we saw a glimmer of light and knew that we were approaching the end of our ride. Feeling my pounding heart and wiping away the tears of hysterics, I was relieved to be away from the spooks and goblins. Needless to say, that was the first and last time I was ever in a haunted house.

    Mari did not seem to feel the after affects as much as I did. I felt and walked like a drunken sailor afterwards, and having cerebral palsy only worsened the situation. The motion of the rides, especially the Whip left me wobbling more than usual. Once I regained my equilibrium, though, I was back to my old self. Even so, we decided to take it easy for the rest of the day and wandered over to a more sedate area to play a game of

Skittle Ball.

Tossing those hard balls into those rings required a certain amount of strength and coordination. Surprisingly, I found it harder to throw with my left hand than my right one. Contrary to what I believed to be true, the problem was with my left wrist, which was much weaker than the right one. Therefore, I was able to toss right-handed. From then on, I needed to choose the hand or arm that would serve me best depending on what kind of activity I wanted to do.

Later that evening as we were sitting in our PJ's and bathrobes rehashing the day's events, Aunt Camille was wrapping Mari's hair around in big, clumsy-looking rollers. I sat there in awe. For some unknown reason, I actually envied Mari having to go through that tedious ritual every night. I was jealous. Even though I had the good fortune to be born with curly hair, I was not satisfied. I longed to have the same hair problem as Mari and Nancy Wysocki who needed to have permanents on a regular basis. At the tender age of twelve, I was displaying all of the classic symptoms of a pre-adolescent.

Thanks to Mari's influence, I developed a healthy curiosity about clothing styles, hairdos and makeup. Actually, I already knew a little something about cosmetics through an introduction by a friend of my mother's, Jackie Gooding. Because Jackie did not have any children of her own, she doted on me, and later on Rick, for whom she was godmother. A native New Yorker who lived on the Upper East Side, she went to her business every day. Since it was just she and her husband, John Rankie, they shared a very carefree lifestyle.

What impressed me most about "Aunt Jackie" was that the top of her dresser resembled the cosmetic counter at Bloomingdale's. She had a vast array of lipsticks, lotions, eyeliners, nail polish, face powders and foundations, perfumes and body oils. You name it – she had it.

Aunt Jackie was one of a kind. In addition to her feminine ways, she also showed a great affection for animals to the point where she considered them her children. I remember her bird, Scottie May, the female miniature parrot who ruled the household. Only after she attended to her business, was Scottie May let out of her cage to roam free and fly about the apartment. She was an intelligent bird and delighted us with her tricks – swinging from the toaster chord, picking up her toys, and so on. Even though I crouched into a fetal position every time the bird flew in my direction, I was quite taken with her.

Despite Scottie May's flying around, we knew that she would only land on Aunt Jackie, or so we thought. One day we were all crammed into the breakfast nook watching Aunt Jackie put the finishing touches on a dish she was preparing, when suddenly the bird came swooping down and landed on my head.

Startled, I let out a piercing scream. Unfortunately, I had been sitting in Aunt Jackie's chair and so the bird mistook my head for that of her mistress. Slowly regaining my composure, I reached up and ran my fingers through my curly hair to see whether I had been blessed or not. Luckily, I had not been.

A few months later we were invited to dinner, and remembering rather vividly the last incident, I asked to have Scottie May retire to her cage while we ate. All things considered, we felt this was a reasonable request especially now that I kept my eyes glued to that bird for fear that she would swoop down on me again. To our astonishment, my simple plea was flatly denied. It was taken as an insult – "How would you feel if I asked your parents to put you in a cage? Scottie May is a child of God and this is her home!" I never meant any disrespect to either Aunt Jackie or her beloved Halfmoon or miniature parrot. All I ever wanted was to enjoy her delicious dinner without the fear of Scottie May flying overhead. However, comparing me to her bird was the final straw that broke the camel's back. Needless to say, we never set foot in her apartment again. On very special occasions, she ventured out of the rat race of the city to our home in the suburbs. Traveling that fifteen or so miles was a tremendous undertaking for someone who never wandered far from her own backyard.

Fortunately, my ego recovered, and I did not develop a phobia of birds, per se; I was only leery of them. However, as long as these feathered friends were confined to their respective cages, I was as happy as a lark.

Later that summer as part of my preparation for the new school term, I had my usual clinic appointment with Dr. Sidney Keats, physiatrist and surgeon. As a rehabilitation specialist, he prescribed and treated patients with various neurological disorders such as cerebral palsy, which was once known as Little's disease.

A thin man in his late 50s and of average height, Dr. Keats had the most annoying habit of talking with his pipe in his mouth. He also spoke in a very soft, monotone voice. Thus, some of his patients and their families had a rather difficult time hearing his words of wisdom. As often as he was asked to please speak up, sooner or later he reverted back to his usual level of intonation.

On a monthly basis, the clinic was held in the physical therapy department where the rehabilitation team convened and reviewed each case that was to be presented that day. Therapists from various disciplines, the orthotic man, the family, and the patient all congregated at the clinic and each child was properly evaluated. To perform an orthopedic evaluation, patients usually wear as little clothing as possible to enable the team to study the physical structure and movement of the involved body parts to determine the best course of intervention. As a child matures and becomes more self-conscious about his or her body, she can wear comfortable pair of shorts and a t-shirt to the assessment.

At the appropriate time, our primary therapist who gave a brief summary of her objective and her strategy to help me achieve it escorted us into the clinic. Naturally, all eyes are on the patient. For me, as somewhat of a shy child, this was a nerve-wracking experience. I always had a stomach full of butterflies feeling as though I was expected to give some sort of performance.

With some apprehension, I slowly walked over to where Dr. Keats was sitting. A therapist helped to position me on the examination table. As Dr. Keats listened to all of the reports, he started to perform his part of the exam. After testing my reflexes with his little rubber hammer he asked me to squeeze his hand to determine my strength and level of dexterity. While I was not receiving speech therapy, he had me repeat a few words, sentences, and phrases to note the formation of certain words and the amount of clarity with which I pronounced them. His favorite phrase was "Peter Piper picked a peck of pickled peppers…"

For quite some time now, the first goal of rehabilitation was to assist me in becoming as mobile as possible and then later, to tackle other areas of development. Even though I had always been able to walk, I had an unsteady gait, which in all probability would worsen as I grew older; perhaps someday I might need a wheelchair. Since physical therapy was ineffectual at this point, surgery was recommended.

The mere mention of the word "surgery" is cause for alarm even in the most courageous of individuals. People imagine the worst when contemplating going under the knife. Probably my first introduction to the antiseptic walls of the hospital as well as the drama of illness and death was through the beloved soap opera. Because I was at a very impressionable age, I mistook everything I saw and heard via the tube as real.

One summer afternoon, my grandmother took seriously ill. As a means of distraction, my mother asked me to watch her soap opera "As The World Turns." On this particular day, a tragic accident took place involving Penny Hughes, a central character, leaving her life hanging by a thread. She lay unconscious as streams of blood poured from every crevice of her face. Background music and other sound effects led one to expect the worst – death.

In the innocent eyes of an eight year old, Penny Hughes was dying and there was nothing I could do to help her. Seeing my panic-stricken face, my sitter started to turn off the set. However, I insisted that I had to continue watching because of the promise I made to my mother. So I kept my eyes glued to the tube. Of course, with my mother not home, viewing all those intense, gory scenes only made matters worse. Even though the sitter explained that the soap opera was only a story and that the characters were merely pretending, I would not buy it. For weeks afterwards, I thought about Penny lying there dying in that dreadful scene. She invaded my thoughts as well as my dreams. Then, several months later, she popped up in another series as bright and perky as ever.

Aside from the graphic hospital scenes I witnessed on TV, I was also was subjected to very descriptive accounts from my mother's cousin who survived twenty-three operations and thrived on retelling the horrors of each and every one. Because she was such a frequent patient, the hospital was her second home. Even when she was supposedly in a semi-conscious state, Jessie gave wild accounts of some of the invasive procedures she endured. Unable to separate fact from fiction, I digested every word. Between the tales involving unbearable pain to those of near catastrophe medication mix-ups, I was completely grossed out and refused to listen to another word.

My own surgery was the last thing I ever expected. All those years, whenever I had an appointment with Dr. Keats, the discussion focused on therapy sessions and how I was coping in a mainstreamed, academic environment. Never was the possibility of surgery ever mentioned.

However, because my right foot was turned in, rendering me with an unsteady gait, I was under consideration for the operation known as a triple arthrodesis. The procedure involved adjusting the chord that ran from the hip to the knee to the ankle. Simply stated, by readjusting this chord, somehow I would gain better stabilization of my right foot which would enable me to ambulate greater distances.

Aside from the time in the hospital for the actual procedure, there would be an eight-day hospitalization and twelve weeks of recuperation. "Nothing to it, Mother," said Miss Nordlin, a former physical therapist who was now Director of the Center.

Since the idea of surgery never before crossed our minds, at first, we were all rather skeptical. Then, as my father mulled it over, he realized that there was not a major organ involved as the surgery only involved the foot. Secondly, without the surgery, the possibility of me losing my ability to walk was that much greater. My parents also consulted my pediatrician, Herbert Poch, who, after carefully considering the pros and cons, gave his consent.

Knowing the consensus proved to be in favor of the surgery, I realized I was trapped. To a twelve year old, going "under the knife" meant doom. Running through my mind were thoughts: Will I live? Or die? Hospitals were scary places. One never knew what was behind those elevator doors or what sights lurked inside the patients' rooms as one passed timidly by.

Would one see someone wrapped in a total body cast resembling a mummy, or a patient with tubes running out of every orifice of his body? I was beside myself with fear, but because I did not want anyone to consider me a coward, I never expressed my concerns. I simply took the attitude of a brave little trooper rising to the occasion.

Of utmost importance to me was the fact that I wanted to begin the seventh grade with my peers and to meet our new seventh grade teachers. Taking my wishes into consideration, the surgery was scheduled for September 25th, three weeks into the semester.

Rosalyn Dorlen, a young, beautiful ambitious blonde was one of the new teachers to join the staff that year. She was bright, lively and full of enthusiasm. Ready to accept the challenge head-on, she was eager to become acquainted with all of her students and especially with me. Unlike some of my former teachers who were anxious and fearful, almost immediately, I sensed how calm and relaxed Mrs. Dorlen was with me. This was a refreshing change. Within a couple of days, I learned the reason for her laid-back approach. Mrs. Dorlen had a younger sister, Holly, who also had cerebral palsy and had been the first in her school district to be mainstreamed.

For the first time in my educational experience, I had an instructor with first-hand knowledge on the subject of cerebral palsy and I was about to miss half the semester. Somehow, that did not seem fair! However, at least I had the chance to meet her and establish a rapport with her before I left to have my surgery.

In the brief first three weeks of school, Mrs. Dorlen handed out her course outline and discussed some of the challenges as well as some of the pitfalls we may face in preparing to enter high school that following year. Her enthusiasm was contagious, and the longer she talked, the more eager I was to try to return to class as soon as I could.

Prior to the beginning of the semester, we notified the school of my impending surgery, and explained that arrangements needed to be made for home instruction. Ever since I told my mother about Mrs. Dorlen and her sister, Holly, she wanted to meet her.

Arranging for a parent-teacher conference was nothing unusual for my mother. However, she was more excited about this one than many of the others she had in the past. As a parent of a child with a disability, my mother quickly learned what a lonely and frustrating responsibility it can be. Very few parents are willing to share their innermost concerns and yet, they have the same ones. The underlying message seemed to be - you handle your situation and I'll handle mine. While families are ready to sympathize with each other, they rarely show empathy, which is the key ingredient, and the one we were seeking the most.

Needless to say, Mom found my new mentor to be charming and informative. Upon learning of my upcoming surgery, Mrs. Dorlen's eyes filled up and a tear slowly rolled down her cheek. Wondering what the cause was for this display of emotion, she explained that her sister went through the same procedure and found it to be very painful – a tidbit of which we were not aware. She also went on to tell Mom some other minor details that the professionals neglected to mention. For instance, do not be alarmed to see a pool of blood at the heel of the cast when Nancy first comes out of surgery. Her cast will run from her foot to her hip and it is immediately put on as soon as surgery is completed for proper positioning. Even though the incision has been stitched, sometimes the wound is still oozing.

Besides relating some other helpful hints, Mrs. Dorlen pledged her full support and promised to explain the situation to my classmates. With a warm hug and strong sense of compassion, my mother came away feeling that at last she had a soulmate and someone who really understood.

Happily immersed in the chaos of seventh grade where we were learning to change classes and gossip about boys, I often found myself thinking about my surgery. Somewhere in the back of my mind, I saw images of myself strapped on a gurney crying out helplessly. As the days drew nearer, the images grew worse and worse, until one day, a transforming sense of inner peace overcame me and I felt more at ease with the surgery and myself.

Because I expressed a strong desire not to discuss my surgery with anyone for fear I would become totally confused, Mom assumed the role of spokesperson and told various family members, friends and Father Moreau. For some reason, I was under the assumption that clergy never set foot out of their sacred domains, therefore, why tell him? Aside from his position, Father Moreau was a caring friend and without a doubt, he would have wondered what had happened to me. I wanted our neighbor, Helen Jago, a former operating room nurse, to know because I knew she would keep my procedure in the proper perspective and try to influence me positively.

Before I knew it, Sunday, the day I was scheduled to check into the hospital, arrived. What to pack? We had already been forewarned not to bring too many personal possessions for fear they would get either lost or stolen. Aside from the usual array of nightwear and slippers, I packed a few Nancy Drew mysteries, some scented dusting powder a friend had given me, and some chocolate candy.

I bade my brother Rick good-bye and told him that I would be O.K. Even though I wasn't too sure of that myself; I put on a brave front. After all, he was my little brother and I did not want him to see me cry. I still remember waving to him through the rear window as we drove off. Secretly, I wondered if I would every see Rick or our house again.

As we sped up the Garden State Parkway to N.J. Orthopedic Hospital where I was to be admitted, I wondered: Would I really survive this ordeal? What about the pain? Would I walk differently than I walked now? Were the nurses kind? What about injections? Oh, how I hated needles. I was so absorbed in my own thoughts that, before I knew it, I was walking up to the admissions desk.

We were pleasantly greeted, and after my parents filled out the necessary insurance forms, we were led upstairs to my room. There was that elevator – the one that set my heart racing even before the door opened. Inwardly cringing, I stepped inside and waited patiently for the doors to close. Oh, how I hated elevators. Finally we reached the second floor. Slowly, the doors parted and I was relieved to find no one lurking on the other side. Once we were off, we escorted ourselves to the nurse's station and then were shown to my room.

Little did I anticipate that I would be sharing a room with five older adolescent girls. Actually, it was a double room, and one of the partitions had been removed so that all the girls could enjoy each other's company. Walking into the brightly sunlit room, we saw that everyone was in traction. Evidently, all of these patients had curvature of the spine and were in various stages of traction depending on whether they were pre-op or post-op. Seeing these bed-ridden young women made me feel fortunate that my confinement would last only a matter of days.

After I was shown to my bed and changed into a nightgown and bathrobe, I was asked to urinate into a little cup. A few minutes later, I was sitting on my bed when a resident came rushing in asking my cooperation as he performed a cursory examination to be sure I was not coming down with something prior to surgery. He listened to my heart, tried to take my pulse, peered into my eyes and ears, etc., and finally pronounced fit for surgery. Within minutes after he left, another nurse came in pushing a cart to draw some blood. "Blood," I thought, "here I go."

With eyes as big as saucers, I watched as she started the needle and prepared vials to collect the blood. Then, she suggested that I lie down and she helped to reposition me in a way that she thought would be comfortable for me. Actually, for me, the position was very awkward, as I had no means to keep my arm still. "No, no, this will not do," I said. Next, we tried a sitting position where I sat on a chair and cradled my arm between the bed and the table. Although rather awkward for the nurse, it seemed to be the best position for my arm. Now that I was properly positioned, it was time for the needle. I could stall no longer. Why do those needles designed to extract blood seem to be so long? "Well, this is it," I thought, bravely holding back the tears. She swabbed the area with alcohol and then poked around for a suitable vein. Once she found it, the needle slowly pierced the skin. I tried not to look, but I could not seem to tear my eyes away. Slightly queasy, I watched as the vials slowly filled with blood – my blood. Beads of perspiration dotted my forehead as I stared as the vials filled with the reddish liquid that was being extracted from my body. At last, the ordeal was over and the nurse withdrew the needle and placed a round Band-Aid over the tiny pinprick. Since I was somewhat wan, she cautioned me to take it easy and to sip some orange juice to restore my color.

A few minutes later, my mother arrived and announced that Dad went home to bring back our portable television. Apparently the security guard stationed at the front desk advised him that he could do this both for the sake of convenience and as a cost effective measure. We all appreciated the kindly gesture and his thoughtfulness.

My parents remained with me until visiting hours were over for the day. Because I checked in on a Sunday, it was a relatively quiet day with most of the departments shut down for the weekend. We tried to keep the conversation light as I became acquainted with my new roommates. Since these adolescents were all older, I think they were more fascinated with the guys across the corridor than their new roommate. But this was only a temporary arrangement, and so I really did not mind.

Before we knew it, visiting hours were drawing to a close and it was time for my parents to leave. The surgery was scheduled for 6 a.m., so we knew that we would not see each other until it was over. With words of comfort and a quivering lower lip, I bravely bid my parents good-bye and wondered whether I would ever see them again.

Sensing my loneliness, a nurse's aide came and sat near my bed. She did not say much, but knowing that she was there was quite comforting. Leaning over the bed, she turned on my television, and within a few minutes she had me laughing at a scene on the tube. Unfortunately, that carefree moment was short-lived. Suddenly, two nurses came barreling in crimson and somewhat shaken. One of them explained that they had been reviewing my file and discovered to their horror that no recent x-rays had been taken. If the situation was not immediately rectified, my scheduled surgery would be postponed.

Startled and shaken myself, I had difficulty comprehending how such a mistake could have occurred. Oh, how naive I was about hospitals! Luckily, they had a solution in mind. Since the x-ray department was closed for the day, the nursing supervisor made arrangements with the hospital up the street. Their radiology department was open twenty-four hours a day.

FITTING IN

Donning my bathrobe and slippers, I was quickly helped into a wheelchair and a light blanket was draped over my lap. Escorted by a pair of nurses, I went through the brightly lit corridors into a dimly lit long passageway connecting the two hospitals. Long, heavy pipes were suspended from every direction lending certain spookiness to already tense atmosphere. For someone like me, who regarded hospitals as sterile places brimming with horror and uncertainty, this little adventure did nothing to boost my impression of hospitals.

Finally, we emerged from the darkened tunnel into another brightly lit setting as we trekked a path to their x-ray room. A technician was awaiting our arrival. Helping me out of the wheelchair, the technician glanced at my chart to note which angles of the foot were needed, suddenly realized that this particular x-ray machine did not reach the floor and therefore could not take shots of my foot. Now what?

After a brief discussion between the nurses and the technician, it was decided that there was no choice but to have me stand on top of the x-ray table. So, with both nurses holding me on either side, I stood on top of the table with my head touching the ceiling as the technician positioned and repositioned my foot to obtain all of the necessary shots. That was scary. When, at long last, the ordeal was over, I resettled into my wheelchair for the return trip.

A sigh of welcome relief swept over me as we reached my hospital room. I was never so glad to see a bed and crawl under its protective covers. Knowing how exhausted and frightened I felt, a kindhearted nurse brought me a mild sleeping pill to help me relax and eventually drift off to peaceful sleep.

Before I knew it a nurse awakened me for surgery. Opening my sleepy eyes, I noticed the room was quite dark and it seemed more like midnight than morning. Actually, it was 5:45 a.m. They needed to have me prepped and ready by 6:30. Pulling down the side rails of the bed, the nurse escorted me to the bathroom and then helped me wash and brush my teeth. After combing my hair, she draped me in a hospital gown and folded my curly hair into what resembled a shower cap. Assisting me back to bed, she gave me another little white pill and within minutes I grew very drowsy. Shortly afterwards, a team of orderlies appeared and whisked me away to surgery.

I remember having to close my eyes to keep from feeling dizzy as they wheeled me through the corridors to the massive doors of the operating room. Once inside the sterile environment, I gazed briefly at all of the machinery and into the bright lights as the anesthesiologist slowly put me out.

I have very little recollection of waking up immediately after surgery or of the few days after, but I do remember the pain. Back then pain management was not as precise or sophisticated as it is today. Pain pumps and other means of control were not yet available. In those days, pain medication was given every four hours, but seemed to only last roughly three. It was that last hour, "the witching hour," as many floor nurses referred to it, which brought tears to my eyes and havoc to the staff. Since everyone's tolerance for pain is different, pain management is not an exact science. Thank goodness, the crushing pain subsided within forty-eight hours to a dull, throbbing ache.

A few days later, I found myself across the hall visiting with the younger children as they watched their morning cartoons. It was so good to get out of that bed. Even though it took two rather large nurses to lift me from the bed to the wheelchair, it was well worth it to regain my mobility. However, once I was situated in the chair, I was forced to remain there until after dinner when the new shift came on duty. While I loved the freedom of being up and about, it made for a very long day, and often resulted in a dull backache that only was relieved by placing me in a prone position.

Sharing a room with a bunch of teenagers brought all sorts of night antics. I remember one night when the natives seemed particularly restless and decided to establish a secret code with the boys on the other side of the wall. Armed with their bedpans, the pranksters began rattling their pans against the bars of their beds creating a powerful racket that alarmed the nurses and brought them running to our room. At first they appeared angry, but then they seemed to reconcile themselves to the fact that the patients were teenagers merely testing their oats.

A hospital is an exhausting place in which to recuperate. Because of the extended visiting hours, taking a nap is virtually impossible. While I loved the attention and most of my visitors, I yearned to go home and indulge in the quietness of familiar surroundings. Friends and neighbors sent lots of cards and other goodies. Aside from my family, Father Moreau came to see me and happened to arrive just in time for lunch. So, he stayed a bit longer than usual to help me with my meal. Feeding myself was not the problem as much as unwrapping everything including the utensils. Unless one is reasonably coordinated, this is an impossible task. Often patients were frustrated and overwhelmed even before they started their meals.

Dr. Keats, an early bird, had the annoying habit of making rounds at about 6 a.m. A few times, he came to see me and my eyes were half open. So, when he inquired about my health, he received a very sleepy, muddled reply. I recall one time he caught me in the middle of my bed bath. I was so embarrassed that I blushed from head to toe. Empathizing with my predicament, the nurse quickly threw a towel over me. After he left, I thanked her for her sensitivity and for her prompt action. Her response to me was, "He should have known better and respected your right for privacy."

FITTING IN

Slowly but surely I was making progress. My incision was healing nicely and Dr. Keats was pleased with his finesse in the operating room. Finally, he announced that I would be released the next day. I was elated and so were my parents. I was finally busting out of this joint!

With my eyes barely open the next day, I had my temperature taken by the nurse, and she found it to be slightly elevated. After conferring with the doctor, she called home to tell my parents of the possibility that I might have an infection and that antibiotics would more than likely take care of it. Alarmed by the words "temperature" and "infection," my parents rushed to the hospital. By the time they arrived, my temperature disappeared. Apparently, I was warm from sleep and a blanket wrapped tightly around me nothing more and nothing less. So, that little fiasco cost us an extra day of hospitalization, not to mention some additional wear and tear on our nerves.

Twenty-four hours later, I was on my way home. With a hip-length cast, maneuvering me into the back seat of our four-door Ford was quite tricky. However, between the nurse and my father, they managed to squeeze me, and my thirty-pound cast, into our car. Thank goodness we only lived ten miles from the hospital, since the ride home was rather uncomfortable. Several minutes later, we pulled into our driveway – I was home!

Running out of her house to welcome me home, Helen

Jago, kindly helped my father get me into the house and upstairs to our living room that had been converted into a makeshift bedroom. The sofa was made up to be my temporary bed and we purchased a commode from our local pharmacy.

After the excitement faded and I was settled, I snuggled down into our comfortable couch for a much needed nap. I was so exhausted from too many nights of interrupted sleep either from the pain or the antics of my roommates.

For the next couple of days, I had a steady stream of visitors – friends and neighbors who wanted to see how I was progressing. Get-well cards arrived by the dozens as well as flowers and other assorted tokens of affection. Faithfully, Father Moreau called on me each week to attend to my spiritual needs. Having our rector come to see me so often made me feel important and much loved. I looked forward to his visits tremendously.

Shortly after I arrived home, I noticed that I had great difficulty controlling my arms. I always had some involuntary movement, but it was never this severe. During the day, it was tolerable, but at night the constant movement of my arms seemed to exacerbate. After two sleepless nights, I was a wreck. By the third night, I was desperate.

It was nearly 11 o'clock in the evening when we decided to phone our pediatrician, Herbert Poch. In his opinion, my body was having a reaction to all of the drugs I had been given in the hospital. These foreign medications were causing an adverse reaction. Dr. Poch prescribed a mild sedative which helped alleviate my symptoms and put me back on the right track.

Slowly but surely we eased into our new routine. A makeshift bedroom in our living room meant that privacy was almost nonexistent with the exception of when I needed to use the commode. I think my worst fear was to be caught on the commode and have the doorbell ring. To my great relief, that never happened.

In the mornings after my father left for work and Rick was off to school, my mother would help me sponge bathe and prepare for the rest of the day. All my meals needed to be brought to me since I was helplessly confined to the couch. Probably, the most difficult meal was dinner because everyone liked to eat together. To work around my setup, we dined on our snack tables, which worked out rather well.

Despite all the efforts to keep my spirits high, there were occasions when I felt rather low. Although these times were few and far between, my temporary dependency and lack of mobility got the better of me, and, at times, the tears just flowed. Fortunately, Bonnie Brae seemed to sense my low moods and she would jump on the couch to try to comfort me. She would nuzzle me in just the right places, and as I stroked her, I reminded myself that my situation was only temporary.

Three weeks after I came home I started tutoring sessions. When a tutor is needed for a homebound student, a notice is posted by the Board of Education. As it turned out, my former fifth grade teacher, Myra Trieber, consented to be my homebound instructor. Since we lived around the corner from the school, she arrived by 3:30 and stayed for about an hour three days a week. While three hours of individual instruction did not seem adequate to accomplish a regular workload, working on a one-to-one basis we exceeded this goal.

I was somewhat nervous about reestablishing our relationship, but once we delved into the books, it all seemed quite natural. We spent about fifteen minutes on each subject. We reviewed reading assignments and worked on projects meant to enhance the material learned. I had a weekly spelling test and a math quiz. All things considered, I did very well.

Several weeks passed before it was time to return to the hospital for my postoperative checkup. If all went well, I would come home with a walking cast. Finally, I would be on my feet. Contrary to my expectations, I was in for a major disappointment.

Waiting in the crowded, darkened hallway for my name to be called, I heard loud shrieks emanating from the plaster room. Alarmed, I could not imagine what was going on. Prior to coming, I learned about the power saw that was used to cut the cast off. Despite the loud noise, the saw only cut the plaster and not the flesh. With this in mind, I could not fathom why this young girl was screaming. Well, sure enough, as the doctor saw droplets of blood seeping through the gauze of the cast he was removing, the nature of the problem became clear. He was cutting into the girl's flesh. After a thousand apologies, a shaken resident discovered he forgot to put the safety gage on the saw.

By the time my turn came, I was extremely nervous. My father accompanied me into the room. Of both my parents, he was the one with the stronger stomach. After they hoisted me up on the table and positioned me, the doctor reassured me that he had the safety latch on the saw so I would not be cut. With the incident still fresh on his mind, he proceeded very slowly.

Suddenly, an ear-piercing sound filled the room as pieces of plaster crumbled and fell to the floor. Within minutes, the teeth-chattering procedure was over and the doctor carefully placed my scaly leg on the table. Was that really my leg?

During the months of immobilization, the leg muscles atrophied and long, dark hairs had emerged where the nurse had shaved it prior to surgery. Aghast by its shrunken appearance, I could not believe that this shriveled up leg was really mine. In addition, it was both stiff and sore. The sensation of pins and needles ran through the limb as it lay on the table. After a semi-sponge bath, the doctor wrapped it tightly in an ace bandage to give it some support. Standing on it was impossibility. In fact, to our dismay, it took months before I could walk again.

Propping the leg up on a couple of pillows, I was extremely careful about moving it. Bending the knee joint was excruciating. Whenever I attempted to bend the knee, I would get it to a certain point and then it snapped and locked. Every time the knee locked, I had to yell for someone to gently press on the knee and pull it down. Sometimes this occurred during the night, arousing me from a dead sleep. Bengay and hot compresses worked to relive the stiffness to some extent, but time proved to be the real healer.

Over the next few weeks, my leg gradually improved and I was able to tolerate it in a vertical position. Because the bottom of my foot was so sensitive, bearing weight on it was agony. With warm soaks and a light massage, I slowly regained the use of my foot. I kept the ace bandage on for several weeks as well as a slipper. With some assistance, I was able to take a step or two. Since I had not walked in almost twelve weeks, I needed to retrain my brain to establish a walking pattern of placing one foot after the other. For some unexplained reason, the most difficult part seemed to be deciding what to do with one foot as I shuffled the other one into place.

Eventually, I was able to walk very short distances

provided I hung onto something or someone. The thought of walking unassisted sent shivers through my spine. As much as I wanted to walk independently, I lacked the confidence to simply let go. At that time, we had a tea cart in our living room and one day I had the notion to try and push that cart. So, with my brother's help, we were able to line it all up and I slowly pushed the cart a few feet. Wow, I was exhausted! As I eased myself into a chair, I could not contain my excitement for now I knew I was officially on my way.

Finally, it was time for my postoperative visit with Dr. Keats. I gingerly walked into the physical therapy room hanging on to my mother's arm. Sensing that we were growing tired with the present arrangement, Miss Nordulyn, a former physical therapist, took me aside and got me walking independently again.

Standing directly in front of me with her hands lightly touching my shoulders, she helped me slowly begin to take off. Together, we ambulated the length of the corridor – I walking frontwards and she walking backwards. So engrossed was I in choosing which foot to put forward first, I had not realized that I was walking completely on my own. I came to clinic needing to hold on to someone, and two hours later, I left an independent young lady.

At last, I had my freedom. Now, I could resume the normal life of a thirteen year old. Even though I still needed assistance to negotiate the stairs, it felt great to be in the privacy of my own bedroom. I loved my bedroom and I took great pride in keeping it tidy and clean. Since I had left my little sanctuary some time ago, I was surprised to find it cluttered with all sorts of token gifts that I had received throughout my recuperation. Nevertheless, I now had the opportunity to go through them and recount all of the memories they held.

For instance, Nancy Wysocki, my backyard friend, was a frequent visitor on Friday nights. Since my life was primarily filled with adults, I really looked forward to seeing her and listening to tales of the gossip circulating around her schoolyard. Nancy attended a private, Catholic school for girls, and I devoured the stories of all the tricks these students tried on the nuns. At times, when the gossip lines ran dry, we resorted to a game of either Monopoly or Rack-o. Of course, we always managed to stuff ourselves with junk food too.

Even though my desk remained empty, I seemed to be on the minds of some of my classmates. One day two of them came to our front door bearing gifts. Apparently, they had taken up a collection and brought me a present and a beautiful card that had been signed by everyone at school, including the principal.

Delighted to have two of my school chums standing on our doorstep, my mother invited them in and led them to where I was reclining on our couch. At that point, I still was in the hip-length cast. Upon seeing me with this monstrosity of a cast, their innocent eyes popped wide open. Happy to see them, I asked them to sit down. Nervously, they accepted my invitation as they practically sat on top of each other. After some fumbling around, they regained their composure and helped me to open the gift they had so generously given me. Since the box was small, I knew that it had to be some kind of jewelry. Managing to get the wrapping off, I opened the box to find a small charm of the Praying Hands fastened to a gold-colored necklace. It was beautiful. Pulling the card out of the envelope, I saw that it had a picture of the Praying Hands too. A bit flustered, I read the front in which a scroll script had, "For you in God's Service." Obviously, the card was for a newly ordained minister and not for someone like me. The person chose the card because it complemented the necklace and not for what it said. It was an honest mistake made by a couple of kids with the best of intentions.

Other presents that were stacked on my bedroom chair ranged from dusting powder and perfume to Nancy Drew mysteries. I also received candy, cookies, and other goodies that never quite made it to my bedroom because they were gobbled up as fast as they came.

At my last postoperative checkup, I had been given permission to return to school on March 1st. I was ecstatic. Even though I had received plenty of attention from my family, friends, and church members, I longed to be back in the classroom meeting the challenges of the seventh grade with my classmates.

Aside from climbing the long tiled staircase to the second floor, I think one of my worst fears was that I would find myself behind in my studies. Happily, I found my situation to be quite the contrary. In some subjects, I was as much as a chapter ahead, and in others, I was right on target. So, my fears were for naught and I felt myself gradually fitting into their routine.

Still rather unsure of myself when going down steps, I held on tightly to the bannister as well as whoever was escorting me. I had a nightmare in which I saw myself tumbling down long flights of stairs. I am not sure as to how a psychologist would interpret a dream like that one, but I understood it as representing my adjustment period with my newly mended foot.

Ask any teacher of the seventh and eighth grade and she will claim that she either loves it or hates it. Her ability to handle a group of emerging adolescents seems to depend largely on her patience, adaptability, and sense of humor. Laughter is the best medicine and when working with preteens who question your every move and test your authority at every turn, a hearty chuckle now and then is a blessing in disguise. Roz Dorlen knew how to make use of laughter.

Because Mrs. Dorlen was our science teacher, she also

acquired the role of health instructor, that is, for the girls in the grade. So, every Wednesday afternoon, the girls would gather in one classroom and the guys in the other to discuss their emerging sexuality and the issues related to it. Believe me, it must have taken a lot of patience to seriously talk about menstruation to a group of immature adolescents. While I believe they were intensely interested in the subject, they felt awkward and embarrassed discussing it aloud. That is, they did until Roz Dorlen vented some of her own concerns from when she was a teenager, and we felt much more at ease.

    I guess I was about eleven when the subject of female sexuality really presented itself. The dog across the street was pregnant and about to deliver. So, my mother thought that it was the perfect time to broach the topic. I remember sitting in my parents' bedroom and I saw a booklet lying on my mother's dresser titled, I Am A Woman Now. When she gave it to me, she encouraged me to read it. I recall I started to browse through the pages and she started to tell me about a monthly "friend" who would begin to "visit." Its arrival was nature's way of preparing my body to perhaps have a baby someday when I was older. With the probability that I would never marry, she really did not discuss the subject of me having a baby. At that point, I was overwhelmed with information, and I had just learned about the menses without bothering to ask about the man's role in conception until much later.

Most parents find it extremely difficult to discuss sex with their children. I think their awkwardness with the delicate subject stems from a number of factors. Perhaps the first major obstacle is not wanting to acknowledge that the child is maturing. Second, especially if the child has a disability, chances are that the family expresses either denial or fear at the prospect of their child developing into an adolescent with a healthy curiosity.

As we listened to our teacher who explained how she felt about the emerging changes that took place within her own body, we started to feel more comfortable and established a level of trust with each other. Probably, the biggest question dominating the mind of every preteen girl is, "Did you get it yet?" No matter what the general opinion is today, menstruation is a big deal. It is the signal of physical maturity and that the body is capable of conception and reproduction. Fully understanding the implications of this process and dispelling its myths is essential to fostering a healthy attitude.

Coupled with a discussion about menstruation, we talked about the importance of good hygiene, breast development, raging hormones, acne, hem length, and hairstyles. We were just filled with questions to be answered, issues to be discussed, and ideas to be shared. Since I was a keen listener and observer, I was absorbing information like a sponge. I was curious enough to want to know, but I was always afraid to ask.

Around my eleventh birthday, I remember our pediatrician asked my mother if she had discussed the facts of life with me yet. Since I was on the verge of developing, it would not be too much longer until I started menstruating. It was both psychologically and emotionally important that I be as prepared as possible. "Because Nancy has C.P., does not mean that she will not be able to bear a child," he said. "While conception and delivery might be more difficult, the possibility of motherhood need not be ruled out."

Through this informal sex education class, we chatted about different brands of sanitary protection, emotions and hormones, handling cramps, and the importance of personal grooming. The underlying message was that we were not alone – every woman in the world goes through the stages of womanhood starting with puberty to menstruation to menopause. It seems too, that the attitude of this monthly occurrence is referenced by the synonym used by a particular generation.

For instance, in my grandmother's day, it was referred to as the "curse," and every young woman dreaded this time of the month. A generation later, women referred to it as their "friend" through which they could now bear children, and which they believed to be the reason they were put on this earth. Nowadays, menstruation is most commonly called a "period" which does not seem to express any particular view one way or the other.

Like every other girl my age, I was looking forward to the day when I became a woman. While I got caught up in the anticipation of this entry into womanhood, I was somewhat apprehensive as to whether or not I would be able to take care of myself. In those days before the advent of protection one could stick onto their panties, women wore sanitary belts, which required a great deal of manual dexterity to handle properly. But, as my mother said, "There was no need to worry about it until it happened."

One Saturday, a few weeks later, we were on our way to Haynes Department Store in Westfield, when I discovered this brownish discoloration in my panties. Excitedly, I called my mother into the bathroom. We managed to find the little kit that we kept conveniently stored for this special passage into womanhood. After Mom helped me, we headed for our scheduled destination. We were in search of an Easter dress and nothing was going to interrupt our plans.

According to the little pamphlet contained within the kit, a monthly cycle lasts approximately three to seven days, and, by this time, I was well into my ninth day. Since I had not experienced any pain or discomfort, I managed to go to school with frequent visits to the nurse. Now that I had officially entered womanhood, I felt very grownup but at the same time, rather concerned that everyone would catch on and wonder why I needed to go to the nurse so often. No one seemed to voice their concern or raise questions – the boys were still too naïve and the girls were too preoccupied with their own agendas to care.

When my period extended into its twelfth day, Dr. Poch grew rather alarmed and sent me to my mother's gynecologist. Secretly, Mom thought I was hemorrhaging and I wondered if I was on the brink of death. I stayed home a day from school to keep my feet elevated thinking that might decrease the flow. By the time we arrived at his office the next evening, my period had stopped. My anxiety may have caused it to stop or it might have been its natural occurrence. Who really knew? All the doctor did was feel my stomach and commented that I had an extended period which occurs in one of every 10,000 girls. Thank goodness, it never happened that way again.

Indeed, I was growing-up. Aside from having to master the trick of putting on a sanitary napkin with spastic fingers, I had to cope with the emotional ups and downs of maturing. Like most other girls of this age, I think my greatest fear was to be caught with a bloodstain on the back of my dress. Heaven forbid!! Of course, I quickly learned the advantages to wearing dark colored print skirt to conceal any noticeable mistakes.

It was not more than a few weeks before I fully acclimated myself to the classroom once again. Although I tired faster and keeping up with the mounds of homework was a challenge that consumed most evenings, I loved being back in the swing of things. With graduation only a few months away, there were several special events coming up which held a particular interest for me. Aside from our class play, seventh grade dance, and the finale of graduation, I had to move on to a new school.

Somehow I had to mentally and emotionally prepare myself to leave the familiar walls of Locust School and enter the chaos of Abraham Clark High School. In our town, the eighth grade was housed within the high school building in a contained area. Fortunately, the overall layout did not present too much of a problem. However, the main concern was that I would be intermingling with approximately 250 kids from various parts of town.

At that time, the principal, Harrison Morson, who was also a member of our church, invited my parents to tour the high school and to get a feel for the layout and the kinds of situations that I might encounter. Aside from the mounds of homework, a daily change of schedules and a different teacher for every subject, this proposed transition would be a cinch.

Contemplating the thought of coping in such a fast-paced environment caused radiated caution signals galore. Even our neighbor, Helen Jago, suggested that I explore the possibility of attending St. Joseph's Girls Catholic High School. While that idea did not address the present problem of eighth grade, it was an alternative thought for the future in case I was not able to cope with the demands of a semi-large high school.

Even though I appreciated our neighbor's concern, I instinctively knew that a parochial school was not for me. After school, I often accompanied my mother on one of our shopping excursions to Malin's, our local five and dime store or to the market to pick up a few items. Undoubtedly, we would meet the kids from St. Joseph's, dressed so prim and proper in their uniforms. One thought they were "little angels," but in reality these students were actually "devils" in disguise. If they did not stop and stare at me while I was strolling down the aisles, they made insulting little comments such as: "Why does she talk so funny?" and "I bet she doesn't know how much two plus two is."

Unfortunately, to many of these kids, I was a freak. Because they had no concept of a person with a disability, they took great pride in mocking and belittling me. Unless there was someone in their family with some kind of limitation, these kids were not exposed to anyone who functioned differently or who had special needs. There were no special education classes in Catholic schools. Students who fell into the category of needing special services simply were not enrolled in that school. Despite my fears and apprehensions, their behavior reassured me that I wanted to make the transition into eighth grade with my classmates. While I knew it would never be the same again, I wanted to have a few familiar faces around me.

As the seventh grade school year wound to a close, in keeping with tradition, it was almost time for our annual school play. This year we decided to put on our own production of West Side Story. Since a blossoming romance was stirring between two of our classmates, Charles Bowden and Marilyn Schultz, it seemed only fitting that they be cast as the star-crossed lovers.

Unlike some other plays where I had a very small role, this time I was part of a large chorus. Even though, I could not carry a tune, I enjoyed the group involvement. Most of all, however, I enjoyed watching the rehearsals and the ongoing private romance between the two love birds, Charles and Marilyn. Between the starry-eyed gazes, hand holding, and those passionate kisses, it was hard to tell where the acting stopped and infatuation began.

Since West Side Story is a musical, we needed to draw on the skill and talent of our music teacher, Marjorie Hoff. A short, stocky widow in her late fifties, Mrs. Hoff was a strict disciplinarian who kept order by frightening the daylights out of little children. We were instructed to sit straight in our chairs with our feet on the floor. If we neglected to sit properly, we would not be able to sing properly. In order to sing properly, one must be able to drop their jaw and enunciate every single syllable.

Aside from her penchant for music, Mrs. Hoff was an

ardent animal lover. So as not to leave her beloved pet at home, Mrs. Hoff would bring her Maltese who would happily perch himself on top of her piano. Needless to say, the class was entranced by the little ball of fur stationed on the piano's edge. I, on the other hand, was scared to death. Since I had yet to completely overcome my fear of dogs, this little dog made me a nervous wreck. Every time the animal moved, I jumped.

As much as I loved singing, I often dreaded the thought of having to go to music class. On rainy days, the class always seemed somewhat rambunctious and their attention span was nonexistent. Instead of yelling at us, she simply banged on those piano keys. Believe me, one never saw a group of unruly youngsters come to attention so fast. In those days, kids still respected their elders and especially their teachers. However, despite her idiosyncrasies, Mrs. Hoff was a dedicated professional who taught students the value of school spirit and team effort.

Whether she was teaching us certain selections from West Side Story or our school song, her instructions were "to drop your jaw and enunciate." Between practicing for the play, Mrs. Hoff always managed to squeeze in the lyrics of our school song. Since the name of our school was Locust, each letter stood for a particular line. It went:

""L" is for Locust in our hearts to always stay.

"O" is for obey which we try to do each day.

"C" is for our colors that are white and bright blue.

"U" is for understanding the lessons we do.

"S" is for the studying we do day and night and

"T" is for the teachers who help us to do right."

Three rounds of this song increased everyone's school spirit and raised morale to its highest.

Contributing everyone's time, talent and energy made our school play a success. I wonder how many of the audience members caught on to the fact that the romance on stage was ever as sweet off stage as well. In fact, the infatuation lasted until Marilyn moved away to attend a private school.

I remember the young couple at our school dance. Despite the visions of grandeur and having everyone pair off to become a couple, most of us still preferred to chat among those of our own sex. While some of us were boy crazy, the rest of us were only in the talking stages. Talk is not only cheap but also often highly exaggerated. The boys hung out in one corner with their hands in their pockets totally immersed in conversations about ball games, hot rods, and pinup girls, while the girls were busy dancing around with each other. Probably the only time that the sexes truly came together was to autograph each other's yearbooks.

Depending on the status of the relationship, some graduates wrote reams explaining how they would miss each other and made unending promises to keep in touch. Time and time again, my fellow classmates penned, "Nancy, you are an inspiration and someone to be truly admired." For the majority of others, this was a chore in itself because most of us had no inkling as to what to write.

Fortunately, I did not have that problem – I had a rubber stamp that only said, "Sincerely, Nancy Jaekle." Needless to say, my message was short and sweet. Foreseeing this situation beforehand, my parents ordered a rubber stamp especially for this occasion. Knowing that there would be yearbooks to sign and aware of my poor penmanship, they were in search of an alternate means in which I could give my John Hancock. While my way was slightly different, I think most of my classmates were impressed by such an innovative solution.

Underneath some of those seemingly cool exteriors, many of us suffered a bout of pre-graduation jitters. I felt this was the beginning of the end. Fear of the unknown seeped in and quickly invaded the very core of my being. After all, Locust School had been my haven for the past seven years and now I was about to embark on new adventures in the less sheltered environment of high school.

Struggling to fight back the tears and to control a quivering lower lip, we rehearsed for graduation. Pairing off according to height, we practiced marching in to the traditional song appropriate for the occasion, "Pomp and Circumstance." Slowly, we proceeded down the aisle trying our best to keep an equal distance apart. As a whole, I think our class did rather well. Even our little mischief-makers seemed to be cooperating.

As June 22 rapidly approached, I found myself besieged with uncertainties regarding my future. Leaving the familiar behind and extending beyond to explore new horizons creates a certain amount of anxiety even for those of us in the best of circumstances. Of course, I worried about being accepted by my peers, keeping up with the homework, taking notes, etc. Needless to say, I had a severe case of pre high school anxiety.

Although I was happy that I had finally achieved this milestone, I longed to return to the days when we did simple projects, spent the afternoon writing short stories or planting seeds in our makeshift garden, or went on field trips and had some sort of crazy adventure on the way. Those were the days. In less than a week, those precious moments would fade into a pleasant memory to be forever imbedded in my mind.

Graduation day finally arrived. Donned in cap and gown, I peeked through the door and saw everyone seated in the auditorium waiting for the ceremony to start. Suddenly, I did not feel as lonely as I envisioned all of my classmates with me at the high school. I knew it was going to be a difficult period of adjustment, but as long as I had someone in my corner, I would manage to muddle through. While I had been offered other educational options, I chose to continue my schooling with my friends.

As we stood on the dais singing our school song, my eyes scanned the audience and I counted my blessings. I realized all of the teachers who shared in the responsibility of preparing me for the future. Thanks to their dedication, I had a solid foundation in which to build on and the determination to do it. Who knew what the future held!

5

Usually by mid-summer, a wave of excitement swept over me as I begin to notice store shelves stocked with loose-leaf binders, notebooks, brightly colored paper, pens, pencils, and racks of school bags and lunchboxes featuring the most popular television heroes of the day. In the final days of summer before eighth grade, I wandered through the aisles of school supplies contemplating what I needed for the coming year. I could not help but feel a rush of anticipation and exhilaration. Selecting new book covers somehow started to mentally prepare me for the new term.

This year, I would be a student matriculating in a different school – a much larger one. Before the official school year got into full swing, Mr. Morson invited us over to see the layout of the rooms and to determine what arrangements could be made to have my typewriter wheeled from class to class. Mulling over my situation, Mr. Morson decided to divide most of the responsibility of transporting the typewriter between classrooms to two honor students. At least, that was the initial plan.

I was also assigned a "big sister" to escort me from classroom to classroom and to lend a hand whenever it was needed. While I appreciated having someone nearby to offer assistance, I also liked the idea of having someone to be friends with even more. In any new situation, the first day is always the hardest. I remember waving good-bye to my mother and reassuring her not to worry while I, on the other hand, had the familiar nervous rumbling around in my stomach, that is until I was introduced to my homeroom teacher, Michael S. He had been briefed on the specifics of my needs before the school year began, and he took charge. With a commanding presence, but sense of humor, he tried to put everyone at ease. He offered a bit of background on himself and then told us about homeroom and what he expected of us. Later, I learned that he was to be my math teacher as well.

After introducing himself, this six foot tall, blue-eyed man with sandy brown hair passed out our schedules and told us that there were eight periods in a day, but only room for seven. Therefore, every day we would be directed to skip one. At first this new system sounded complicated and somewhat asinine, but it did have some advantages. Probably the most important, as far as we were concerned, was that if we did not like a particular subject or teacher, we would have a day's reprieve every eight days.

Since I really loved English, I was really looking forward to fourth period. When I entered the classroom, there stood my typewriter already plugged in and ready to go. Surprisingly, it was situated in front of the classroom adjacent to the teacher's desk on a rather long table that ran almost the length of the room. We were given our first assignment, to write out the Pledge of Allegiance word for word.

While the assignment sounded simple enough, it really wasn't. True, all of us knew the Pledge of Allegiance by heart - by rote. However, typing or writing it out proved to be a different story. There I sat ever so carefully pecking out the words, inserting commas and periods wherever I thought they were needed. Finally, I had finished. Smiling at myself for doing what I thought was a decent job, I raised my hand for our new teacher to come and mark it. Within a matter of seconds, a petite woman in her late twenties with shoulder length brown hair and a rather firm expression started to correct it. Heartbroken, I sat there and watched her as she rapidly drew big, red circles around what seemed like every other word and punctuation mark. Without a word, she passed the paper back to me. Written in bold, red magic marker was the grade "40." I could not believe my eyes;

never in my life had I gotten such a poor grade. Watching the teacher record it in her grade book, I was both humiliated and embarrassed. Until then, I always considered English to be one of my best subjects. Now, I had a "40" next to my name.

I had failed my very first assignment. Lying awake that night, I began to have doubts as to whether I was eighth grade material. I knew I was undergoing a period of adjustment and that it would take time before everything worked itself out. Perhaps I just needed to try a little harder and to have a bit more patience. After all, I realized that it was much too soon to declare the move to Abraham Clark High School a mistake.

While I appeared to be flunking English, I was, surprisingly, excelling in math. We were studying our multiplication tables and our teacher challenged us to memorize them up to the fifteenth times table for extra credit, which I did. Besides the extra credit, I was doing very well with multiplication and division. That marking period I received a "90" – my first ever in mathematics. For some reason, I had done a complete, unexpected about face – English "75" and Math "90." My parents were flabbergasted. My emotions, on the other hand, were mixed. I was delighted with my math grade, but perplexed as to why I was doing so poorly in English.

So, for my first term, I received three 75's and one 90. While it was not exactly a bad report card, it did indeed call for improvement, and I was determined to do something about it.

Meanwhile, I experienced my first official indoctrination into the social scene of high school when I attended a pep rally to get into the school spirit. The name of our football team was the Roselle Rams and they were good! Trying to be kind, a teacher escorted my Big Sister into the auditorium and told us to sit in the third row. Not really knowing what a pep rally entailed, I felt rather honored to be seated so close to the stage. Shortly thereafter, a stream of enthusiastic cheerleaders carrying red and grey pom-poms came prancing in to do their cheers. Screaming at the top of their lungs, the girls recited their cheers, and with each one the spirit of the fans mounted and soared until the noise was deafening. For someone with sensitive hearing, the vibrating loudness was overwhelming. At one point, I thought my eardrums were going to burst and I could not wait to get out of there.

Finally, I was able to escape. While I appreciated the school spirit and the admiration for their team held by my classmates, I wished it could have been demonstrated in a quieter way. By the time I reached home, I was so drained and worn out that I could barely hold up my own head. The minute I came through the door, I collapsed on the couch. I was just exhausted. I had had enough team spirit for one day.

After the first few months, everything began to settle

down and fall into place. My particular schedule started with gym class from which I was excused for obvious reasons. So, I had a study period that I spent in the library reviewing notes and preparing for my day's classes. This temporary arrangement worked out well as it gave me time to become acquainted with the librarians and their policies.

The head librarian was a very tall, thin woman with long brown hair and big, dark rimmed glasses. Indeed, Mrs. Romanisky did appear to be the studious type, which aptly matched her position. She was sharp but soft-spoken. Although at times it did not show, she loved kids and never failed to take the extra minute or two to assist someone in finding what they really needed.

On days when I had spare time, I wandered over to the autobiographies to make a reading selection. My interest in reading self-accounts of people with various disabilities managing to seek ways of overcoming them, was just as acute as it is today. I remember the book Karen and the sequel With Love From Karen about a girl who had cerebral palsy. The books recounted the numerous obstacles she and her family overcame. I loved that book. For once, I had found someone with whom I could identify and admire.

As a way of broadening my reading appetite, the librarian introduced me to Louisa May Alcott and her famous novels,

Little Women and Little Men. Like millions of other girls my age, I laughed at the antics of Meg and Jo and cried my heart out when Beth died. For extra credit in English, I remember writing a paper comparing and contrasting the two novels.

Submerging myself into the rhythm of high school life, I found myself forming some new friendships. My first friend was Linda Hargrave, a friendly but shy girl who had a big crush on our homeroom teacher. Since she had a brother the same age as mine, my family managed to befriend her entire family, thus turning our relationship into a family affair. Unfortunately, Linda's mother had several health problems and she passed away a few years later.

Through Linda I became acquainted with Madeline (Mattie) Mandell, a short, petite, sensitive girl who was serious about her schoolwork, and who had a mischievous side too. Mattie was just plain fun to be with.

The last person in our foursome was Carol Aspell. Carol was an albino and had the whitest hair and eyelashes that I had ever seen on such a young person. Despite her beautiful blue eyes, her visual acuity was so poor that she often held her book within inches of her face. Even though she sat in the first row of every class, copying notes from the blackboard presented a real challenge. Trying to be as inconspicuous as possible, Carol inched herself up close to the blackboard practically coming nose to nose with it to read what had been written. If mimeographed copies of supplement material were passed around, the teacher always made sure she received the darkest one.

In an awkward way, Carol's visual handicap turned into an advantage for me. For some odd reason, our science teacher, Mr. Frederick D'Antoni, seemed to confuse Carol's visual handicap with mine and he would offer to read me the questions. While in some cases of people with cerebral palsy vision is affected, mine was not. So, I always politely declined and reminded him to pose the same offer to Carol.

Of average height with brown hair and big green eyes, Mr. D'Antoni was soft-spoken and even-tempered. Still, in his early thirties, he related well to his students and brought the fascinating subject of science to life for us. Learning about light and color and the evaporation of water were some of the topics we explored. Unfortunately, science was not until the last period of my school day, and by that time, I was tired and not functioning at my best.

One of the hardest tasks for me was learning how to take good notes. In grammar school, we merely copied what was on the blackboard. However, now we had to try to figure out what was noteworthy and what was not. To do so, we not only had to rely on what was written on the blackboard, but also we had to focus on the lecture in order to recognize and jot down the main points. Even though I had taken a mini course the previous summer on that very same subject, I soon came to the realization that I did not have the manual dexterity needed to keep pace with someone's voice. This posed quite a dilemma.

At first, I thought of bringing in a tape recorder to record the lectures and then transcribe them at home. Of course, with that arrangement, I would be typing into the wee hours of the morning. Obviously, this would not do. Lack of sleep made my physical condition worsen, not to mention how it negatively impacted my mental state.

After posing the problem to my occupational therapist, we came up with the viable solution of carbon paper. This was in 1968 and computers were not as much a part of everyday life as they are today. Easily slipped between two sheets of notebook paper, carbon paper proved to be the answer. Thereafter, I looked for a student in each class who took comprehensive notes and had legible handwriting. While there was some anxiety over using the inky side of the carbon paper the right way, eventually everyone got the hang of it. In fact, some students volunteered to be a note taker because they felt that by taking notes for me they were taking better notes for themselves.

Thanks to the surgery I had on my foot, I was walking with a good, steady gait and mobility posed less of a problem. Therefore, we thought that it was time to concentrate on another area of development – my speech. Until now, the crux of all of my therapy centered on the physical aspect and more specifically my arms and legs; however, now that I was older, communication and the ability to make myself understood held top priority. Even then, I had high hopes of having a job someday and so it was imperative that my speech be as clear as possible.

With a written order from my physiatrist, Dr. Keats, for speech therapy, I was scheduled to receive a half-hour weekly session at Children's Specialized Hospital in Mountainside, New Jersey. Since my speech pattern had already been established coupled with the fact of my age, therapy might prove difficult, but working on my breathing patterns and certain sounds could be doable.

Prior to the start of speech therapy, a routine hearing test was administered to see if there had been any hearing loss. It stands to reason that if one is unable to hear certain sounds, then their ability to speak will be affected too. However, this was not the case with me. My hearing had always been acute, and I often overheard tidbits of conversations that were not meant for my ears. So, in my family's opinion, this hearing test was a mere formality.

Seated in a tiny soundproof booth with headphones on, I listened to each sound and indicated in which ear I heard it.

Whether high or low, sharp or dull, I heard them all. In fact, the test indicated that my right ear was keener than my left. Perhaps this is not surprising especially since my right side is much more involved than the left one.

In the next session, I was tested on my ability to articulate different sounds. Seated opposite me, the therapist held a packet of flash cards and I was to give the name of each object. We did this a few times. Then, these words were extended into phrases or sentences. Finally, we concentrated on groups of sounds. According to the results, my greatest difficulty seemed to be in forming the sounds: s, m, p and b.

Part of any evaluation included an examination of the oral cavity or the mouth. The therapist noted the number of teeth, size of the tongue and palate, as well as the structure and movement of the jaw. Any impairment or abnormality of these structures would affect my speech and ability to articulate.

One day I came home close to tears because my speech therapist told me that I had a big tongue. Being thirteen, I was super-sensitive to learning that I had another handicap. After all, I was just starting to cope with the erupting blemishes dotting my face and now I had a big tongue! What next?

Overridden with anger, I refused to work with that therapist again. I was not about to subject myself to another insult. Within a few days, my anger subsided. With some coaxing and a little psychology, my mother got me to return to the therapist's office the next week. After my mother had explained the problem, the therapist immediately suggested that there had been a misunderstanding – my tongue itself was not big but rather I had a big tongue muscle. This realization was merely a fact of life, not the end of the world.

Once we cleared up our little misunderstanding, it was smooth sailing until our next hurdle. In the meantime, I was making steady progress. With the use of a mirror and a tape recorder, my sounds were becoming clearer and more distinguishable. Instrumental in therapy, a mirror is useful in helping the client see the formation of her mouth as she is forming certain sounds. For instance, I have very expressive eyebrows; when I am nervous and under stress, my eyebrows seem like they are going to jump off my forehead! Through some relaxation techniques, I have learned to overcome this tendency and to control my facial expressions better. I remember one therapist tried ice as a means to help me calm my grimaces, but rubbing an ice cube on specific areas of my face only temporarily relieved the spasticity.

Like a teacher, every therapist brings her own philosophy and methodology and passes it on to her client. One therapist had the notion that I should try to situate myself so that the person speaking to me would be on my left side. It seems that my speech is clearer from this side. Granted, in most instances this arrangement could be easily worked out. Since I have a tendency to talk with my head tilted upwards, another therapist wanted me to ask everyone who wished to converse to please sit on the floor. Of course, this included family members, friends, teachers, and any other acquaintances. While I am sure the therapist had the best of intentions, her suggestion was impractical. I could not fathom asking authority figures to sit on the floor when conversing with me; this would really make me stick out like a sore thumb. Fortunately, since I saw the value of speaking with my head at a lowered position, I attempted to incorporate this mannerism into my routine lifestyle.

Altogether, I estimate that I had about four years of speech therapy. Unfortunately, my therapy was interrupted several times in the span of eighteen months. Three therapists in a row left because they had become pregnant. After the third one gave notice, I decided to quit. Just as I had begun to establish some sort of rapport with one, she went on maternity leave. While I had learned some valuable pointers, I was becoming increasingly aggravated. One therapist wanted me to sit in a certain position. Another speech pathologist recommended that I have everyone sit on the floor. I knew that suggestion would go over like a lead balloon. Yet, a third one claimed that the secret was in my breathing pattern.

Actually, when I thought about it, there is a direct relationship between speech and breathing. Oftentimes, a small child will go through a stage where his brain will go faster than his tongue and his speech will be a garbled. For this particular common problem, the best action is to help the child to take a breath and slow down, but in some cases, this is easier said than done. It is a learned technique that requires plenty of practice.

This concept of learning to slow down was also applied to me. I remember how one therapist would take a sentence and draw a slash between every two or three words. At every slash, I was to pause and take a breath. We did this for several weeks until I was able to incorporate this technique on my own. Learning to pause naturally coupled with practicing a few troublesome sounds enabled me to articulate with greater ease and hopefully, be better understood.

Like most very young children, every once in a while I stuttered. One proven method to overcome stuttering or some other similar speech difficulties is through song. Amazingly, some people who have been terrible stutterers have conquered their handicap through singing. Some stutterers even sing their conversations. I love singing. So, for one brief semester, I attended a music class.

Our teacher, Mrs. Pierce was a tall, buxom woman who loved her craft as well as her students. She was also the first black instructor I ever had. Our school was integrated, and many of the students were thrilled to be introduced to such songs as

Mr. Bo Jingles as well as a few Negro spirituals.

The year was 1968. At that time, the beloved leader and civil rights activist, Dr. Martin Luther King Jr., had come on the scene. Every time anyone turned on the TV, there he was, preaching and lecturing on issues regarding discrimination and equal opportunities. With hard work, these obstacles could be overcome. Without a doubt, Reverend King had a strong impact on the black community, and in keeping with the times and his message, I remember learning the words to the famous song, "We Shall Overcome."

I remember vividly the day Martin Luther King was shot. Upon learning of the tragic news, a hush came over the students. One of the most influential figures of the black community was dead. As the initial shock wore off, anger set in. Some black students were so enraged that they started screaming and running up and down the halls; teachers scrambled to maintain order. A sense of fear overcame them as they struggled to try to regain control. Never had I felt such a sense of confusion and bewilderment, and I truly embraced the safe haven of home that night.

Father Moreau called that night and suggested that I stay home from school the next day. Apparently, Harrison Morson had called him for counsel and in the process Father Moreau learned of a rumor of possible violent outbreak by some angry and hostile students. So, I remained home. Contrary to what they expected, the students were relatively quiet and calm. Later, the next evening, Father Moreau called and apologized for having "cried wolf," but we were thankful for his concern.

After the murder of Dr. King, the remainder of the term was uneventful. Since I was about to enter my freshman year, I needed to meet with my guidance counselor to determine my course schedule. Ever since I can remember I had longed to go to college. I watched with vested interest the expansion of buildings at Union County College, and every time we rode past I would announce, "That's where I will be someday."

Prior to officially starting high school, I took some vocational tests to determine my aptitude in various areas. According to this test, I scored high in two specific areas: the arts and the helping professions. Under the arts, I showed an interest in the following: writing, music, poetry, painting, and interior decorating. In the helping professions, I excelled in positions such as: social worker, counselor, religious leader, teacher, nurse, and librarian. At that age, I was open to almost all areas and practically wanted to pursue each and every one. Naturally, I was being idealistic. However, somewhere along the line, I needed to be realistic with myself in terms of what I would be actually capable of doing.

No matter what field I chose, a profession in that area

would require a college education. With that thought in mind, I chose a college preparatory curriculum, which meant taking courses in algebra, language arts, and the sciences. These were not Mickey Mouse courses, but I was determined to succeed. After some discussion and input from my counselor, my freshman schedule consisted of English composition, algebra, history, Spanish home economics, and I. For obvious reasons, I was excused from physical education and so I had two study periods. My concerns about how to utilize this extra time quickly dissipated; I had to focus all my efforts on my studies.

To mark my thirteenth birthday that year, my mother decided to give me a surprise celebration luncheon and invited my three best friends Carol, Mattie, and Linda over to share a small feast. We had platters of cold cuts, salads and the traditional birthday cake and ice cream. I remember coming home that day to find balloons and streamers tied to backs of chairs as well as a large banner draped across the dining room curtains that read, "HAPPY BIRTHDAY." Little did I know that this occasion was to be the last time all three of us would be together. Unhappy with the impending racial turmoil at the school, Carol and Linda decided to pursue their education at other academic institutions. Carol was accepted at Mother Seton Regional High School, and due to unfortunate circumstances the dynamics of Linda's family changed and they relocated first out of town, and eventually out of state.

Of the three, I probably was closest to Linda who had a cousin with cerebral palsy. Even though I never met her cousin, this common link brought our families together in friendship and support. By coincidence, they had a son, Billy, who was the same age as my brother, Rick, so this even strengthened our relationship. On several occasions all of us got together for dinner or met at the pizza parlor for a family evening out.

As we got to know the Hargrave's better, we learned that Linda's mother, Jean, was not well. Aside from diabetes and glaucoma, she was harboring another more serious illness that eventually cost Jean her life. I think Bill knew his wife was dying because suddenly they were spending money like crazy. The couple went on cruises and trips to Las Vegas. They just lived for the moment since Jean's days on this earths were numbered.

Meanwhile, I entered my freshman year. Even with the official change in dress code to more relaxed, causal attire, I preferred to dress as I had been dressing in either a skirt and blouse or an appropriate dress for school. I was raised with the belief that obtaining an education was the equivalent of a full-time job, and that in order to acquire the necessary skills to later qualify for a position, I had to concentrate on my studies first and foremost and to squeeze a little fun in here and there when I could. As far as my style of dress was concerned, I felt that if I dressed like a lady, I would have the respect of one. And believe me, in that changeable, unpredictable atmosphere, I needed all the respect I could get.

Of all my classes, algebra proved to be my biggest bug-a-boo. Fractions and decimals were relatively easy, but setting up the equation to do a word problem was entirely another matter; I was sunk. As much as I wanted to throw in the towel, I did not dare. If I could not pass algebra, my dreams of college would go down the drain.

My instructor, Mr. John Donner, a bachelor in his mid-sixties often came to class a bit disheveled, wearing the traditional white shirt that grew more soiled and stained around the cuffs as the week wore on. For a man his age, he had a marvelous spirit of adventure, which he proudly displayed through a twinkle in his eye every time he spoke of his favorite vocation – flying. He owned his own airplane and spent his weekends flying the friendly skies. Oftentimes, he would use his knowledge of aviation and apply it to an algebraic problem to capture the kids' attention. The boys were spellbound as I'm sure some of them dreamed of someday owning their own planes too.

Sensing that algebra presented a real dilemma for me, Mr. Donner wanted to help me but was perplexed as to how to do so. Something just was not clicking and I could not get a handle on it. My inability to get the numbers in the right columns only intensified the problem, which compounded my frustration. Fortunately, in one of my study halls, I befriended a sophomore,

Bibliana, who took it upon herself to tutor me. So, every day we would review my homework as she re-explained each step of each problem. Without her expertise, I never would have passed that course.

While algebra blew my brain, I loved English, home economics, history and Introduction to Spanish. Contrary to algebra, home economics had many practical applications. Aside from the excitement of being in a class with all upper classmen, I loved learning about nutrition, meal preparation and cooking. Our teacher, Anne Prout went to great lengths to instruct us on proper eating habits. One assignment required us to plan a well-balanced menu and then go to the market and price the needed ingredients. We also were taught the value of color, size, temperature, and taste when planning a meal.

On Fridays, we either cooked or baked. We started with simple desserts such as brownies and eventually advanced to more elaborate entrees. One of my favorites was lemon meringue pie with the meringue about two inches high. We always took home the leftovers and believe me, sometimes those delicious morsels never did quite make it home.

As we mastered the fine art of cooking one by one, we learned how to work with various appliances. The stove was our biggest challenge as we were constantly grilled on safety measures before using it. We also were taught about the blender, mixer, etc.

Aside from being a stickler about cleanliness, Mrs. Prout had the most annoying habit of questioning the girls about their home and personal lives. Every so often tempers would flare and she knew she had overstepped her boundaries. One of my pet peeves about her was that she constantly reminded me of my limitations and suggested that I was a burden on my parents. I just let her insinuations roll off my shoulders because I think she meant well but lacked the diplomacy to express her meaning clearly.

Even with her questionable temperament, Mrs. Prout was overprotective where I was concerned. For instance, when my classmates were cooking, I was allowed to observe but not to participate. Extremely fearful of burning myself, I did not entirely mind foregoing what my peers were doing. Perhaps if Mrs. Prout had had the time or the interest to learn more about my abilities, I would have been encouraged to participate a little more.

From home economics, which was held in the basement, my "big sister" and I trekked up to the second floor to my next class – history. Always warmly received by Miss Coffee, a frail, older woman close to retirement, I somehow looked forward to her class even though history was not a favorite subject of mine. Memorizing a myriad of names, dates, and places was a little bland for my taste. However, some of her personal stories, especially those involving her grandparents, added a certain appeal and charm to an otherwise boring subject. Miss Coffee made many historical events come to life, and because of that we learned to appreciate all that our forefathers went through.

Fully acclimated and enjoying the high school scene, we put the major racial tension behind us, not ever anticipating that something was brewing among the black community. The year was 1968. Till this day I do not know what prompted the outburst, but I suspect that it had to do with the death of Martin Luther King, Jr. In the middle of class one day, a messenger came to the classroom door with a note asking that I immediately come to the principal's office. Baffled by this strange request, the messenger quickly grabbed my belongings and off we went. Seconds later, Miss Coffee appeared. Just as we were ushered into the principal's private sanctum, the fire alarm went off.

Enclosed in the safe haven of our principal's office, we listened to the piercing sound of the fire alarms and then the scurrying and rapid footsteps of several hundred youngsters as they made their way to the nearest exit and out of the building. In the background, we heard the sirens of several police cars coming to a screeching halt. By this time, my heart was beating so violently that I half expected it to beat right out of my chest. Glancing at the clock, I saw that it was almost lunchtime and knew that soon my mother would arrive to pick me up. Panic-stricken, I fought back the tears.

Meanwhile, as mom drove through the streets towards the high school, hordes of petrified students were running in all directions. Her first thought was of a bomb scare, which seemed to be a regular occurrence those days. But then she caught sight of the police cars milling about and knew it was much more. Not knowing what to do as she approached the building, she decided to remain in her car with the doors locked and the windows rolled up tight. Luckily, a member of the faculty recognized our car and sent a police officer out to escort her inside.

Frantic, my mother hurried in and grabbed me. Sensing my relief, she began to pose what seemed like 101 questions. At this point, there really were not many answers. Everyone, including faculty, was still trying to recoup as well as regroup after this violent outburst among students. Gradually, as the chaos died down and the building emptied out, gathering our wits about us, we attempted to go home. Since it was a Friday, everyone hoped and prayed that over the weekend tempers would cool off.

A couple of days later, we learned what had actually happened. Apparently, some enraged black students from a neighboring town wandered over to provoke our students into a brawl. I'm not even sure the black students knew why they were at odds with those particular students. Nervous and edgy over the weekend, I wasn't keen on returning to my classes. However through the church grapevine we learned of some security measures that were to be put in place.

Even on Monday morning, it was clear from the general attitude of the administrators and the students that everyone was still recovering from Friday's incident. An overwhelming sense of disillusionment pervaded as students fought their way back to normalcy. Most of the students, including myself, were tiptoeing around uncertain as to what to expect. For days afterwards, I was literally afraid of my own shadow.

Unfortunately, that isolated incident was only a small taste of what was yet to come. About a month later, as we were returning from lunch and upon reaching the building, we were beckoned by the vice principal who was standing in the parking lot waiting for us. Word of trouble brewing had reached his ear via the Roselle Police Department, through a tipster who informed them that students from neighboring Linden High School were on their way over to ignite some tempers.

After quickly explaining the situation, he ushered us into a small office claiming there was no time to escape. Time was of the essence. Entering the ominous darkened hallways, we were escorted into a small office with a locked door. Anxiously sitting in this locked room, we attempted to mentally prepare ourselves for another outburst. Moments later, we heard what sounded like a herd of elephants running overhead. Enraged students, supposedly from Linden, carried long, metal pipes as they ran through the deserted corridors. Through the windows, we saw backup police squads arriving, armed with bats and megaphones. They also brought teargas to be used as a last resort. Some of the perpetrators were handcuffed and hauled off to juvenile detention and others were ordered to go and evacuate the building immediately.

As soon as the authorities were assured that the school had rid itself of any lingering perpetrators or students, we were free to leave too. Escorted by a couple of policemen to our car, we were thankful that it had not received any damage. Surveying the parking lot, we had noticed some smashed windshields and slashed tires. Bits of glass were scattered over most of the pavement as well as pieces of rubber. Timidly, my mother drove through the lot with extreme caution.

Even the streets seemed deserted. Turning into our driveway, we noticed my grandfather waving at us from the front door. He had been temporarily staying with us, and from the expression on his face he was still unaware of what had transpired. Before we left, mom had told him that she had some shopping to do and not to worry. In a way, we were grateful that he was oblivious to the riot because we had the chance to break the news to him gradually so as not to overwhelm him.

Having witnessed the intensity of student violence, I was unable to watch any news segments about racial upheaval for several months. In fact, if I even heard the segment being announced beforehand, I got up and turned off the TV. To let seething tempers dissipate, members of the Board of Education voted to close the school that Friday and reopen the following Monday. We all needed a breather. During this time, members of the Board of Education had come to grips with the fact that our modest, suburban high school had fallen prey to violence and would never be the same again. For those who were lifelong residents of the community, this was a bitter pill to swallow. Not only that, but recent events had prompted them to seriously question the safety of the school and what measures could be taken to ensure that safety.

When school reopened, we were astounded by the kind of transformation that had taken place. No longer was our school typical of those in the past where students were free to roam and gossip and chatter and mill around in the carefree fashion of adolescence. Our corridors were now filled with police officers and security guards stationed at every exit. While some of the members of the law enforcement team were armed with guns, others were equipped with walkie-talkies. Whatever their rank, their main task was to keep abreast of any minor squabbles that could escalate into further attacks within the student body. So, overnight, our typical suburban high school was transformed into a mini-prison.

Generally, I think students felt relieved that we now had tight security and school authorities had taken the necessary steps to circumvent further commotion. In the past, several teachers as well as students had received minor abrasions and were treated accordingly. Probably, this was one of the few times when having a disability proved to be an advantage as I was taken to a sheltered environment and not left to fend for myself.

During this tumultuous freshman year, I did manage to make a few new friends. Actually, it was surprising that I established any relationships at all, especially since I had spent so many hours under lock and key in the principal's office. Be that as it may, I did form two close friendships with two girls who had first volunteered to be my "big sisters".

Marlene Hooper came from a lovely black family and was a very bright, studious person with a winning smile. Marlene was a dedicated and compassionate "big sister." Walking hand-in-hand through the halls together as she escorted me to our next class, we exemplified racial harmony. Seeing us stroll through the halls together, no one would have thought that there was racial tension in our school.

As close as we were in the classroom, we only once stepped over that fine line and entered each other's private domains. I invited Marlene over one Saturday afternoon. She accepted my invitation graciously and rang our doorbell promptly at two o'clock. We had a pleasant afternoon exchanging anecdotes about teachers, mutual friends, and some of the more colorful characters to cross our path. Even though we vowed to get together again, we never did so. Unfortunately, I think that invisible color barrier intruded and drew a silent line that highlighted our racial differences. Although this divide never interfered with our relationship in school, it did seem to prevent us from forming a friendship beyond school grounds.

On the other hand, Carol Lutwin and I built a strong relationship that extended far beyond the classroom. Carol was the middle child of an all-girl family. A very bright, well-rounded individual, Carol was always in the top ten percent of her class. Raised as a reformed Jew, Carol and her family kept a kosher home and observed all of the main religious holidays. I would often be at their home on a Friday night where a lit candle would be in the window in observance of the Sabbath. In keeping with Jewish law, meat and dairy products were always served separately and on different plates. At first, I found this custom very difficult to follow, but eventually I fell into a pattern where I almost automatically separated the meat from the dairy when I was in the company of the Lutwins. Surprisingly, one of the reasons we so frequently visited Friendly's was because the restaurant chain served kosher ice cream.

I think that perhaps one of the reasons Carol and I got

along so well was that we were so respectful of each other's religions. I have often heard that Judaism is not only a religion but also a way of life. Perhaps this is not as evident in the liberal and reformed customs, but religion is most certainly a way of life for the orthodox Jew where there are over 900 laws to follow.

Despite Carol's adherence to her religion, she dated a Catholic guy for a brief period while we were in high school. He was a tall, rather lanky youth, lightly freckled and with dark rimmed glasses. Like Carol, he was quiet, studious, and definitely college bound.

Trying to remain as unobtrusive as possible, the young lovers would seek a semi-darkened corner to exchange a brief kiss or two. Almost inseparable, they often walked down the corridor hand-in-hand between classes. When not in school, Carol and her boyfriend studied together, attended football games, or went to the movies. Even though at that time Carol was my best friend, I was neither jealous nor envious of their relationship. While I may have fantasized about having a relationship of my own, I knew I was not ready for one, plus Carol and I still got together on a regular basis despite her relationship.

For several months, Carol and her boyfriend were a hot item. Despite their religious differences, the couple somehow managed to stick together. I think both sets of parents were wise enough not to interfere and let nature take its course. Although I am certain that a few chosen words were expressed as to the possible dilemmas of a mixed marriage, there wasn't any lingering resentment for either party.

As probably predicted, this infatuation eventually died out. Perhaps, some harsh words were spoken and some tears shed, but as the cliché goes, "time heals all wounds." I think I rather enjoyed sitting on the sidelines and watching a full-blown romance take place before my eyes, but I was not yet ready to participate in one.

Dating was not a top priority with me. Either my hormones had not fully kicked in or I was preoccupied with too many other projects. While I liked and respected boys my own age, I thought of them as brothers. Many of them I had known since grammar school. Besides which, I think most high school age boys who are into the dating scene are very conscious of a girl's appearance. It is a male ego type of thing. Let's face it; in the eyes of an immature adolescent, the ideal dating partner needs to have the most perfect body and an outgoing personality. Need I say more? While I had a trim, shapely little figure, my involuntary movements and facial grimaces detracted from my appearance. Therefore, I do not think the boys thought of me in a sexual nature.

At home, the topic of dating was seldom discussed or

even mentioned. I once asked my father if he thought I was attractive. His reply floored me. He told me that I was the offspring of two rather average looking people and so, therefore, I was average. He even went to further say that compared to some others with cerebral palsy I was quite pretty. I think my father missed the point. I was searching for some sign of approval and recognition of my emerging womanhood. While he was trying to be realistic with me, I was not expecting such a blunt answer, though it did address what he thought of me as his daughter.

My mother, on the other hand, downplayed the subject of dating and romance by simply denouncing the theory that all women need to have a monogamous relationship with a man to be happy. She emphasized that some women are career-oriented and find enormous fulfillment in the professional arena. Even back then, I guess my mother intuitively knew that somehow I needed to explore some means to find contentment within myself whether it be in a profession, a vocation, or a hobby.

Since my heart was set on going to college, I needed to try to explore some career options. Even though, I was only about to enter my junior year, I needed to at least start thinking about my future. Like many kids, I went through a phase where I thought I was destined to teach. When Nancy Wysocki and I were little girls, we were forever playing school. We fought over who was to be the teacher, a by-product of the Catholic School

System, Nancy insisted, the stricter the teacher the better. Of course, the school day was incomplete unless your knuckles got slapped with a ruler once or twice.

While my friend was accustomed to a more rigid environment, I had been exposed to a more lenient, carefree one. By the time I had reached high school, I had been challenged by a number of teaching methods and styles. While some of those worked, others left me cold and dry. As much as I may have thought I wanted to be a classroom teacher then, the voice of reality kept inching its way in and let me know that I lacked the assertiveness necessary to maintain order and discipline in a classroom.

My second choice was a career in library science. Aside from my literary and studious nature, I loved the quiet atmosphere of the library. Being constantly surrounded by classic and more contemporary works of literature, I could never die of boredom. However, upon a rather thorough investigation of the responsibilities of a librarian, I realized that one needs quite a bit of manual dexterity to shelve and code books, to effectively use the card catalog, and to research topics of current interest. While the idea of meeting and assisting students with their various assignments appealed to me, I wondered if the strain of always having to use the fine motor manipulations of my hands would be too much.

Not only do books inform and entertain, but once they capture the imagination of the reader, nothing seems impossible. I remember a phase I went through where I read nothing except romanticized versions of stories about doctors and nurses. No matter what the situation, the doctor or nurse always came out the hero. I loved the thought of healing people, alleviating their misery and saving lives. Carried away by the heroism of the profession, I neglected to consider the blood, the guts, and the gore, not to mention the sometimes-frantic pace that usually is involved in saving a life. In most instances in the healthcare profession, time is the enemy.

While I was engrossed in learning about textures of fabrics, styles of furniture and color schemes, I briefly considered becoming an interior decorator. To my amazement, I discovered I had an eye for color as well as an artistic flair. I liked putting together colors and coordinating furniture pieces. I also realized that it was possible to liven up a room with a few modest touches of creativity here and there. I visualized myself working in a furniture store like Huffman-Koos and assisting customers on how to redecorate either a room or an entire house on a budget. Dressed in the appropriate attire, I saw myself sitting behind a rather large, impressive oak desk imparting my wisdom on the subject to weary customers seeking the advice of a professional, me. Indeed, I suspect that I was having delusions of grandeur over what someone with my disability would be capable of doing, but at least I was open to a number of possibilities. Of course, whether or not any of those careers ever materialized was another matter.

If one happens to be so brave as to ask others what to choose as a career, nine times out of ten, their suggestion will be to work in a field where you can serve as a role model for others with physical disabilities. I remember, our neighbor, Helen Jago, suggesting that I become a social worker and give encouragement to others with cerebral palsy. For a while I explored that possibility, but it did not feel quite right. Aside from the fact that a master's degree was required, chances were that I also needed to be able to drive. At that time, I did not see driving as a realistic possibility for myself.

I am of the opinion that one need not be expected to pursue a career in the field of rehabilitation to be an effective role model and inspire others. I was determined to try to break this stereotypical suggestion and enter a field that held interest for me. Despite the fact that I had no idea what might be a realistic direction to pursue, I knew that eventually I would either find it or it would somehow find me. However, I knew for sure that whatever career path I chose, I needed a college education to reach it.

Why is it that some of us know instinctively, almost from the day we are born, what we want to do with our lives and others simply flounder about hoping that someday we will stumble on the answer? I was only a sophomore in high school when I was making a decision of this magnitude. This kind of decision requires life experience, of which I was in short supply. With the exception of a few rare occasions, I seldom had the opportunity to escape the vigilant eyes of my parents. However, the adventures that I did manage to have, shaped my approach to the future.

All throughout out childhood, Rick and I had the advantage of traveling on family vacations with our parents. In the early 60s, my paternal grandparents, who had been residents of Cranford for over forty-five years, decided to pull up stakes and retire to the Seminole section of St. Petersburg, Florida. Prior to contacting a realtor, my grandparents were in agreement that their new home must meet two requirements, namely, a suitable eat-in kitchen and a backyard filled with trees. With a little help from a realtor, they found a small, two-bedroom ranch with an enclosed patio and carport.

The Jaekle's shared a wonderful retirement. Every year, a few weeks prior to the holidays, United Parcel would deliver this crate filled to the brim with handpicked oranges and grapefruit from their very own trees. "When I'm in the mood for an orange, I simply go out in the backyard and pick one," grandpa would exclaim. Nothing delighted them more than being able to grow their own fruit. Living among friends, many of whom they had known all throughout their married life, afforded them social opportunities that enhanced their health and well-being. Aside from joining friends two or three times at the beach, they dined out at least three times a week. Restaurant prices were so reasonable retirees would have been foolish not to take

advantage of them.

    Because we lived over 1200 miles apart, we saw each other only once a year – one summer we would go down and the next year, my grandparents traveled up North. Some years, the weather would be so beastly hot in Florida that we never had the air conditioner off, and other years, the temperature was so mild, we never turned it on.

As small children, my brother and I always looked forward to going to the beach and swimming in the gulf. With my rubber tube around my waist, I would ride the waves on a calm day. Every once in a while, I would swallow a gulp of salt water or get my toes tangled in a web of seaweed, but that was part of the surf experience. I loved it. Rick, on the other hand, felt very differently. He was timid and fearful of the enormous body of water and of being swallowed up by it. So he needed to be gently coaxed into the calm surf. Of course, two years later when we returned to Florida again, he jumped right in.

By the time my parents lured me out of the water, my fingers and toes were shriveled and prune-like. After a few minutes to towel off, catch my breath and reapply the sunscreen, I was ready to search for seashells and other treasures along the water's edge. Armed with my little plastic bucket, I wandered several feet of the shoreline looking for perfect seashells – ones that had been spared being crushed by the sand trucks. Stomping through the mounds of sand was hard work, but marvelous exercise to strengthen my weakened leg muscles. Since I had my heart set on adding to my collection, I did not mind the extra effort. Catching my enthusiasm, eventually the whole family became involved and then my collection really mounted. I could hardly wait to get back to my grandparents' home to rinse off the sand from my precious gems.

Peering inside the plastic bucket, I noticed how much of the moist sand still remained on them. So, I decided that the best way to remove the sand and other matter was to soak and clean them in the bathroom sink. Nonchalantly, I carried the bucket into the bathroom and proceeded to rinse the sand particles from my newly acquired treasures. Then, I carefully dried each small wonder with paper towels.

Later, as we were sitting around the dinner table munching the last morsels of our evening meal, I happily relayed how I had cleaned my seashells. As I excitedly gave a blow-by-blow description of how I accomplished my task, I happened to glance in the direction of my grandmother and could not help but notice her reaction. To everyone's amazement, she removed herself from the table and ran into the bathroom. The next sound we heard was the tap running in the bathroom sink. Perplexed by this sudden action, we anxiously awaited her return to the table. Somewhat relieved, she finally returned with a glimmer of a smile on her face. Hearing me explain how I had taken care of my seashells, she was fearful that the sand combined with their hard water would force their pipes to clog causing a disruption in their sewer system. Fortunately, it had not. With a quivering lip and a guilty conscious, I apologized to her. That was the first and only time I was ever in trouble with my grandmother.

Every other summer when we ventured south, it seemed as if my grandparents had some new sport that they were dying to show us. One particular year, the Jaekle's had purchased an adult-sized tricycle which had increased in popularity especially with the senior set. Not to be ridden in heavy traffic, my grandparents bought it for the exercise and the occasional ride to the 7-Eleven.

As a young child, I had a red tricycle and eventually learned to ride it rather well despite my wobbly posture. I remember I rode it up and down our block and often captured quite an audience of overprotective mothers who stood with noses pressed to the window anxiously watching me. Every so often I fell off and scraped a knee or two or bumped my head on the pavement, but my injuries were minor compared to the sense of achievement I felt from doing the same thing as my peers.

Now, several years later, I was about to take on that challenge again. However, this time my desire was mixed with some trepidation. In my flashbacks of previous falls, I imaged the worst. As I was more aware of the consequences of falling, I was fearful of getting hurt. Even so, I managed to muster up the courage to get on that bike. My father and brother stood on either side to gently coax and support me as I struggled to mount myself on the seat. Finally, I boosted myself onto the high seat. Once on, I cautiously felt for the pedals and ever so slowly began to push them down and around. From not performing that motion for quite some time, the muscles in my legs were stiff and tight. At first, every push on the pedal produced pain. By the second day, I was more relaxed and at ease on the bike, so much so that I was able to maintain an erect posture as I slowly began to ride a few feet. Rather proud of myself, I rode further each day until I was able to ride around the block displaying confidence and pride. So, each night after dinner, I took a couple of spins around the block, and in doing so, I imagined the possibility of myself riding my tricycle to various places in my own neighborhood. I envisioned myself riding to the library, to my friend's house, and who knew where else this three-wheeled vehicle could take me in the future!

Some might refer to my imaginings as wishful thinking, but I, like most adolescents, was in search of ways to become more independent. I was reaching the age where my friends were counting the days until they could obtain a learner's permit and head for the roads. Instinctively, I knew my chances of getting behind the wheel were rather slim because of my startle reflex. I remember once asking my father if he thought I could drive and he replied, "If you just had some more control in your arms, perhaps driving would be a possibility. I think that it is too big of a gamble." Disappointed, and also relieved, I never questioned his opinion again until several years later when one of my graduate professors suggested that I at least explore my chances with a pre-driving test administered by rehabilitation professional.

As the months rolled around and my friends turned 17 and got their driver's permit and eventually passed their driver's tests and became licensed drivers, I felt pangs of envy. Deep down I knew the mobility gap was ever widening between my able-bodied peers and me.

Fortunately, as soon as my friends felt confident behind the wheel, some of them began taking me places on Saturday or Sunday afternoons. I remember my first car trip with Carol Lutwin. Only weeks before, she had received her license, and therefore, she was still a novice behind the wheel. Prior to coming to fetch me, her parents gave her a million and one instructions so that by the time she pulled into our driveway, she was a nervous wreck.

Earlier in the week, we had decided that our first destination would be Friendly's for an ice cream sundae. Finally, Carol arrived at the appointed hour somewhat frenzied, but obviously pleased with herself that she had made it this far. Sensing how anxious my parents were, I quickly climbed into her car, and after a quick wave, we drove off.

Fortunately, I had been securely belted in before we hit our first red light. Not very familiar with brakes, Carol stepped rather hard on the brake and we both fell forward. Startled by this sudden jolt, we somehow found the courage to continue on to our destination. By the time we reached the restaurant, we both paused long enough to catch our breath and offer a silent prayer of thanks for getting us there in one piece.

Upon entering the franchise, we were shown to a booth and handed menus. Of course, we were not in a rush to order.

Instead, we just wanted to bask in our moment of glory, for Carol had proved herself as a capable driver, and I was discovering my wings of independence.

Indeed, I was growing up and displaying the normal qualities of adolescence. Like most teenagers, I yearned to explore the world a bit apart from my family. As much as I wanted to cut some of the apron strings, I knew that some of them still needed to remain intact and probably would indefinitely because of my disability.

As it turned out, an opportunity for independence presented itself during the summer of 1971. My paternal grandfather had died of cancer of the stomach the year before, and prior to his death, my grandparents had decided that grandmother sell the house and move to Arizona to live near their daughter Carol. So, six months after my grandfather had passed away, my grandmother ventured out west and re-established herself in an adorable little apartment in Tempe, which was approximately five miles from her daughter in Scottsdale. Even though I had not seen my grandparents very often in my childhood, I established quite a rapport with my grandmother as I grew older. In the past, she had been rather domineering and overprotective where my grandfather was concerned. Since his retirement and the onset of diabetes, she more or less took charge of all decisions on household matters etc., to the point where she infantilized him. I'm sure she felt this was for the best, but I'm not so sure. Now, since his death and the responsibility of his illness was off her shoulders, she was a much more mellow and flexible person.

Once she settled into her new surroundings and adapted to her new status of widowhood, she began broaching the subject of me flying out west for a few weeks in the summer. At first, we did not take her invitation very seriously. However, as weeks passed, her insistence grew more intense, and we gave it more thought. After all, I was sixteen. While in some matters I still lacked some emotional maturity, this trip would be an experiment in my emotional growth and independence. With a little persuasion and serious thought, my parents and I agreed to her idea.

It was not until we purchased my plane ticket that it dawned on me that I was really on my way. For two weeks I would be away from all that was familiar. Even though I had traveled every summer, this time I would be without my family or their emotional support.

As my departure date drew closer, I was on an emotional roller coaster. One hour I was elated at the prospect of my adventure while in the next hour, I experienced pangs of intense anxiety. In my mind's eye, I saw myself in situations I knew I would not be able to handle and came down with a case of the "what ifs." In the next three weeks, I imagined the worst scenarios possible, everything from dying in a plane crash to scalding myself in the shower.

Finally, the day arrived, it was bright and sunny and without a cloud in the sky. Since this was to be my first flight alone, my parents made arrangements with the airline to have a stewardess accompany me on board and provide assistance throughout the flight. The thought of taking off and soaring through those soft, white clouds thrilled me to no end. It was only a matter of hours until I was airborne.

After a last minute check to see that I had packed everything I would need, we headed for the airport. Since my flight was scheduled for midday, traffic was relatively light. By the time we arrived at the designated terminal, I'm not sure who had achieved a higher state of anxiety my folks or me.

When at last we found the gate, my parents entrusted the stewardess to oversee that their precious daughter was safely delivered to her grandmother some 2300 miles across the country.

As a person with a disability, I received the V.I.P. treatment and was allowed to board first before all of the other passengers. In fact, the airline even allowed my father to accompany me and see that I was settled before takeoff. Within minutes, the rest of the passengers began to board including a high school student who was about my age who had the seat next to mine. Fortunately, for my sake, she was a wonderful traveling companion and she gave me the assistance I needed, especially with my lunch. Dining at 30,000 feet presented some difficulties for someone with limited dexterity. With cartons that required opening and utensils that needed to be unwrapped, eating became a real chore.

Except for an occasional air pocket, the plane ride proved to be a rather smooth one. Of course, those air pockets made me feel like I had a butterfly doing a somersault in the pit of my stomach. At first, this odd sensation really frightened me, but when I realized that everyone on the plane experienced the same feeling, I laughed.

If I had not had such a delightful traveling companion sitting next to me, the five hours would have seemed endless. She was a bit shy and hesitant in the beginning, but as the flight progressed, she was quite talkative. Eventually, she confided to me that she had never encountered anyone with my disability before and that she was afraid that she might unknowingly do or say something that might offend me. I assured her that she should just relax, and that she need not worry so much.

At last, the sign to fasten our seatbelts went on and we knew we were about to land. Taking off is one thing, but landing is something else entirely. As the plane descends and the wheels drop down to touch the ground, the plane does a little bouncing.

Finally, the plane is gliding on the runway and eventually comes to a complete stop. The light goes off and people start moving about collecting their belongings. I remained in my seat as I watched passengers prepare to disembark from the plane. Prior to landing, I was informed by the stewardess that I would be one of the last passengers off and so there was not need to hurry. When my turn came to disembark and descend the steps which were temporarily affixed to the plane, they positioned one attendant behind me and another one in front, and together we slowly made our way down the stairs.

At the end of this rather steep set of stairs, there was a wheelchair waiting to transport me to the terminal where my grandmother and the rest of the Arizona clan were eagerly awaiting my arrival.

"You've made it!!" exclaimed my saucy, redheaded Aunt Carol.

"Welcome to Arizona!"

After some excited chatter, we collected my luggage, and the stewardess accompanied us out to my aunt's station wagon. Even though I was well able to walk, I was glad to have the convenience of a wheelchair, especially in a crowded airport terminal. With sincere gratitude, we thanked her for her services. I slid out of the wheelchair and into the car and away we went!

My grandmother lived in a garden apartment in the town of Tempe. Upon first sight, Grandma fell in love with the apartment. "It's as cute as a doll's house and just the right size for me," she commented. From the moment she saw the place, she was enchanted with its size, layout and certain special touches that added to its charm. When I saw it, I thought to myself, this would be the perfect setup for me, if only it were in New Jersey. In the idealistic mind of a sixteen year old, I thought and daydreamed quite a bit about having my own apartment someday. Even at the age of 71, my grandmother was extremely independent and drove herself everywhere in her little Volkswagen bug. Today, these cars are considered relics, but in those days Volkswagens were quite popular. We toured most of Arizona in one.

Although the humidity is not as high in Arizona as it is in the east, some days the temperature can exceed 120 degrees. Even without humidity, that is hot and stifling! Except for an occasional cactus tree, the terrain is flat desert. Tempe was a sharp contrast to the changing seasons of New Jersey.

A few days after I arrived in Arizona, my grandmother and I decided to visit a Mormon Temple. The architecture was magnificent with tall white pillars and a domed roof. Beautiful stained glass windows dominated the temple. Inside the air conditioned building, guides led guests around to a special little theater where they were showing a film on the Christian view of death. Since both of my grandfathers passed away only months ago, I was a bit hesitant about watching it. My grandmother, however, was rather persuasive.

With approximately twenty others we sat in this dimly lit theatre. Contrary to my expectations, I found the film to be both uplifting and comforting. The film was about an average extended family whose grandfather is stricken with a heart attack and eventually dies. Finally, the man is free of pain and at peace. Like a white cloud moving across the sky, the soul leaves the body and floats up to heaven. Once there, the family and friends who have entered the kingdom before him lovingly greet him. While my interpretation of the film may seem a bit simplistic, I thought it took the mystery out of death and made the process seem less frightening. As a firm believer of the Christian faith, I found a great deal of comfort in the testimony that there is indeed an afterlife.

Aside from our jaunts here and there, grandmother loved to introduce me to her friends. Like most grandparents, she took great pride in her grandchildren and was especially proud of me who flew out there to spend some time with her. Having to move several times in her life, she had little trouble re-establishing herself and she seemed to be able to form new friendships rather quickly.

One of her new companions was Rose Rice, her identical

twin as everyone lovingly called her. People say that everyone has a double; well, Rose Rice was certainly my grandmother's. Both women exhibited the same body type. That is they were short and round in stature. Their mannerisms were strangely similar. Skin coloring and personalities were almost identical. Backgrounds and lifestyles were alike. No doubt about it, the resemblance between these two ladies was uncanny. The three of use went out to lunch one day. We were not in the restaurant more than five minutes when someone came up to our booth and asked if they were twins. People were stunned to learn that they were not even related. Fate had somehow just brought them together.

As much as I loved visiting my grandmother and receiving all sorts of attention, I did experience a few twinges of homesickness. The change in water and diet caused me to have a slight case of constipation, and so, for a few days, I wasn't my usual cheery self. Thinking that a laxative would relieve my irregularity, I took one. However, I made the bad mistake of taking it the night before I was to go on a family picnic with my cousins. Since the laxative had worked before our planned outing, I put the whole issue out of my mind. On our way to the picnic site, we had to stop, and once we got there I had severe cramps and broke out into a sweat. Then, on the way home, I had an embarrassing bout of it again. By the time we returned to the house, I was a mess and the car had a foul odor, which everyone endured because they simply had no choice.

The sight of grandmother's apartment and bed never seemed more appealing than on that rotten day. Weary and ashamed, I hardly made it past the front doorstep before I had another little accident. Several hours later, when I regained my dignity and self-worth, I apologized to everyone for my error. I was not thinking rationally when I took the laxative and promised to join the others on a picnic the next day. After the cramps subsided, I called my mother. Teary eyed and homesick, I relayed my tale of troubles. How I wished I was home and safely tucked into my own bed that night. But I wasn't. Exhausted and humiliated by the days' events, I finally drifted off to sleep that night. Knowing the worst was behind me, I slept soundly, and, by the next morning, I felt recharged and ready to take on the world once more.

Despite that one minor, embarrassing incident, I had a wonderful trip and a memorable summer. Because of my experiences away from home, I gained a new sense of maturity. With my growing confidence, I felt ready for my junior year of high school.

Only two more years until college! I was both excited and apprehensive about my future. Ever since I was a little girl, I wanted to attend college and work towards a career, but deep down, I wondered if I would be able to handle the pressure and the social scene of the university. I also was in a quandary as to what sort of career to pursue. Unfortunately, I had no role models or people with similar disabilities to advise me. I was hopelessly lost as to what to do with the rest of my life.

I had completed my math requirements, so I entered the academic year relieved and with one less stumbling block ahead. For years, mathematics had been my nemesis, and I had endured endless hours of tutoring just to get a little bit better than a passing grade. In lieu of math, I studied three years of Spanish to prepare for college.

For the most part, I liked Spanish. Since a lot of it required memorization, I did rather well. Pronunciation was another matter. My teacher, Mrs. Nugent, was not that concerned with my ability to speak the language, but wanted us to be exposed to another culture and to gain a sense of appreciation for it. I think one of the hardest rules of the language for me to remember was that the adjective came after the noun. Despite the fact that I was unable to insert the accents with my typewriter, I managed to pull an 80 for the course, which meant that I had made the honor roll.

As a junior, I wanted to branch out somewhat from the traditional courses, and so after discussing it with my guidance counselor, I decided to take Introduction to Journalism as an elective. At the time, I was not very interested in newspapers, but since they were always scattered about the house I thought that I had better learn about them.

    Catherine Bradley, a tall woman in her mid-fifties and a seasoned professional, was kind but somewhat reserved in her judgment about having a student with a disability in her class. There was no doubt that I would need to win her over. In her class, we gained knowledge of the fundamentals of the makings of a newspaper as we actually formed the staff of the school paper, The Rampage. As a low person on the totem pole, I started as a typist who typed copy for publication and eventually worked my way up to columnist where I wrote my own column every month.

    Through some turn of events, of which I cannot recall, we managed to obtain a professional typist who claimed to be the fastest one in the world to come and address our student body. Awed by the fact that a man could type a whole page within a matter of seconds, I was assigned the scoop. I think Mrs. Bradley had an ulterior motive when she gave me the story and so I just ran with it. "A story! Mrs. Bradley wants you to actually interview someone." Rather stunned by the news, but delighted that I was given the opportunity to tackle a real assignment, my parents were behind me all the way.

    Since she knew that I was unable to take notes, Mrs. Bradley suggested that I use a tape recorder. I was familiar with recorders because I had used one in speech therapy. Armed with my recorder and a list of questions, I sat within a few feet of this incredible man whose finesse with the keyboard was a marvel to witness. Nervous at the thought of speaking before an entire audience, I waited patiently to see what kinds of questions were forthcoming. As it turned out, all of my questions had been addressed and therefore, I could concentrate solely on recording the interview. My main task now was to push the right buttons so that my taping would be clear and sharp.

At home that night, I carefully typed out the interview and topped it with an appropriate lead ready to turn in the next day. Rather pleased with myself, I handed in my story. Of course, there were many changes and corrections, but that was to be expected. After all, I was only a greenhorn learning the ropes of a well-established profession. Over the course of the semester, I gradually improved to the point where I now had a column and wrote about a specific issue each month. In one column, I wrote on the Beadleston Act and how it affected the education of handicapped children. Although I'm not sure it was a topic of interest to my peers, the education of children with disabilities was a hot issue among various educators and parents alike. To everyone's complete amazement, I won an award for that particular column.

Taking Introduction to Journalism and working on the school newspaper changed the course of my life. Not only did a regular byline increase my self-esteem, but it allowed me to prove to myself as well as some doubtful others that perhaps there was a respectable place for me in society where I could make a valuable contribution and possibly even a livelihood. For so many years, I had encountered scores of doubting Thomases, and now the attitude of these people was slowly changing. Classmates like Jeffrey Meyers and Evelyn Brody were starting to see me in a new light. I was no longer someone to be pitied and cast aside with the "dumb" ones. Instead, I was possibly someone to admire for having the determination to succeed.

Feeling rather pleased that I had now established a name for myself as a contributing member of the Class of '73', I really started to blossom. Through my association with The Rampage, I found a refined identity that helped me emerge as a total person and not the little girl with cerebral palsy.

However, while the prevailing attitude among some students and the local community seemed to have shifted to a more optimistic one, I still encountered my share of prejudices. I recall an incident that occurred in Hahne's Department Store in Westfield. It was a typical Saturday. If I was not going out somewhere with my friends, I would accompany my mother shopping – a favorite pastime among us women. On this particular visit, we stopped by the perfume counter because my mother wanted to purchase some Chantilly. As my mother was fumbling through her handbag in search of her charge, the saleswoman asked for her name and address. Since mom was obviously preoccupied at the moment, I volunteered to give the necessary information. Well, after I had recited the last digit of our zip code, the saleswoman turned to my mother and replied, "Isn't it wonderful that she knows her name and address." Seeing RED and the smoke steaming from her ears, my mother responded by saying, "Yes, it is especially since she will be entering college soon." With her expression unchanged, the saleswoman replied, "Very well" and walked away in a huff.

Grabbing our parcel, we headed for the door. I was more annoyed than angry. While my ego may have been temporarily bruised, I knew it would recover. I had encountered ignorant people before and undoubtedly I would run into them again. My mother, on the other hand, was outraged. Like a lioness protecting her cub, she was not as willing to forget the incident. Previous encounters had taught her that once a person's mind is set any further explanation only falls on deaf ears. It is only through education that their attitudes will change.

A perfect example of this comes from a series of episodes that occurred in the Coach & Four Restaurant in Cranford. One of our frequent haunts, we dined there usually on a weekly basis. In fact, we had been regular customers since my booster seat days. As a well-established family restaurant, most of the waitresses had been working there for years and years. As a result, many of them watched me grow up.

FITTING IN

I was about seventeen or so and one night after the meal when our waitress brought our check, she handed me two red lollipops. At first, I thought it was some kind of joke. Staring at the sucker, she handed them to me and told me, "You were a good girl". Horrified by her ignorance, my father tried to explain that I was only months away from graduating high school. She looked up and replied, "Would she like another lollipop - perhaps a green one?" Again, the reply fell on deaf ears. While we could have made an issue out of it, what would be the point? We did not want to embarrass her because we knew she meant well but, unfortunately, she lacked the proper tact to express it.

Despite that incident, we still dined at the Coach & Four quite often. Experience had already taught me that I would encounter such situations all throughout my life. Because of my disability, I was a member of a misunderstood minority. This minority encompasses over 30 million people nationwide and continues to grow at an alarming rate. Some of us are members from birth and others join as a result of injury or illness. Unlike most elite groups, no one is exempt. One can join at any age and at any time. In my case, I joined shortly after I was born. In some instances, one's disability does not show and their membership comes without any stigma attached. However, in my circumstances, I cannot conceal the fact that I have slurred speech and involuntary movement; I can only accept it and continue on from there.

As I was soon to be a senior, college was very much on my mind. I had already taken the PSATs and I had not done all that well. When it comes to standardized tests, I am a poor test taker. Even with a mentor and extra time, my scores remained quite low. In lieu of that, I was thrilled to discover that, at that time, most institutions of higher learning did not place all of their emphasis on these tests, but rather viewed the overall academic performance of the student. Therefore, college officials review a student's record to see what courses were taken, their GPA, involvement in school activities, and special awards and honors.

In my case, my GPA was 3.3, I was on the staff of the Rampage, and I was a member of the National Honor Society.

Because of my disability, I was not interested in going away to college. The thought of me depending on college roommates for assistance did not bode well for either me or my parents. Besides that, I needed my sleep, and, as most of us know, dorm life is anything but quiet. Even though I had expressed a desire to attend Montclair State University, once I saw the campus, I knew I would not be able to handle the hills and dales of the terrain. I was ultimately only interested in fulfilling my dream of attending Union County Community College.

At that time, Union County Community College was among the three highest ranking two-year colleges in the state. While the college had an "open door" policy and accepted almost everyone who applied, the second semester told the real story. By this time, approximately one-third of the class was invited to leave – the immature students were weeded out and the serious ones continued to matriculate.

Because I was only interested in two schools, I applied for early acceptance. I will never forget the day that I received my acceptance letter from Union County Community College. The letter was lying on the stereo waiting to be opened as soon as I arrived home from school. I was thrilled to see that I had a reply from the college. With trembling hands, I opened the letter. I had been accepted. I was so proud of my victory that I was eager to share the news with everyone. Of course, my mother was delighted. My father was surprised and a bit skeptical as to whether I would be able to handle a full course schedule. The rest of the clan and all of my friends offered me their sincere congratulations.

Now that I knew in what direction my future lied, I was free to enjoy the rest of my senior year. While I still continued to work on the Rampage, I did not participate in any other after school activities. By that time, my mother was working part-time as our church secretary and I was being transported from school in a van provided by the Special Services Department of the Roselle School System. Apparently, this was a free service extended to all children with special needs, and so every day I was among three girls to be picked up at 3:06 and driven home. While it gave me a sense of independence, it gave my mother some slack to do as she wished.

Though I was on the right track and headed for graduation, I still needed to keep up my grades especially since I was invited to in the National Honor Society. Being inducted into the National Honor Society was indeed an honor of which I never expected to attain. Actually, it was more happenstance than anything else. For several consecutive marking periods, I had made the honor roll. Then, one day I received a letter congratulating me on my most recent accomplishment. I was overjoyed. I never considered myself to be among the "brains" of my class, but there was my name printed in black and white as one of the newest students to be inducted into the National Honor Society. None of my classmates were more stunned by this announcement than Jeffrey Meyers and Evelyn Brody – those notorious class snobs.

Each candidate received several announcements about the induction ceremony to be sent out to family and friends inviting them to be part of that special evening. Since we did not have any family in the area, I decided to ask Father and Mrs. Moreau to attend, and they graciously accepted. A few days prior to the big night, they held a rehearsal for 2:30 in the afternoon so that all participants could practice marching in and accepting their pin. Unfortunately, I had to leave in mid-rehearsal to catch the van provided by special services to take me home. As a result, I was not informed about the proper way they decided to exit. So, when the ceremony ended, I exited via the center aisle and walking the entire length of the auditorium and left by means of the side exits. Embarrassed for the moment, I wanted to crawl into a hole and hide. Then, I realized that my mistake was an honest one. Since I was not present for the entire rehearsal, I naturally assumed we would leave the same way we entered. To this day, I regret that no one thought to tell me otherwise. Even so, I was not about to let a minor faux pas dampen my spirit.

Whether my error was really obvious or not, no one every stated. Everyone was just delighted that I had earned such a distinguished honor and their pride shone forth in their remarks. Aside from the principal and several teachers congratulating me, Jeffrey's parents extended a sincere word or two that made me feel that I had finally gained acceptance.

Years later, as I finger the remains of the petals from that red rose still pressed in my scrapbook adjacent to it the prestigious announcement of honor, I feel an enormous sense of pride. As a senior, I felt relieved that I would now have two major accomplishments to list under my picture in the yearbook of '73': Member of the National Honor Society and columnist for The Rampage, our school newspaper.

Ever since I started taking the van to school, I also needed assistance with opening my locker and hanging up my coat. While we still had plain clothes security guards scattered within the building, several teachers were assigned to various posts for hall duty. For convenience, my locker was located directly outside of the main office. After I climbed a flight of stairs, I only had a few feet to walk until I reached my locker.

Because the halls were so crowded with kids at that time, Mr. Potter, my former geometry teacher who had been assigned hall duty, assisted me with my belongings and opening my locker. As any normal seventeen-year-old young woman, I appreciated the extra attention especially from this rather handsome man. A few doors away was a language arts instructor by the name of Mr. Sohm. In his mid-fifties and a bit flirtatious, he started teasing me about leaving him for Mr. Potter. Thereafter, I was bestowed with the nickname of "the two-timer." Still somewhat naive, I was unaware of the connotations of the phrase, but I loved the attention.

With all of this inane bantering amongst the three of us, it was important to remember that it was done in jest. In a sense, these two men were preparing me for some antics that take place between the sexes. At that time, I was submerged into a world of adolescent boys who were too preoccupied with their raging hormones to give two hoots about me. Nevertheless, I think these two teachers saw that I needed a little encouragement in relating to the opposite sex. Whether I chose to marry or not, I would definitely need some expertise in establishing a good rapport with men in both the workplace and society at large.

Because I had made such a diligent effort to complete all of my required courses ahead of schedule, I now had the opportunity to take a few electives. At that time, the Interfaith Council of Roselle and Roselle Park approached the Board of Education with a proposal. In an effort to expose students to various religions including Christianity, several clergymen in our community got together and decided to offer a course titled, Religions of the World. A non-credit elective, each student would be given the option of attending this lecture series in place of their study hall. Every few weeks, a cleric from a neighborhood church would come and discuss such religions as Buddhism, Islam, Hinduism, Judaism, and of course, Christianity to name a few.

Not well received at first, the course started out with only a handful of semi-interested students. Discussing religion is at best a tedious task, especially when the particular one in question is not your own and you are presenting a body of information to some rather narrow-minded callow adolescents. Coupled with the fact that many of the clerics found it trying and difficult to relate their material to the youth, some of their key points were totally lost.

Frustrated and confused, the class dwindled until it reached its all-time low of four students. We were almost to the point of withdrawing ourselves from this seemingly boring course when we were rescued by the Reverend J. Max Creswell whose topic was Christianity, a religion that most of us knew rather intimately and of which we still yearned to gain a deeper understanding.

So, the next Friday, a tall man with greying temples and striking features greeted us as we came through the doorway. In his mid-thirties, Reverend Creswell was fairly new to the area having arrived from a small parish in Pennsylvania only a few years before. Aside from his warm and friendly personality, he had a real presence, one that people could feel whenever he was in the room.

It did not take us long to discover that he had a gift for storytelling. Somehow, through his choice of words and inflexion in his voice, Reverend Creswell had the amazing ability to make a story come alive. Like many of my classmates, I had heard many of the parables either in Sunday school or at my mother's knee. For the most part, I regarded these tales as ones Jesus Christ had told to his disciples and nothing more.

Now, thanks to our great preacher from the Presbyterian Church, I saw these stories with a moral in a whole new light. One time, he read three parables from the Good News Bible: The Lost Coin, The Prodigal Son, and The Lost Sheep. However, before he read the parables to us, he asked the class two questions: - how many of us had ever been lost and how many of us had ever lost something? Whether the object might be as insignificant as a pen or as essential to us as a loved one, the point was that we had all endured a loss of some kind. So when these questions were proposed to us before the parables were read, they were the instruments, if you will, that got us into the proper frame of mind to help us relate to the message that Christ wanted to convey.

Captivated by his ability to make Christianity come alive,

our class slowly grew. Reverend Creswell's enthusiasm for what he taught was highly contagious. Unlike his colleagues who stayed the minimum time allotted for their part of the course, Reverend Creswell remained with us for several weeks and enjoyed every minute of it.

Digressing a bit from his subject matter, Reverend Creswell took the time to share some of the memories of his own high school, college and later those precious days spent in seminary. Much to our amazement, he still wore his college ring, which symbolized his past accomplishments of which he was so proud. Above all, Reverend Creswell shared his own testimony of faith with us and told us how he strove to fulfill his lifelong desire to become a servant of God's church.

At the time I met Reverend Creswell, he had just completed his master's degree and was eagerly waiting to start the lengthy process of writing his dissertation. To our surprise, he chose the topic of Roselle, our town. As someone who only had plans to attend a small community college, I was impressed by his long-range ambitions.

In the weeks that followed, our class had become a close-knit little group with Reverend Creswell not only as our leader but our "surrogate" father as well. Aside from teaching us nuggets of the Christian faith, he emphasized the importance of fellowship within the church. Coming from a church where I had only experienced occasional fellowship from my peers, usually at the insistence of a higher authority, I felt somehow as though I had missed an essential ingredient in the fabric of my faith. Oh, how I yearned for it. I remember thinking that perhaps this unmet need would somehow find fulfillment as I grew older.

True to his word, Reverend Creswell took a personal interest in each one of us. Unlike some of his colleagues, who were there to fulfill an obligation in the form of a commitment made by the Interfaith Council, I think Reverend Creswell came because he genuinely wanted to share the Good News with us. And, his genuineness was real in his desire to remain with us for as long as possible. I recall how he surprised us by not only coming to our baccalaureate but our graduation as well.

My association with the First Presbyterian Church actually started when I was a youngster and attended their Summer Bible School for two weeks several summers while growing up. Because of this connection, I had formed relationships with some of the Presbyterians that still remain intact today. In fact, for many years, Reverend Creswell referred to me as the "adopted" Presbyterian.

A few years after Father Moreau resigned to accept another pastorate, our new rector, the Reverend William Kenneth Gorman, a devout Christian and intellectual, eventually formed a friendship with Reverend Creswell which later led to the joining of both congregations for Bible studies, special projects and annual Maundy Thursday services. Thereafter, whenever I met Reverend Creswell, he always greeted his "adopted" Presbyterian friend with a warm hug and a sincere interest in my well being.

As the day of graduation approached, the hype surrounding the event intensified. For reasons that escape me, our class decided to forgo having a prom but we did have a wonderful class night. Open to everyone, regardless of their social status, it was the last time we would be together as the class of '73. We reminisced about the past and we projected into the future. Who would succeed and in what capacity?

Proud of myself that I had accomplished so much, I faced my future with uncertainty and trepidation. Was I really college material? Would I be able to adjust to a life outside the world of high school? What kind of future would I have? I faced severe fear of the unknown. Indeed, I had a case of pre-graduation jitters. Unfortunately, I was not as convinced as everyone else as to my success in college, but I certainly was willing to give it a try. Scattered all throughout my yearbook were message of encouragement and support. Every now and again, I pick up that yearbook and feast on the many memories it holds. Next stop: College!

6

I was officially accepted to Union County College, and I felt that a weight had been lifted from my shoulders. The next step I would take would be seeing a counselor, Violet Wilmore, at the college. Fortunately I had known her from Girl Scouts and I felt at ease with her. When I told her about my father's idea of having me take one course per semester she asked me, "how long do you want to be here?" I said as long as I can successfully complete my college education.

She asked, "How many courses did you take when you were in high school?"

I replied, "Five."

"While college is a bit harder and more is expected of you as a student, why don't we compromise and have you take three courses per semester and see how that goes?" she suggested.

I was relieved that she was on my side. Mrs. Wilmore was a very compassionate person, and because she knew me from Girl Scouts, she had a better sense of what I was capable of doing. So, she pushed me to achieve and to reach my potential.

My first course was Introduction to English taught by a very nice older woman who, like many English teachers, had us write part of an autobiography. I have come to realize that this exercise has two purposes, first, to give the instructor a glance at our writing styles, and, second, to allow the instructor to learn something about their students. With a class of 30 to 35 students, there simply isn't time to get to know everyone. This writing activity kills two birds with one stone. I enjoyed her class. Most of it, however, was a review of grammar and the basics of writing. For me this was all review, but for other students this was a much needed course because most classes required writing a thesis of some kind.

I also enjoyed my Introduction to Psychology course. This is where I met my first college friend, Phyllis. She was a nontraditional student in that she was a little bit older than the others and she was already out in the working world. She wanted to further her education in the hopes of someday securing a better job. We discovered that we lived about five miles apart and we got together maybe about once a week. We enjoyed talking about classes, doing homework, and discussing our life experiences. Phyllis lived with her parents who were elderly, and she had most of the responsibility of caring for them. Unfortunately, this was a short-term friendship, as Phyllis seemed to think I was holding her back from meeting "Mr. Right."

Like nearly every student, I found the cafeteria to be the central meeting place and I enjoyed having my lunch there. If I needed any help (which I did) carrying my tray from the line to my table, I could always ask the student in front or behind me if they would assist me; nine times out of ten, they were glad to do so.

During my first semester in college most of the sororities had displays set out inviting students to join. I was particularly impressed with one display because it seemed to be a service sorority where the members would involve themselves in fundraising for various charities and local organizations in addition to socializing with each other and having a good time. The sorority I chose to pledge to was Gamma Sigma Chi. To pledge, our memberships we had to make a wooden paddle featuring the name of the sorority, our name, and our intentions. Of course, my father helped me with this. He was glad that I was entering the college social scene. We also hosted a sorority get together at my house with tea and cookies, etc. It was there that I met the two young ladies who were to become my best friends, Kyle Barnum and Sue Clay. Both girls lived within five miles of each other. Sue had her mind set on becoming a psychologist and Kyle wanted to be an occupational therapist. Eventually Kyle transferred to Temple University in Pennsylvania. I think her desire to work with people with disabilities attracted Kyle to me. I remember many times I served as a guinea pig when she had projects to do for her classes. For example, I remember sitting outside in the beautiful backyard painting. She asked me to paint a picture of what I saw and with my CP, and I painted what I thought looked like trees. She had other ideas of what they might be. On another occasion, she and I made pizza and I rolled out the dough to give my hands some exercise. Kyle always had very creative ideas and I did not mind at all being her guinea pig.

    Once, when Kyle's parents were going to be out of town for the weekend, she asked me to come and stay with her. She did not want to be in the house alone all weekend. Kyle lived in a large ranch in Scotch Plains in an affluent community. Before I accepted the invitation, I asked my parents what they thought, and they encouraged me to go and stay with her. So, for the weekend we were bachelorettes. Sometime that weekend she confided to me that she suffered from bipolar disorder. While she was on medication for this mental disorder, it seemed to bother her more during the fall. Sometimes Kyle could not get out of the bed in the morning because she felt so down. Other times she felt so high and excited she would not be able to control her enthusiasm and would do some strange things. Since then I learned that bipolar disorder seems to present itself in people in their teens and early twenties and can change the course of one's life. Kyle was fortunate to have parents who had the means to get her help right away. However, this too is a lifelong disability that one must learn to accept and cope with.

As for Sue Clay, she had her heart set on becoming a psychologist. She was always citing different experiments and things that she had read. She was very friendly and talkative and enjoyed engaging in deep conversations. Her parents were very down to earth and opened their home to us; on Friday nights that would be our flophouse. As we became acquainted with each other, we realized that we really were not interested in the sorority but in something more meaningful such as Christian Fellowship. Unfortunately, the sorority that we pledged to turned out to be more invested in partying and drinking rather than having social get togethers and encouraging the formation of intimate friendships. Therefore, the three of us decided to leave the sorority life and get more involved with Christian Fellowship and learning about our Lord.

At this time, I also took an Introduction to Sociology course taught by a man who seemed to love four-letter words more than anything. I soon learned that his method of teaching was not for me and decided to drop that course and pursue Sociology at another time. That was the best decision I ever made because that very next semester I signed up for

Introduction to Sociology again with a wonderful man, Paul Evans, who became my mentor and friend. We still maintain a relationship today that has endured 45 years. I have watched this man with his children, grandchildren, and now, great-grandchildren and seen him enjoy each generation. Unlike his colleague, Paul Evans is a man of faith. He is an ordained Methodist Minister, and he also served as a missionary in Nigeria where he and his family spent three years teaching the people about sanitation, education, and, of course, about Jesus. I remember going into his office where he had a photo cube on his desk showcasing pictures of his family, his wife, his biological daughter, his Chinese daughter, and his adopted son; he was very proud of his family.

I think Paul Evans was intrigued by me because of my disability. He realized quite quickly, though, that I was a young woman with a disability and not a disabled young woman. He always had a lot of questions pertaining to how I became disabled, how I got through school, how I managed with homework and more. He was very interested in my life. In fact, he brought his wife, Mary Ellen, to my college graduation. She had heard so much about me that she wanted to meet me. I attended the weddings of their children, baptisms of their grandchildren, and several other social occasions where we celebrated with their family.

A year later, I found myself taking a music appreciation

course with Mary Beth Evans, Paul Evans' biological daughter. She had many of the same characteristics as her mother, but the height and body mass of her father. Mary Beth was in love with her high-school sweetheart and planned to marry him someday. Of course, I think it was more an infatuation than true love. Absence can either make the heart grow fonder or it can reveal what the heart lacks. As Mary Beth and he were going to separate colleges, so their hearts went separate ways, and, eventually, Mary Beth met Tommy. They fell in love and married and had a family together. In fact, my parents and I were even invited to their wedding. At Union College, Mary Beth helped me in our music appreciation class. She took notes for me, and we sat and listened to all genres of music from the Baroque era to present day.

As I became better acquainted with Kyle and Sue, I learned of another friend that they wanted me to meet. Her name was Betty Jo Shepherd and she lived in the same town as Sue not far from me. Betty Jo was a quadriplegic due to a fall from a second story window. Unfortunately, she tried to commit suicide, broke her neck and ended up in Kessler Rehabilitation Institute for several months. This is a heartbreaking story. Fortunately, her parents were able to convert their home to meet Betty Jo's special needs. For instance, the dining room was converted into a first floor bedroom with an adjoining bathroom. The girls introduced me to Betty Jo, and she and I became very good friends and stayed friends for over 35 years.

Prior to my meeting Betty Jo, my mother had met her through an extension course she was giving on raising a child with a disability. She was a master seamstress and made several of her own blouses. She even altered her pants to accommodate her catheter. She really had a lot of creative ideas to share with people in similar situations. Betty Jo was endured so much and yet she did so much. After her accident, it took her several years to get her life back on track, but eventually, she married, lived in a senior citizen apartment with her new husband, and eventually had a house built with 40 living accommodations to meet their special needs. Her husband Ed, who was also confined to a wheelchair because of polio, worked as postmaster for the Dunellen Post Office in New Jersey. He held this position for over three decades and retired at the age of 65. Before Ed came into the picture and everything changed, Betty Jo and I used to get together once a week and play Scrabble. She and I enjoyed words and we liked to challenge each other. Both of us were quite good and so we were well matched. Betty Jo was a source of inspiration to me and gave me counsel when I needed to make decisions regarding my disability. She was very encouraging and supportive.

Betty Jo was also interested in furthering her education and from time to time took courses at Union County College too. She was also one of the first people to take part in the tele-a-college program where students who were unable to attend in person could attend classes with a special device over the phone. Of course, this does not replace the actual college experience, but it does give people who otherwise would not have the opportunity to pursue higher education the ability to do so.

We tried to include Betty Jo in as many social activities as possible. I remember one Christmas it had been quite warm and there was no snow, so we bundled up Betty Jo and went caroling door to door around her neighborhood. Then we returned to her home where her mother had hot chocolate and homemade chocolate chip cookies for us. Because of her disability, Betty Jo had a different lifestyle than we did. Through the years, she had several aides who would help assist her with activities of daily living, do the grocery shopping, and complete everyday cleaning. By this time her parents were well into their 70s and they needed some physical help as well. Her father was a retired lawyer and her mother a retired social worker, so they had the means to afford the extra help. Betty Jo received disability, which, combined with her father's pension, enabled her to get the help she needed.

Several years later, Betty Jo met Ed Gill and they started dating. She had told everyone that they were just friends who shared some common interests. We believed her and we were glad she was pursuing another friendship. Well, three months later Betty announced she and Ed were engaged. Ed was 20 years older and had endured his own trials and tribulations. Aside from being a remarkable guy, he brought out the best in Betty Jo.

They decided to have a private civil ceremony, at her home with both sets of parents in attendance. This was to be held on February 24, 1986. After their wedding, Mr. and Mrs. Gill moved into a senior citizen complex three miles from his job. With all of their special equipment, it was a tight fit in their apartment, but later they had a home built to accommodate their special needs. As postmaster Ed was very dedicated to his job and got up at 5:30 a.m. to be able to complete his personal hygiene and to get to work by 8 a.m. He drove himself in his specially equipped van.

The more Sue, Kyle, and I bonded and became more comfortable with each other, the less my disability seemed to matter. One summer we decided as a group to go down to the beach to see the sunrise. It was a 30 mile trip from Sue's house, so we all spent the night there and awoke about 3 a.m. to get dressed, pack the car, and head on our little adventure. Driving down to Ocean Beach we catnapped until we arrived at our destination. By 4:30 a.m. we were sitting on the beach awaiting the sun to rise.

As we witnessed the beautiful sunrise, we realized the wonder of what God had created. We stayed on the beach until about 7 o'clock and then we went to breakfast at a pancake house. By about 9 o'clock we were back on the beach. The guys were playing Frisbee and the girls were wading in the water; I decided to take a nap. I just couldn't keep my eyes open any longer. So thinking I was under the umbrella, I turned on my side and fell asleep. About an hour later, I woke up and, oh, was I a sight! One half of me was red, and one half of me was white, but that's the price you pay for doing something out of the ordinary. When I returned home later that day, my grandmother took one look at me and she said "we'd better get you in the house and lather up with Noxzema." Needless to say, I was uncomfortable for a few days, but it was worth the experience to have a day out with my friends.

By this time, Kyle had met Doug West who was also a devout Christian and they started going together. Doug became part of our little circle of friends who were now in Christian Fellowship, and we all met weekly during the college social hour. Our group expanded to about twenty people who would read a portion of scripture and pray together. This was a very cohesive bunch and soon we were attending Friday night coffee houses together. I enjoyed these times and felt a real sense of community.

Back in college I soon realized that I needed to take a science to meet my curriculum requirements. I decided to take Biology, the study of living things. In our lab, we were assigned partners. Mine was a young man by the name Bill, and, for obvious reasons, he did all the cutting. We dissected an earthworm, a bullfrog, and a chicken. I found this to be very interesting while others found it to be very gross. Some students found the odor of formaldehyde nauseating. Despite all our hang ups, this was a very interesting and intense course that I think made me realize just how complex, and yet how beautiful, the human body is.

As time went by I loved the freedom of going from class to class unaided knowing that no one was going to try to throw me down the stairs or try to push me like I feared in my high school days. In time, I chose the major of Liberal Arts Urban Studies. I loved most of my courses except for History and Government, which I found to be quite dry and rote. Memorizing a bunch of facts and recalling them was not my cup of tea, but like everyone else I had to fulfill the requirements for my major. While enjoying the college scene, I always had thoughts in the back of my mind about what I would like to do when I completed my education. Many ideas entered my head, but I did not know how realistic they were. I liked interior decorating, library science, and, obviously, I liked writing. However, I could not see myself as a journalist because of my speech. My counselor with vocational rehabilitation discouraged me from occupations where I had to verbally interact with other people because of it.

I soon learned that most rehabilitation counselors did not take into consideration the individual person but, instead, put people in groups according to their disability and special needs. This was a sort of stereotyping. In many cases, these counselors really did not have experience with any particular disability and they acted based on what they felt was best. They were not taking into consideration the individual person's strengths and weaknesses. Obviously, it falls back on the person themselves to choose what they decide is best for them. There are no crystal balls and no one can predict the future, but it has been my experience that much depends on the motivation and the determination of the individual. To succeed, a person must have these two ingredients plus the support of family and close friends.

As my years at Union County College were drawing to a close, I now had to decide where I wanted to continue my education. I knew I needed a four-year degree if I wanted to purse anything worthwhile. Sue was still intent on pursuing a degree in psychology and was accepted at Montclair State University. I had toyed with the idea of going there too. However, when I went to tour the campus I learned how far apart the buildings were spread and what a wind tunnel it was in the winter. I also toured a dormitory and noted how noisy and carefree it seemed. As a person who needs a lot of quiet, I could not see myself in that situation. Back in those days, they did not have the accommodations for the physically disabled that they have now. Therefore, I was very hesitant to transfer to a school where I would need to stay on campus. So, I decided to transfer to Kean College, which is now Kean University, about a half-mile from my home. This may have short-changed me the full college experience, but it allowed me to complete my education, which set me up for the career of my dreams.

7

After debating whether to go away to finish college or not, I finally decided to go to Kean College, which is now Kean University, formerly a teachers' college that has, through the years, expanded to offer many more career options. Since Kean College was only a half-mile from my home I decided to attend, which seemed to me to be the best decision at the time. I just did not feel right about moving away from home, especially when I could access the courses I needed within a mile of home. While I envied Sue and Kyle, and even my high school friend Carol, their ability to test their wings away from home, I really did not feel comfortable doing so. I enrolled in Kean College as a junior with a major in Sociology and a minor in English. I realized this was quite a combination, but I really did not know what major to choose.

When I went to new student orientation, I was pleased to learn that the two buildings that housed most of my classes were adjacent to each other. This would eliminate a lot of unnecessary walking. At this point, the furthest building I would need would be the library and perhaps on occasion the cafeteria. This I could handle. Instead of taking my usual 9 credits a semester, I expanded it to 15. This was a full load, but I was determined that I could handle it.

My first semester, I took three Sociology courses and two English courses and all of them required some type of writing. I spent many a weekend typing my fingers to the bone working on these papers. Some were short, others were long and more detailed, but I managed to get them all done and turned in on time. I am pleased to say that most of them came back with either an A or a B, and so I was delighted.

I remember my first English course at Kean required a lot of writing. I really liked my teacher, Mrs. Scotto who was very kind and understanding. Later, I learned that she was also my advisor. She pointed out that I almost had enough credits to make English a second major. I only needed two more classes and I could have a BA in English as well as in Sociology, and so I said "my goodness, why not? After all, two majors are better than one!" Had it not been for Mrs. Scotto, I might not have ended up with a career in journalism.

FITTING IN

As far as Sociology was concerned, I was adding to my knowledge by taking courses such as the Sociology of Religion, the Medical Sociology, the Sociology of the Family, etc. These were very interesting courses, but I do not know whether they would have led to a career or not. However, the background that they gave me would always be useful, especially in my work in journalism.

During those days, my mother worked as a church secretary for our church. Even though this was a part-time position, she spent many evenings on the phone with various parishioners who voiced their complaints about our new minister Reverend William Kenneth Gorman. He succeeded Father Moreau who left to take on another church. Of course with a change in ministers comes a change in leadership style. For some parishioners, especially older ones, this can be hard to accept, but it is a fact of life.

Father Gorman, his wife Bobbi, and their little son, Scott were a welcomed sight. I think because my mother was secretary, I probably got to know them a little sooner than everyone else did. As most young women, I loved babies, and Scott was no exception. He was almost two and was fascinated by certain words. For instance, if he heard the word "spaghetti" he would laugh and laugh. I got a kick out of his behavior and I just loved to hear him talk. It seemed like every week he was learning a new word or two.

As the Gorman's became more comfortable with me, they eventually asked me to babysit Scott. It seemed that Bobbi wanted to participate in an afternoon Bible study and needed someone to stay with the baby, and she asked me if I would do the honors. I was very touched and surprised by her request. I was nineteen and no one had ever asked me to babysit before. I think probably because of my disability people did not think I could handle this responsibility. I was about to show them.

At the time, I was driven home from campus by Red Cross who picked me up from school and dropped me off at home. However, on Wednesdays they would drop me off at church so I would be able to babysit Scottie. I would get there by one o'clock and Bobbi would have my lunch on the table. Scottie would be napping. Usually I would soon hear a little voice and know that someone was up and ready to play. Scottie would be able to get himself out of his bed with help and he would love to give me all his toys and surround me with them. He liked to entertain me as well. Sometimes he would bring me five or six of his favorite books and would want to be read to. He loved Dr. Seuss. I bet I read Cat and the Hat fifty times.

As Scottie got older I began to babysit in the evenings as well. The Gorman's trusted me and I trusted them. I remember a funny story when Scottie was two and a half and learning to uses the potty. He had the crazy idea that he had to take off his shoes and pants and step into the toilet. Since the toilet water was so cold, he quickly started to cry and learned that it was not for him. I helped him out of the toilet and dried his tears and told him he could stand beside the toilet to go and that was the end of that. When his father came home I told him the story and he got hysterical. I think his father still needed to show him how to go like a big-boy.

My babysitting days lasted about two years. It gave me a wonderful opportunity to learn confidence and trust. I knew with

the right child I could do a reasonably good job as a sitter. As Scottie grew older and his vocabulary expanded and he learned that different words rhymed he soon referred to me as "fancy Nancy." As a matter of fact, to this day, I can still hear him calling me "fancy Nancy" as I came down the church aisle. Even though his mother tried to curtail his excitement he still sought to get my attention, and he did.

Juggling 15 credits did not give me much time for a social life. However, I did mingle here and there. It was in my English course, the Bible as Literature, where I met Kathy Cronin who became my friend and later my sister-in-law. We sat on opposite sides of the room, but somehow we got together and she became my note taker for that particular course. As we got to talking, we also realized we both loved the water and swimming. Kathy was a certified lifeguard. She volunteered to take me swimming at the Olympic sized pool on campus. I was thrilled. I loved the water and I could not have been more pleased than to have a friend to go swimming with every week.

Kathy came from West Orange and she commuted back and forth to school on a daily basis. Because she received financial aid, she worked in the counseling office as a secretary so many hours a week to offset the costs of her schooling. Coming from an Irish-Catholic family, she had one sister and two brothers. They lived in the armory because her father was the maintenance man and as part of his salary he received housing there. Kathy was interested in becoming a special education teacher, while her sister Patty was also interested in teaching but at the high school level. They were a very religious family and a very intact one.

Even though Kyle was studying in Pennsylvania I still heard from her quite often. One weekend she invited me to come to Temple University. I was elated. I spoke with my parents about it, and even though they were hesitant about me taking a train, they both agreed it would be a wonderful experience for me. They trusted Kyle and knew she had my best interest at heart. So we bought a train ticket and off I went! I was nervous and excited at the same time. I had flown to Arizona by myself, so I guess I could handle this two-hour journey as well. My father helped me onto the train and made sure that I was seated and comfortable before the train took off. When I arrived at the train station in Temple, Kyle was there to greet me and we had a wonderful time.

We went to a dance at a seminary that Saturday night. I am not much of a dancer, but there was one seminary student who decided to give me a whirl, and he did. For some reason, there was a shortage of young women that night so I never got a chance to sit still. My handicap didn't matter. That night I was just one of the crowd. True, I was tired, but it was an experience I will never forget.

Meanwhile back on the home front, Rick was getting ready to graduate from high school and thinking about his career options. He had decided from the get go to be an engineer. As my mother always said, he had "golden hands" and could fix anything. Many a Saturday he spent under the hood of a car tinkering with all kinds of parts. That seemed to be his passion, and so it was not a surprise to any of us when he chose Mechanical Engineering as his major. We visited Lafayette

College in Pennsylvania and several other schools. He finally decided on Stevens Institute of Technology in Hoboken, New Jersey. He too wanted to stay close to home, but unlike me, he decided to live on campus. At the tender age of 17, Rick left home and started his college career in engineering. While he did not know what kind of engineering he was truly interested in, he finally decided on Mechanical Engineering and that served him very well.

While he was at college, Rick met a girl named Cindy who he briefly dated. Unfortunately, we did not like Cindy and saw some definite flaws, but we had to let Rick have his fling and figure it out for himself. Meanwhile, back home, I was getting together weekly with Kathy who seemed to be spending more and more time at my house when she would drop me off after swimming. It seemed the talking was not just with me but with Rick as well. We noticed that these two never ran out of things to say to each other, and their chemistry was really starting to become quite evident. Soon, Cindy was out of the picture and Kathy was in. I remember that Rick invited Kathy to a dance and she accepted. That was the beginning of a romance that has lasted their lifetimes.

I had some unusual, but rather funny, experiences during my college days. I remember when I was negotiating around Kean College one windy day, and I got stuck on a little bridge across a narrow creek. For some reason, the wind would just not let me move and I was hanging on for dear life. Fortunately, an instructor happened to be lecturing and saw me frantically trying to hold on and balance myself so that I would not fall into the creek. He was my rescuer. He sent two of his strongest male students down to rescue me from the windy bridge. Thank goodness someone was looking out their window! I thank God he intervened and saved the day. Another time, I got stuck in an elevator between floors. Everyone else was able to jump down and out as the doors were opened, but I could not. Several young men had to help me and lift me down and out of the elevator. That experience was scary. If I had not been with other people, I am not sure how long it would have taken me to get help.

Meanwhile, Rick and Kathy were starting to seriously date. Their friendship was turning into a romance. One date turned into several and they continued this relationship for several years before they started to think about marriage. Of course, they were both eager to finish their studies and to begin their careers before even thinking about a wedding.

Kathy's first job was in Newark, New Jersey at a Day Center for the mentally and physically challenged. It was not a high-paying job but she had to start somewhere. Most everyone has to start in the trenches and work their way up and Kathy did. On the other hand, Rick had a year to go at college and he was offered a position at Ingersoll Rand in New Jersey. Like Kathy, he had to start somewhere, so he got his own small apartment and saw Kathy on weekends.

Summer was vastly approaching, and I, like my peers, wanted some type of summer employment, not so much for the money but for the experience. Aside from my education, I really had nothing to put on my resume, and I thought if I had some working experience that it would help me in the long run to secure a good job. So, I went back to my counselor at the Division of Vocational Rehabilitation in Elizabeth. This time when I went back, I discovered I had a new counselor. It was time to start all over again with questions about my disability, what I wanted to do, what I could do, etc. By this time, I was really getting frustrated because I had been through all of this so many times before.

I told her my reason for coming was that I was seeking summer employment and I needed a little extra help finding a job. She said that she would take down the information and get back to me. Although she never specified when she would get back to me because she never intended to. Unfortunately, a DVR has so many clients that they are just inundated with visits and paperwork. Instead of being honest and saying that she did not have time to find summer employment for me, she just strung me along. Every week I would call up and I would get the same answer that she was still looking. Finally, the summer was about to come to a close and she said that they do not do summer employment. I was furious and disappointed, and I lost a lot of my faith in "the system."

I was about to enter my last year in college. This was going to be a turning point. I had a lot of trepidation about graduating because I had no idea what I would be doing if anything at all. That experience with my counselor really soured me on trusting people that were supposed to help me. However, that was about to change as I was assigned a new counselor. Although I had reservations about giving the DVR another shot, my father said I had nothing to lose. I still had not had a job, so what was the worst that could come out of it?

Contrary to my past experience my new counselor, Jim Lape, he was tall and thin with dark wavy hair, had an entirely different approach and he really seemed to believe that I was employable. While he couldn't quite pinpoint it, he knew that because of my intelligence, college education, and determination that I could have a career. I felt he believed in me and that was a big plus. It just so happened that he had a connection with another counselor, Rita Lang, who ran the Screening Unit. This unit was comprised of people with some sort of disability in Newark, New Jersey, which wasn't too far away from home. Jim gave me the connection and I called and set up an interview. My father took me down for the interview and I could tell right away that Ms. Lang was a no nonsense type of person. After asking me a few questions, she said the job was mine if I wanted it. She explained to me the ins and outs of the job and she said it was not the most glamorous one, but, she said, I had to start somewhere and that this was a good starting point. As far as salary was concerned, this was a CETA position, which was an alternative for people with some kind of disadvantage, so wages were not high. This was an 18-month program, which could be expanded depending on how well I did and their funding. I also could take a Civil Service test and depending on how well I scored on the test, I would be able to keep the job. My father waited in the hall, and when I told him that I got the job, he couldn't believe it. He couldn't wait to tell my mother the good news. He was very surprised but he was also very happy for me. Now that I knew I had a job waiting for me, I was looking forward to graduation.

Graduation day was looming and I was growing more and more excited. We were planning a small party with my grandmother, my godmother, a few close friends, and my favorite professor, Mr. Evans from Union College. I received many cards and presents including one gift that was really special, a wood carving of the Lord's Supper that was made in Nigeria where Mr. Evans was a missionary. My friends were all at the party including Carol from high school, Kyle and Sue from Union County College plus my family. I was about to start a career like everyone else!

8

Like many people, I was nervous the first day of my job at the Screening Unit. Arriving on the job site about five minutes early, I was dressed in a well-pressed suit carrying my pocket book and my lunch. Miss Lang greeted me at the door and pointed out the desk and where I would be working. Happily, I noticed that I had a typewriter as well as a chair with arms to make me as comfortable as possible.

I met some of my coworkers who were there not by choice but because of their disabilities. In time, I learned that the Screening Unit was created for people who were capable of working but who had other hidden and not so obvious disabilities. These disabilities ranged from physical to psychological to just plain hitting the bottle too hard. At the Screening Unit, we reviewed files of cases of people seeking disability because of a condition that they felt prevented them from successful gainful employment. For instance, someone in their late 50s might injure their arm and that may have impaired their ability to carry boxes. A reasonable accommodation could be made where they did not have to carry boxes but were asked to perform another task that they were capable of doing instead.

We made determinations based on the information presented in each case. Sometimes this was rather difficult because we never got to meet the person face to face. The criteria for making a determination were based on age, disability, vocational history, and motivation. Motivation was a critical factor. After being injured some people just give up and say they have a legitimate excuse to collect disability. Other people are very eager and determined to be retrained for some other kind of employment. Those in the latter category are much more successful because they choose not to give up, and these were the candidates that we wanted to help.

As for the staff, Rita Lang, our supervisor, was there for a specific reason. Rita was kind and caring and she arrived early at 7 a.m., well before the staff got there, and she would leave at noon. I think this arrangement maybe gave the staff too much freedom and certainly some of them took advantage of it. For instance, three workers were alcoholics. Every Friday they would claim that they needed to go to "the bank" and make a withdrawal. It did not take me long to realize that the bank was a bar and the withdrawal was alcohol. Therefore, about three hours later, they would return to work quite happy and quite drunk. They were kind people, but they just had an addiction to the bottle.

Probably my best friend on site was Jean Ware who also had athetoid CP. She was in her late 40s and had slurred speech and difficulty getting around. However, she was a kind person and very interested in showing me the ropes. Her husband, Don, also had CP, but was not as involved as his wife. He worked upstairs as a vocational supervisor for the Department of Rehabilitation in Newark. They were happily married for over 30 years. Because of their physical disabilities, they agreed not to have any children, but they were very close to their nieces and nephews. Both of them loved their jobs and enjoyed a very active social life as well. For the first time in my life, I had a real role model, someone who had the same disability, and someone who I could call on for advice and guidance.

Another coworker whom I befriended was a woman in her early 30s named Evelyn. She had red hair and was more attractive than she realized. Unfortunately, she had suffered a stroke. It was during her gym class at the young age of 11. Needless to say, she scared her teacher and her peers, as well as her family, half to death. It took her several years to recover. Even though she lost the use of her left arm and walked with a limp, she did quite well. However, she seemed to make herself more handicapped psychologically by avoiding contact with people. She was a loner. She liked to take long walks. She followed a very strict diet. As a matter of fact, one time, she decided to only eat carrots, and believe it or not, Evelyn turned as orange as her red hair. She claimed she followed a special diet, but we felt it did more harm than good. As far as her role as a coworker, though, she was very conscientious and always eager to express her opinion.

Since the work site was located about eight miles from home, I was going to have to learn to take public transportation. Of course this was a big step toward independence. I first took the bus with the help of a young woman my father hired to accompany me. Her name was Karen and she was a high school senior. My father knew her from an insurance client that he serviced and felt that she would be a good match for this type of job. She met me at the bus stop and rode with me to the job site. She did this for the first couple of weeks until I felt comfortable riding by myself. By this time, I had acquired the aid of a few of my fellow passengers and they would look out for me and make sure I was seated before the bus took off. Noticing my awkward gait, the passengers were very protective and made sure the driver was alerted to my special needs. In time, we all became friendly and we all looked out for each other.

After about six months of taking the bus, we realized I could travel faster if I took the train. Since Penn Station was only a block away from my building, we thought that was the fastest and most direct way to travel. Taking the train posed some concerns and fears. However, after I had taken the train twice, the conductors were very conscientious about making sure that I was seated before the train took off. Of course, sometimes this did not happen, and once I landed in a man's lap. Some people might say I fell for him. I don't know who was more surprised, he or I, but he was very kind and helped me to a vacant seat.

I also got myself into some other rather unusual predicaments. It was three days before Christmas and many of the companies were having were having office parties. That day it had snowed and it was slippery under foot. Even though I tried to be as careful as possible I slipped and fell right in front of Penn Station. There I was sitting on the cold ground with both my shoes off. I guess I looked like I had had one too many, and people passing me by thought I was drunk. So there I was sitting on the cold ground and unable to get up when finally two young men came along and saw my dilemma. They quickly put on my shoes, helped me up, and I was on my way. Finally, I reached my train and the conductor took one look at me and asked what happened? I explained to him that I fell, scraped my hand, and probably bruised my ego, but that other than that I was ok.

Another time I happened to be walking through Penn Station and a woman approached me and asked if I could give her some money. She was in her mid 50's dressed in a raggedy coat and didn't smell that great. When I refused, she cornered me and said that I had a very nice coat and therefore I should have money to give her. Again I refused, but this time she became a little more insistent and would not take no for an answer. Fortunately, a man passed by and overheard the altercation and decided to intervene. He managed to pull me away and escort me to my train. I was very thankful!

Back at the office, Jean and I learned that we were both Christian, and we decided to participate in an interdenominational worship service about a block from our office. It was held on Wednesdays. We would go and then have lunch in a little restaurant, which was inside a hotel and directly across from the small chapel where this worship service was held. It was only about a half hour, but we liked the minister and the type of message he gave. Sometimes we would even meet Jean's husband and he would join us.

My other coworkers were also rather interesting people. For instance, our secretary, Rose Marie Corio, was a young woman, age 26 who often was very depressed. She lived alone and was concerned that her life was going nowhere. However, at this time, the state offered college courses and Rose Marie chose to enroll. Overall, she liked going to school and she enjoyed the challenge. Eventually, she chose to major in English. After several months we became good friends and we got together during the weekends on a regular basis. I think Rose Marie chose me to be her confidant and she would complain to me about her lack of dates. She had a poor self-image and this contributed to her depression. She was close to her family and even though she lost her father ten years prior, she still relived those memories on a regular basis. Sadly to say, she never seemed to get over her father's death.

In addition to Rose Marie, I worked with Josephine who was in her fifties, a Polish gal, who liked cooking her favorite dishes and liked bringing samples to her coworkers. She was the official "mother" of the group. She was always the one to lend an ear and offer advice. Then there was Peter who was the other counselor. He was well liked but he was also loner. He had some family problems and more or less kept to himself. I liked Peter and I would often engage him in conversation especially regarding his ten-year-old daughter. As far as work was concerned, Pete was very frustrated working in the Screening Unit and hoped that someday he would return to a more challenging job.

Everything was going well. I liked my job. I now could get there independently by riding the train or taking the bus. I was making friends and I felt as though I had a place in the work force. I was truly happy and proud of my accomplishments even though I had to convince people of my capabilities. Then one morning, everything changed. My world as I knew it turned upside down.

It was a Saturday morning, October 6, 1979, when I was leisurely lying in bed trying to find the energy to start my day. I remember hearing my father call upstairs and say, "Nancy get up I need you down here." I couldn't imagine what was going on. I got downstairs as fast as possible and saw that my mother was sitting at the breakfast table with coffee coming out of her mouth and a cigarette on the table. "I think your mother's had a stroke," said my father. He called 911. I looked at my mother, she was red faced and looked like she did not know what was going on. She was dazed and her eyes were half shut. The ambulance came within three minutes.

They carried her to the stretcher, took her vitals, and then they were off. My father took his car and I stayed home to make some very necessary phone calls. My brother was at college. Fortunately Helen Jago came over and stayed with me until someone came. At that point, I didn't know what to think. I was upset, but I was able to carry on. I called my Godmother and I also called Kathy. They both came right away.

Meanwhile, in the emergency room, the physician said that my mother had had a severe stroke. Unlike today, there was no TPA, the medication that is a clot buster, which can help to decrease the effects of the stroke. Instead, it was a waiting game. They placed Mom in intensive care so that she would be monitored to see what course the stroke would take. The next three days were critical.

FITTING IN

My father made some calls from the hospital and my brother was on his way home. It is amazing how quickly people can gather in the wake of an emergency. Even though we could not do anything to physically help my mother, we, the family and friends, needed some kind of support system. My grandmother who was in her 70s and now living in South Jersey was also notified and she offered to come up and stay with us for a while. We also called Father Gorman. As our priest he needed to be notified, and as my mother's boss he needed to know that he would have to make arrangements as far as coverage for the church office.

The next three days were a wait-and-see game. Doctors wanted to ensure that the stroke was over and to note any residual symptoms that would erupt from the episode. That was a long three days. Because it was Columbus Day weekend, I had an extra day off. That Tuesday, I called Rita Lang and explained to her what happened. She was very sympathetic because her mother had also had a stroke. She told me to take all the time I needed and to keep the faith.

Meanwhile, my neighbors had learned of the tragedy that befell my mother. Unknown to my father and me, they were making arrangements amongst themselves to get me to and from the train station. This was so kind of them. There were five neighbors involved and each day a different one came to the train station and picked me up and brought me home. This went on for months. My father was very grateful to them. As the breadwinner, he needed to do his job as well. His boss was also very understanding and sent flowers. However, in sales, production is everything and if you do not produce, then the paycheck suffers.

My father was always a pessimist. He was ready to put my mom in a nursing home, sell the house, and just be done with it. Fortunately, none of this materialized. After the three day waiting period, we could see that my mother was a fighter and she was determined not to give up. While she did loose the movement in her left arm and had difficulty with her left leg, there was nothing wrong with her mouth. However, she did suffer from aphasia and she had difficulty remembering our names. For example, I became "Natalie" I think because Natalie starts with N. My brother was referred to as "the boy." She could not remember his name for anything. However, the one name she did remember was my father "Dick." The speech therapist was soon involved and taught her different tricks to help her cognitive functioning.

Any type of communication disorder is very difficult for a patient to accept, especially if you love to chit chat. For my mother, not being able to communicate properly was extremely frustrating. She knew what she wanted to say but could not express it. She knew the words but they just would not come out. It was like playing charades trying to figure out what she wanted to say. I remember one night visiting her and she wanted the cup and she said all the words around the cup but we couldn't get "cup." So, we were both frustrated. Finally, when I realized what she wanted, I was drained.

In addition to the speech therapy, physical therapy became involved. They had her sitting up and starting to walk within a matter of days. It is vital that this happens for a number of reasons. The faster patients are able to get up and get moving, the quicker those abilities return. The more patients stand and are able to put their weight through their legs with the help of the physical therapists, the more patients are able to feel their own weight and get back to functioning again.

Every patient is different in how they recover from strokes and every stroke is slightly different. Since the left side of her face had been affected, she had trouble swallowing and liquids would just pour out of her mouth. Fortunately, after working on it, that ability to swallow returned in a few days.

After a two week stent in the hospital, Mom was transferred to Kessler Rehabilitation Facility in East Orange, New Jersey. Because the doctor wanted her to have the best chance for recovery, he made arrangements for her to be in-patient there. Since she went directly to Kessler via ambulance from the hospital, Medicare covered the trip. Some patients choose to return home for a couple of days just to reunite with their loved ones, and they loose coverage of the transportation to the rehabilitation facility by insurance.

Since my mother was recovering nicely between the hospital and the rehabilitation facility, I returned to work confident that she was well taken care of and that everything was progressing well. I was glad to be back to work and with the support of my coworkers. My spirits were up because I knew my mother was getting the best of care. Being the fighter that she was, I knew that she would bounce back as quickly as she could. I accepted that everything may not come back and that she may not, in some ways, be the same woman that I once knew, but that was something we would all have to adjust to. We all had to accept the new Gwen, and, looking back, I think, for the most part, we all did.

She entered Kessler Institute on October 20, 1979, and came home to stay on December 20, 1979, just in time for Christmas. During her two months at Kessler, she learned how to bathe herself, dress herself, feed herself, socialize, walk independently, and she learned a little bit about cooking. I remember the day when she told me she made breakfast for herself at Kessler. They had a little kitchenette and all the patients who were capable made a meal for themselves before they returned home.

Before they released her, they sent a physical therapist

out to the home to do an assessment. They wanted to know the arrangements of the house, the number of stairs, the bathroom set up, if the bathtub is accessible, if the bathroom has grab bars, etc. Needless to say, they did a very through evaluation. This is for safety and to help my mother to be as independent in her home surroundings as possible. For instance, if there are any scatter rugs lying about, they are a no-no and they have to go so that the patient does not trip over them.

After about six weeks into the rehabilitation program, she started coming home weekends just to get adjusted. Not only does the patient have to adjust, but so does the family. The family now has a chance to realize what the patient can and cannot do for themselves and the patient has a chance to figure out how they are going to adapt. It is not always an easy adjustment for the caretaker to become taken care of by her family.

For me, this was going to be a complete adjustment. Now the tables were turned. Instead of my mother taking care of me, I now had to take care of my mother. For example, I needed to show her some of the tricks that I learned in occupational therapy to help dress myself. I also had to show her the best way to handle the shower. At Kessler they had walk in showers, but we had a shower with a bar across the front so that I could grab onto it and lift my feet over the bathtub edge. We had a shower chair for my mom so that she could be seated while she washed herself.

As time went on, the aphasia seemed to disappear. She was back to her old talking self. Of course, she had to resign from her job and that took away of some of her social interaction. However, we found other ways that she could socialize. Unfortunately, it was during this time that her best friend, Dolly Beaver, moved away to Maryland. Her husband was transferred and they packed up and left shortly after my mother's stroke. This was a big loss for my mother. She spent many, many hours on the phone with her friend Dolly. They also played cards together and were on many of the same church committees. However, a lot of other people stepped in and tried to fill the void.

Back at the Screening Unit, the longer I worked there, the more frustrated I became. I liked working on different cases and making determinations based on what I read. However, some days there were not enough cases to go around. So there were many hours with nothing to do. It wasn't long before I brought a book to read, and, some days, I read quite a few chapters. Sometimes, I felt rather guilty taking the taxpayers money to sit there and read, but when they did not supply enough work, that was the only option. One day, after looking at the newspaper, I got an idea. I remembered that there was once a column that was written for and about the disabled by a disabled woman herself. That woman was Jean Ware. She no longer wrote a column and I asked her why. She said she ran out of ideas and working at the Screening Unit took much of her time.

I had a brainstorm. If Jean did not want the column, why didn't I see if I could write it? So, I wrote a well-crafted letter to the editor asking if a column such as Jean's could be reinstated. Approximately two weeks later, I received a call from the social editor of the Daily Journal saying that they were impressed with my letter and that if I wanted the column reinstated, I was the one that would need to do it. That was my entre into journalism. That letter changed the course of my future.

When I told my parents what I did, they were shocked. "You did what?" my father asked. I said I wrote a letter and said that as a matter of fact I think it was in yesterday's paper, and I got it out and showed it to him. He said, "My goodness, wow! Now you have a second job." After conversing with the social editor, we decided that I would write this column once a month and that I would get paid $25.00 per column. Granted, it wasn't much, but it was a start in the right direction. So, I think I can truly say never underestimate the power of a letter-to-the-editor. In the right hands, and at the right time, it can change the course of someone's life -- it did for mine.

My coworkers were equally amazed. I guess they did not realize that I had the spunk to take the initiative to help myself and to create a job that would be meaningful to me and helpful to others. I felt that now I had seen both sides of disability – as a disabled person myself looking out and as a caregiver looking in. I was in a unique position to really help others understand both sides of disability. Where I could help the disabled person himself as well as their loved ones who stand by and watch. Now, I could see both points of view.

Although it was a monotonous job at the Screening Unit, keeping the job was a different story. Regardless of my ability to do the job, I had to take the civil service exam. I am not a good test taker and keeping the job depended solely on passing this exam. I failed at passing the test with a score high enough to keep the job. However, maybe that was a blessing in disguise. Therefore, after the CETA contract expired, I would be jobless. I should explain that CETA was a government program designed to help the disadvantaged, including the disabled, to find some sort of employment. In many ways it did, however, in my case, I just was not able to pass the exam with a high enough score to secure a government job. Fortunately, I had already discovered my true calling to become a journalist.

9

Unemployed and disabled is a combination that I would not wish on my worst enemy. Because of my physical limitations, I knew that I would need to prove myself once again to the working world. However, to my dismay, I found it even more difficult proving myself to those who had known me most of my life.

Most employment counselors agree that networking is an important part of the job search and that one should not leave any stone unturned. Keeping this in mind, I began asking those whom I highly respected for help. I sought the counsel of a former professor, a minister and several others. Even my godmother offered her assistance. A widow and a very private person, she asked to have a copy of my resume to give to a friend who worked in the personnel department of Hoffman La-Roche, a well-known pharmaceutical company.

After several weeks, I finally received one of those standard form letters stating that there were no positions available at this time, but that my resume would remain on file. Of course, I always wondered whether or not that meant the circular file! While I appreciated my godmother's efforts, I realize now that nothing would have ever materialized. Even though she lived not more than 30 minutes from us, we saw her on a very limited basis. Years ago, she was a close friend of my mother's, but our relationship had somewhat drifted apart.

We usually got together twice a year on a Saturday afternoons for lunch and some light shopping. After about 2-1/2 hours, my godmother would excuse herself saying that she needed to get home to do some mending etc. Interestingly, when we did see each other, she would always ask about my job. Sometimes, she wanted to know things such as how I got my ideas, how I landed interviews, and how I managed to get around since I did not drive.

Indeed, she did have an interest in me, and many of her questions are the same on the lips of most who know me. However, time and time again she would make remarks such as "wouldn't it be easier if you worked at home? Who helps you? Do you really write it all yourself?" For some reason, she could not picture me as a working woman. I think she was too focused on the things I could not do instead of the things I could. Perhaps, subconsciously, she still thought of me as a child and did not see me as the young adult that I had become.

Even though I have heard the very same statements from a professor whom I have known for almost twenty years, they still baffle me. A generation or two ago, people with disabilities were not considered employable for the most part. And, if by chance we were hired, our jobs usually involved doing something in the back office away from the public eye. While I may have started out working in a small, sheltered office in the state, I certainly was in the limelight now. As a medical writer, I interviewed as many as eight physicians and/or other health professionals a week, recorded and typed volumes of copy, and completed various other tasks. Finally, I had the career I always dreamed of, but never really expected.

Reflecting back over my fourteen months of unemployment, I can wholeheartedly say Sunday nights were the worst. It seemed that everyone had a place to go on Monday morning except for me. Of course, the first few weeks were great – an extended vacation! I watched television, read a few good books, and started grocery shopping with my mother, which was a good thing because she was still recovering from her stroke.

Then I had my first experience with the unemployment office. While few people ever expect to need to file a claim, it is amazing how many of us do. Even though I had known for quite a while that my job was ending and the funding was running out, I never imagined myself on the unemployment line. We moved like a herd of cattle from one line to the next, filling out one form after another, and answering question after question. When scanning around the facility, it appeared as though I was the only physically challenged person there. Although I am sure that I wasn't, I was, however, the most visible. I sensed that the interviewers were somewhat surprised, but managed to hide their feelings and proceed with business as usual.

When one collects unemployment, he is supposed to be actively looking for work and must go on a number of interviews each week. For me, this was an impossible task to fulfill especially since most employers would not even grant me an interview in the first place. So, instead, I listed the number of places where I had sent a resume.

Weeks rolled into months and time hung heavy on my hands. During that time, I enlisted the help of the Division of Vocational Rehabilitation (DVR) as well as the Union County Office of the Disabled. I soon learned that the DVR counselor who had placed me with the Screening Unit had moved on to bigger and better things. I had to start all over again with someone new. Insisting that I get the job myself, Carol

Berkowitz was of little help. Although she came highly recommended by my former counselor, Carol seemed overwhelmed by her caseload and proved to be a disappointment.

I also tried the Union County Office of the Disabled, headed by an older man, Roy Rusk who supposedly had years of experience in job placement. After a relatively short time, Rusk proved to be more talk than action. He came to the house several times and suggested various ways that he would help me. He even promised to take me to meet his cousin, the infamous Dr. Howard Rusk of Rusk Institute in New York City where I was first diagnosed with cerebral palsy as a baby. Needless to say, that meeting never took place. At that time, I was very interested in an interview with Schering-Plough, a large pharmaceutical company in Kenilworth. Time passed and that never came to be. In fact, I never had one single job interview through either of these "experts."

As the search continued, I felt even more discouraged and depressed. The world seemed to wiz by while I stood still. During this time, I decided to volunteer at Rahway Hospital, a small community facility not very far away. I met the director of volunteers, Phyllis Adelman, who was very charming and decided to give me a chance. Because of my background at the Screening Unit, I acquired knowledge of a lot of medical terminology. So, she placed me in the medical records department where I needed to review cases and see that all the paperwork was in the correct order. I also took a course in medical terminology, which aided in my career development. It is probably one of the most beneficial courses I could have taken.

Now that I was volunteering at Rahway Hospital, I had that work as well as my monthly column to keep me busy. At the same time, I continued to help my mother with her rehabilitation. She was beginning to feel very lonely and isolated. She no longer worked and had many empty hours to sit alone and feel sorry for herself. We were beginning to see a need for her to do something productive and to find some way for her to socialize. One day, I had a brainstorm. If I could do some type of volunteer work, why couldn't my mom? By this time I had gotten to know Phyllis and some of the other volunteers pretty well. I made an appointment to see Phyllis and to ask if just by chance she might have something for my mother to do. She said she would love to meet my mother and if my mother were anything like her daughter, then she would have a volunteer position for her as well.

After talking to Phyllis, I went home and I said to my mother, "How about you doing some volunteer work at the hospital? You probably will not be in the same department as I am, but I guarantee that you will get to be out and about." With some hesitation, my mother called Phyllis and a week later she was sitting in front of her deciding what she could and could not do. Phyllis placed her in the outpatient department as a receptionist. By this time, her speech was back to normal and the only residual effect of her stroke was a nonfunctioning left arm. Amazingly, she learned to do most things one handed, and because of that Phyllis thought that she was a good source of inspiration for others. Of course, Mom was hesitant at first because she had lost a lot of her self-confidence. However, Phyllis somehow managed to convince her that she could do almost anything she wanted to do as long as she had the determination to do it.

As the weeks went by, I could see my mother's self-confidence returning. She was a much happier person because she was productive. Slowly she began to interact with people and make friends. It was good to see her come home and to be excited about life again. My father drove her to volunteer the first few times and then she was able to make connections with other people who offered their services to transport her to or from the hospital.

The summer months were busy enough with our membership to the Roselle Swim Club, and I joined two friends on a cruise to Bermuda with some of the savings I had accumulated through unemployment. Even though I felt guilty on spending money so extravagantly, I knew I needed a change. We were an unusual threesome. Blind since birth, Carol worked as a receptionist for the Department of Human Resources, which incorporated the Office of the Disabled. Sharon worked as a clerk for a local insurance company. She also had cerebral palsy, which limited her somewhat physically, but hampered her more emotionally. Personally, I do not think that Sharon or her family ever emotionally adjusted to her condition.

Of the three of us, Sharon was the most sheltered. Although we were both mainstreamed in the public school system, Sharon remained in a cocoon shielded by her parents and isolated from her peers. Her personality was very unpredictable and sometimes aloof. Therefore, people found her difficult to befriend. However, her one redeeming feature was that she was able to drive and Carol and I, on the other hand, could not. For Carol and myself, Sharon was the key to our independence.

Because of her unpredictable moodiness, Sharon had not established a real friendship until age 26 when we came along. Even though Sharon was one of four siblings, she remained a loner even within her own family. In many ways, Sharon was spoiled. Upon high school graduation, her father landed Sharon her first job. This meant that, unfortunately, she really had little idea of the frustration I was going through trying to find work.

During the winter, we had discussed the possibility of traveling to Bermuda via ship. We even went as far as getting estimates and brochures from a local travel agent. By this time, our trio had gone out often enough to dinner, the movies, etc. to build enough confidence within ourselves to function rather independently. We saw this cruise as a stepping-stone to test our independence. Our parents were hesitant but encouraging. I think they knew that if we really ran into trouble we would know how to get help.

In the weeks prior to our adventure, we were all besieged with well-meaning advice especially from our mothers. In the past, I had flown to Arizona by myself to visit my grandmother and Carol had gone away for a few years to attend a special school for the blind. This time, however, we were really on our own. It wasn't until we put that final deposit down that I think we finally realized we were on our way. Of course, I had mixed emotions – what if I fell or got sick? However, deep down I knew I really wanted to go – to test the waters of independence. I swallowed hard and off I went.

We certainly attracted a lot of attention on the ship. It is amazing how many sets of adoptive parents we had acquired within ten days. People were astounded by the fact that we all were employed in some capacity and that the government was not financing this vacation in any way, shape, or form. True, I had lost my full-time job with the state, but by this time, I had started a regular column in the local newspaper, The Daily Journal, and I was writing freelance articles for the NJ section of The NY Times.

Of course, it is every writer's dream to be published in The New York Times. Somehow, I managed to have a connection with someone who wrote for the New Jersey Section of The Times and called him. He told me to send some samples of my writing. Even though I thought my chances were slim, I sent the material anyway. One thing about having a byline is that it automatically opens doors. Everyone seems to question the mentality of someone with a speech problem, and being able to display one's talent through the written word dismisses any doubts.

My first article in The New York Times was "Understanding a Misunderstood Minority." Later that day my doorbell rang and it was a delivery from the florist. It was from a proud church member who was also an author herself. She had just published her first book, and she sent flowers after she had read my article to wish me success in my future writing endeavors.

While we were in route to Bermuda, I took part in the ship's version of "What's My Line?" Beforehand, I was briefly interviewed and told that I would follow another New Jersey resident who worked in a factory and helped to manufacture Pamper diapers. As it turned out both of us stumped the 400 member audience, and we each received a prize.

That night all three of us – Carol, Sharon, and I - became instant celebrities. If anyone had been curious to begin with, they were even more so now. As people got to know and accept each one of us, we acquired more and more sets of adoptive parents. I met one woman and her husband who had recently adopted a little boy without arms, and that family became the subject for my next article.

Once we docked in Bermuda, we went shopping and to Horseshoe Bay Beach. The water was beautiful different shades of blue and green, and it was sparkling clean. The sand was pink and unlike any sand I have ever seen. We held hands and waded in this clear crystal waters. We sat on the beach and sunbathed.

Then, that evening, we went on a horse and buggy ride. Getting up into the buggy was rather interesting but we had a helpful guide who saw to it that we were safely seated. In fact, this ride turned out to be a bit of an adventure. Our driver, who was very knowledgeable, would get off the buggy to show us different things like flowers and animals. Unfortunately, however, one time he got down from his post and the horse mistook that signal and decided to go off on his own with the three of us still in the buggy. Realizing the predicament, the driver went running after us and finally caught the reins and pulled the horse over. We were all frightened and grateful that Sharon was able to grab the reins. Unfortunately, the horse misread the driver's signal and decided he could just take off. After giving this threesome a near heart attack, the rest of the ride was rather uneventful, thank goodness!

All too soon the cruise came to an end and we were forced back to reality and, for me, that still meant unemployment. August came and still no job in sight. I decided to enroll in a creative writing course at Union County College. At least I would be doing something productive with my time, and, who knows, I just might happen to be in the right place at the right time.

Since I had graduated I had kept in touch with a professor who took a personal interest in me. Through the years, we had always gotten our families together for summer picnics and special occasions. While I was a student, we often got together on a weekly basis for a talk. During these sessions, Paul Evans discovered a lot about me, my upbringing, my family, and my dreams and ambitions. As a former church minister, he did his homework well. However, as a byproduct of my parents' generation, in many ways, he had a narrow-minded view of what a person with a disability could do. I believe he saw my limitations as something that would always hinder me in whatever area I pursued.

Affectionately nicknamed "Uncle Paul," I remember asking him to write a letter of reference. Unfortunately, after reading his letter, the interviewer was completely baffled as to my qualifications for the available position because Mr. Evans focused on all of the challenges I had as a disabled person. For instance, he neglected to mention that I was a conscientious person, etc. Needless to say, that was the first and last time I had him write a letter of recommendation. Sadly, I realized that he never understood me as well as I thought he had.

Even though I was granted two extensions, eventually my unemployment ran out. Thank goodness for my small savings account. As time passed, we could see that I was getting nowhere with either the DVR or the Office of the Disabled. Throughout this period, I had been sending resumes accompanied with cover letters out, but to no avail. While I did have a few nibbles, I had no one to help me land the position. Unfortunately, the Americans with Disabilities Act had just been passed and few people were acting upon it. In fact, most employers were finding a way to get around it. For instance, they would interview someone with a disability for a job but with no intention of hiring them. It looks good on paper, but in reality they had no intention of offering a job.

By this time, my father was convinced, more so than ever, that employment for me was an impossibility. My poor coordination and my speech were indeed a definite turnoff to any prospective employer. In fact, he was in the process of contacting a lawyer to have me declared "disabled" so that I could collect long-term disability. Of course, the mere prospect of this was even more discouraging and I fought bitterly against it.

Once I was on disability, I thought my life would be over.

All the college courses and long hours of studying certainly did not help me now. I was depressed and disappointed with my father for not having a little more faith in mankind and in me. Just when I thought the inevitable would happen, I received a call from Carol, who worked as a receptionist for the Office of the Disabled, and she promptly notified me that they had received a request from The Daily Journal for a tearsheet person. At that point, I did not even know what a tearsheet was but I was soon to learn.

Jim Johnson, the business manager was looking for a disabled person to fill this position. Because he himself had a disabled daughter he wanted to expose the company to what a disabled person could do, and he also wanted to help the company fulfill its Affirmative Action requirements. This was in 1981, during the time that the United Nations had declared the International Year of Disabled Persons.

Eagerly, I called and made an appointment for the interview. After 14 months, I was a little rusty. As it turned out, a tearsheet person cuts all the advertisements out of the newspapers and sends them to either the store owner or agency for payment. While it was a messy, inky job, it was an important one. Without proof that their advertisement ran, store owners refused to pay the bill, and unless their bill was paid, we would be unable to collect a paycheck.

I had plenty of mixed emotions about this job. First, I had a college education, which was not needed for what I was about to do. Second, the position required a lot of fine manual dexterity, which is certainly not my forte. Even so, my parents encouraged me to take the job because it was a foot in the door. By the way, at the same time my column "Being Independent" was still running strong.

My first day of work at the Daily Journal was August 3, 1981, and when I returned home from my first shift, I was exhausted. Being the new kid on the block isn't easy, but I survived. Even though I worked for the Business Office, I sat in the Editorial Department, which proved to be a good source of inspiration. While I struggled with the daily tearsheets, I got to watch young reporters scooping stories. The Daily Journal was another step towards my aspirations as a journalist.

10

Being the first disabled person to work at the Daily Journal, the oldest county newspaper in New Jersey, I am certain that I was the subject of discussion among the staff. I could tell these people were watching me with fascination at first, and, later, with admiration.

One of the first people who really befriended me was a young reporter named Frank Scandale. Frank is a tall, Italian string bean and liked by everyone. He was everyone's friend and confidante and I affectionately referred to him as my big brother. He was also the guy who threw the best parties.

As I became more sure of myself, I really opened up and blossomed. People eventually knew they could kid me about my disability and that I would not take offense. In fact, one day, I remember my co-worker, an Irish, freckled kid by the name of Bill Murray, who sat opposite from me asked what would happen if I ever got drunk. With a light chuckle, I replied, "I'd guess that I would walk straight for a change." That snappy, honest answer gained me more acceptance and laughs than I ever would have imagined.

Of course, the true test of whether one is accepted or not is being invited to the parties. And party-hardy this gang did. Liquor seems to be the big thing with young people and these greenhorn reporters were no exception. Friday night, when the final copy was sent to press, it was time to let loose and have a few belts.

Most people think that writing for a newspaper is a glamorous profession complete with one's own byline. Depending on the type of newspaper and the amount of prestige it carries, the caliber of the writing can vary. Of course, meeting daily deadlines, coping with editor's quirks, and all the other snags one can encounter makes reporting a very stressful occupation. Another bugaboo is the long hours. For instance, it is not unusual to work a 10 or 12-hour day and return the next day for round two. So, for this gang, getting drunk was a means of releasing stress.

I was only at the paper three months before I was invited to my first get-together – a Halloween costume party. A reporter by the name of Lisa Prezzio invited me. I was thrilled because this meant that I was officially accepted. Eventually, I decided to go as a clown. A friend of ours was a kindergarten teacher and owned an adult clown suit complete with a wig. So, now I had a costume and I was set.

My parents dropped me off and I was soon to learn that I was the only clown. Great, I had no competition. Other people came as geisha girls, someone dressed as Houdini, and Frank came as an Italian woman in mourning. Dressed in black and wearing a long veil, Frank's only problem was his sister's high heels, which he soon discovered were not to his advantage to wear.

With the party in full swing and food galore, people were really at ease and having a good time. Having only known these people a few months, I felt this was an opportunity to get better acquainted. Then, a man approached me that I did not recognize. Unalarmed at first, I started talking to him. I noticed that he was without a costume and I thought that was a bit odd. However, the straw that broke the camel's back was when he asked me to step into the bathroom because he wanted me to try his new "stuff." Fortunately, someone overheard this strange conversation and signaled Frank to come to my rescue.

I was frightened. This was my first party and now this. As it turned out, the unknown intruder was a "crasher" who thought he would be able to get kicks from toying with me. Little did he know, he was barking up the wrong tree and that I had a small army to protect me. After the initial encounter, I was fine and my buddies were the ones who had to recover. It was the shock of the event that really got to people. A few hours later, Frank offered to take me home. Even though the crasher was long gone, I think that scene will forever remain in our minds. After all, the party could have ended in tragedy, but, fortunately, we looked out for each other.

Imagine riding down a quiet, residential street and suddenly, close by appears a woman dressed in black holding the arm of a somewhat wobbly clown. Good thing it was Halloween night!

Even though my parents were happy that I had been invited to Lisa's party. I think they had some reservations about me attending. Up until then, I had been sheltered, so to speak. Most of my friends were "Christians" so they did not participate in "wild times," which included drinking. While I do not believe in downing the bottle either, I think being part of that group was an important part of my growing process. Despite their drinking habits, my co-workers were an extremely caring bunch. For instance, if someone needed help moving they were there. If someone needed to paint the quarters, these good people, armed with supplies, would be at your doorstep.

After that unfortunate incident on Halloween, I wondered whether or not I would be included in the next party. Of course, the crasher was not anyone's fault and I realized that. However, I could not help but wonder whether they felt that I was too much of a responsibility for them. Aside from transportation, I really did not need any help. Well, any doubts were quickly cast aside. Frank hosted the next extravaganza and I was there!

Several months had elapsed and there I sat day after day cutting these tearsheets. What a monotonous job! With the help of a steak knife, I would cut the newspapers – several copies of each issue because advertisements dominated both sides of the paper. While some agencies requested only one copy, others asked for several, which then had to either be stuffed into properly addressed envelopes or stored to be sent with the monthly statement. Of course, as an excuse to delay payment, some advertisers would claim that they never received tearsheets. Just like anyone else, I made mistakes and I rectified them.

While I was happy to have a job and be working with a congenial bunch of people, I was miserable. Even though I had my monthly column, my career was going nowhere. This was a dead-end job with no future in sight. For some reason, I could not fathom how editors could sit there watching my struggle with these unending tearsheets and at the same time, print my monthly column as well. I think that it was a case where they did not want to get involved or that they did not know how to become involved. Perhaps it was a bit of both.

FITTING IN

By coincidence, Frank had a friend who was then a vocational rehabilitation counselor for Kessler Rehabilitation Institute at the East Orange facility. By that point, I needed some guidance as how to either advance at The Daily Journal or to pursue training in another area. As my closest friend and confidante, Frank knew I was discouraged and growing more so every day. Therefore, he made arrangements for me to meet Maria.

A few weeks later on a warm summer evening, Frank stopped in and introduced me to his lifelong friend, Maria. A tall, blonde and rather large-framed woman, Maria had been employed with Kessler for about four years. Her caseload consisted of people with a variety of disabilities. Sitting on our patio sipping glasses of iced tea, Maria educated me about their unique vocational testing and job placement services. I was impressed with what I heard, and yet I was cautious. In the past, so many of these counselors had gotten my hopes up only to result in bitter disappointment and feelings of betrayal.

After mulling the concept over and discussing it with my parents, I saw an inept counselor with the Division of Vocational Rehabilitation Services and the business manager who was my boss at the newspaper, and I decided that I had nothing to lose and everything to gain. While giving me the opportunity to work, I think that Mr. Johnson, the business manager of The Daily Journal knew that I was unhappy and frustrated because I was not utilizing my potential. I had a college education and there I was cutting up newspapers for a living. After I assured him that I would still complete my work on time and I explained to him how much I wanted to take advantage of this opportunity, he supported my plight.

Scheduled for this two week period of intensive testing, I began commuting to Kessler via my father in early October. Prior to the date, I had to meet with my vocational counselor, Carol Berkowitz, at the DVRS office in Elizabeth, New Jersey. After telling her about Kessler's program, she applied for a $2000 grant to pay for these services. The Division of Vocational Rehabilitation is a state-funded agency for helping people with various disabilities to eventually gain some kind of substantial gainful employment. The agency provides funding for education, assistive aides, job coaching, and training. Serving a wide variety of people with disabilities ranging from emotional to physical to mentally retarded to the deaf and hearing impaired, these counselors are met with every conceivable challenge.

An average caseload ranges somewhere between 150 to over 300 cases per counselor. With the exception of the deaf and hearing-impaired population, each caseload is a "mixed bag" with each client representing different needs. Of course, not all clients are at the same level at the same time, but each person is served for a reason whatever it may be.

FITTING IN

Because I have cerebral palsy with severe motor involvement of my limbs and speech, my case was supposed to be given top priority. In other words, if a counselor is fortunate enough to convince a company to take a chance and hire me, it really is a feather in his cap. To date, only a half of one percent of persons with a variation of cerebral palsy are in the workforce. I dare say that most of these people got their big break from knowing someone, either a family member, close friend, or a political contact.

I remember my supervisor in the Screening Unit claim that the only way I would get a permanent placement within the system was if my parents become politically involved and I worked my way in the door. My parents responded with a big, fat "NO" to that one.

I was thrilled that the request for the tidy sum of $2000 was granted. I had expected some opposition especially since the DVRS had not funded my college education. As I reflect back, I realize that we were mistaken. At that time, my father was a very successful agent with John Hancock Mutual Life Insurance Company. In fact, he had received a citation from the president of the company for having written over 1 million dollars in policies that year. Shortly thereafter, my maternal grandfather had passed away leaving my mother a considerable inheritance. As a result of our financial situation, my parents felt that since they had the means, they should finance my college education.

While their intentions were honorable, I think they should have let me apply under my own name for financial assistance from DVRS. If the DVRS had financially invested in my education, the agency would have taken a greater interest in seeing that I found suitable employment.

Now that several years had passed since college and I was employed part-time, the DVRS was willing to invest a couple of thousand to possibly help me advance. After all, I had now proven that not only was I capable of employment, but also I had convinced the private sector that I could be a success. Since I worked 25 hours a week, I was not eligible for health insurance. Therefore, I had to pay for it on my own, which was a substantial amount of my income.

Sitting opposite Fred Quinn, my vocational counselor at Kessler, I wondered what was in store for me over this two-week period. I was both excited and a little anxious. Deep down I knew I was doing the right thing. I also knew that if I had made an error in career choice I was still young enough to rectify it in some way. A large-framed man in his early 40s, Quinn was eager to help me explore some other possible vocational avenues. But first he had to get to know me.

A comprehensive battery of tests designed to specifically measure one's abilities and interests provided Quinn with some of the answers. These tests included measurements of: dexterity, tolerance, strength, endurance, and stress levels. I was examined on everything from my ability to add a column of numbers to how quickly I could put different sized pegs into different sized holes. Next, I took the vocational inventory test to try to determine my vocational interests.

Administered in many colleges and employment agencies, this test measures one's vocational aptitude for a particular field. Since my interests seemed to be in writing and working with people, I was not surprised to learn that I leaned toward journalism, social work, research, medicine, and art. At first, this might sound like a broad diversification of interests, but when one really analyzes them, they are not.

Beginning in toddlerhood, I always loved books and enjoyed having someone read to me. During my adolescence, I read my fill of novels about doctors and nurses. While I may have been caught up in a world of romanticism, I was genuinely interested in medicine. Fortunately, I did not need to go to the doctor any more than the average kid, but, like others in my peer group, I enjoyed the soap operas.

For the most part, medicine and social work have a strong link, especially if one is interested in helping disabled people or disadvantaged youngsters. Because of my personal situation, I always read biographical books about disabled people and how they coped with their challenges. As a source of inspiration, these true stories proved invaluable. One common theme ran through all the hundreds of pages and that was to never give up no matter what the adversity.

Like most youngsters, I loved to color pictures of whatever fascinated me. Always attracted to the bright, vibrant colors of my Crayola's, one Christmas set gave me the deluxe box of 92 assorted colors. I was in crayon heaven. Since I was also a fan of the infamous Flintstones from Bedrock, I loved their coloring books. When we visited my grandparents in Florida, I would always bring my coloring books and crayons. My grandfather and I would sit together every night and color one picture. Taking this task very seriously, my grandfather would even add a dab of color to the complexions of Fred and Barney so that these pals would look more life-like.

To encourage my artistic talents even further, a lifelong friend of my mother's, an art teacher, would bring packages of bright colored paper when we got together. Every color of the rainbow came in those precious bundles. Merely, eyeing the array of assorted colors set my imagination wild.

Because my parents enjoyed a healthy social life and Mom was active in the Parent Teacher Association and church work, my brother Rick and I had a number of babysitters. We loved these teenage girls who would come and not only watch over us, but entertain us as well. One of our most lively babysitters, Patty, who lived two houses down the street, was our favorite. Rick and I would always marvel at the fact that she was able to get her hair to stand up so straight in her beehive hairdo.

Fortunately, Patty possessed an artistic flair too. As soon as my parents would leave for the evening, we would pullout the colored paper, shears, paste and crayons and have a wonderful time. We would make all sorts of creations and decorate my bedroom closet door. I remember one holiday we made a Christmas tree about six feet tall and garnished it with ornaments we created. I loved it so much that mom did not take it down until it almost fell off my door three months later.

Now that Mr. Quinn had an idea as to where my interests and aptitude lay, the next step was to try to determine what kind of job I could realistically handle to hopefully bring home a decent livelihood. In order for us to find this information out, I remember Mr. Quinn arranged a series of interviews. Some of the people I spoke with were right in the hospital. I spoke with a social worker, the Director of Volunteers and a Client Patient Representative. All of the women proved very sincere and helpful as they carefully outlined the duties of their job and what was expected of them. I was both impressed, and yet, somewhat doubtful as to whether or not I would be able to handle all of this responsibility.

My counselor and I also went on a few field trips as well.

Since I was interested in counseling parents of disabled children, he took me to a local Cerebral Palsy Center to meet with a teacher's aide and a psychologist who ran a support group for parents. I was impressed with everyone there and thought that I could even be of greater benefit especially since I had C.P., too.

Since the day I graduated from college, I always kept the possibility of graduate school in the back of my mind. I definitely had the potential. However, through the years, I had come across enough people with disabilities who went for their Masters only to find themselves with a beautiful plaque decorating their wall and nowhere to go. Employers now told them that they were overqualified. Perhaps, this was another excuse not to hire someone with a limitation.

Even before I was officially a freshman, my father felt that I should only take one course per semester. Of course, at his rate, I would still be an undergraduate on my 40th birthday. Probably the only student who would be turning gray. Thank goodness I proved him wrong.

Surprisingly, both my parents were thrilled when I decided to give graduate school a try. But my pessimistic father wondered about my ability to keep up with those "brains". I must confess that I had my doubts too. After working for so long in an unchallenging and unstimulating position, I wondered if I would suffer from a sudden overload of information coming at me.

However, once Mr. Quinn and I visited the Counselor Education Department and its Director at Kean College, Drew Cangelosi, many of my fears were alleviated.

Since I was an alumnus of Kean College, I was familiar with much of the campus. I knew the layout of the grounds and some of the professors of my past. The library, one of my regular hangouts, was still one of the mainstays of the college scene. Even with an advanced degree there is no guarantee of a job. Still, I would be a cut above the rest, so to speak. And personally, I looked forward to the chance to hone in on some skills and perhaps, develop some new ones. Most importantly, I would have the opportunity to learn about someone very special – myself.

On one of our many field trips, Fred and I rode over to Campus School East and met with Drew Cangelosi, Ph.D., the head of Counselor Education (formerly Student Personnel Services). Prior to our meeting, Fred had explained our intent and that we were exploring many avenues. Dr. Cangelosi, a warm-hearted Italian man in his mid-thirties wearing sneakers and jeans, greeted us with kindness and compassion. Genuinely interested in helping me explore vocational possibilities, Dr. Cangelosi told us about the program. He explained the objectives, the core courses, the advanced seminars, and of course, the thesis.

However, before I went any further, I had to take the Graduate Record Exam (GRE), which is a standard requirement among most institutions of higher learning. As I do not test very well, I was very apprehensive about it. With the GRE Manual, I got an idea of the types of questions included on the test and what the administrators of the exam were looking for. Until I glanced at the vocabulary section and word associations, I always thought that words were one of my greatest assets. Then, I turned to the math portion and really felt that I was in a foreign country.

I felt completely overwhelmed. While it was necessary for me to take the exam, my scores did not matter to this particular college. In fact, the department placed more emphasis on a student's overall academic achievement as an undergraduate than the GRE and their rank.

Throughout my academic career, I never performed well on standard examinations – the GRE, the SAT, or the high school placement tests. I guess I am just not a test taker.

Even though, I did not perform well on the GREs, Dr. Cangelosi agreed to unofficially accept me into the program based on my previous academic record as an honors student, my work experience, and my motivation. Prior to his appointment as department head, Dr. Cangelosi had been a special education teacher and taught the emotionally disturbed and perceptually impaired for several years. Through those rather, at times, trying experiences, he developed sensitivity to people in all situations. In fact, as I advanced in the program, I discovered that most of his staff had a similar background.

My first course, Community Relations taught by Frank Backhi, Ph.D., a personable man with a wealth of experience, or so it seemed, tried to show the myriad of services within each community. His assignments were classified as "busy work" by most of his students, but his field trips were great. Never without connections, we went to places like a spice factory, a local hospital, Engine City and the University of Medicine and Dentistry in Newark, just to mention a few. No matter where we went we were always served food. I think food was his secret agenda for every class – I never came home hungry.

After completing Community Relations, I went on to Introduction to Counseling, one of the core courses and taught by Dr. Cangelosi. A very demanding course filled with theory and memorization, his assignments were thought provoking and really provided a means of self-examination. We were a very small department and the average class consisted of 15 students. Counseling provided a means to communicate, at times on a deeper level than one might ordinarily do in another curriculum. To be able to effectively counsel others, one must be able to engage in self-discovery and exploration in terms of feelings, emotions, and thought processes as well as to be able to share these feelings.

By this time, I had befriended two other graduate students. The first was Mary McGovern, a tall, freckled-faced, Irish redhead, who was still coping with the death of her mother due to cancer. A fifth grade teacher, Mary had enrolled in the Masters program with the purpose of salary advancement in mind. Second was Georgia Lane, a tall, thin mother of three, who constantly struggled to hold together her difficult marriage. Her husband was eventually arrested and imprisoned for drug possession and selling. Georgia and Mary met when they were both going through a particularly trying time and therefore, developed a growing dependency on each other. Both shared the same classes and virtually the same assignments, which meant they could study together. On occasion, when they took different courses, Mary would volunteer to babysit for her friend so that she could attend class.

Despite their troubles, both women were good company and excellent note takers. Whenever we were working on a big project, we went to the library together. I guess we felt that three heads were better than one. I remember one Saturday afternoon when we as a threesome, trekked on down to Rutgers's library to gather resource information for our thesis. On the way home, after spending hours researching our topics, we stopped at a Jewish Deli in Highland Park for sub sandwiches. For some reason, we all felt that we needed to share our innermost thoughts. Perhaps, unknowingly, we were preparing for our next course – Group Process.

As a course, Group Process provided a simulation of the group counseling experience. It also gave each student an opportunity for self-discovery and self-disclosure in a controlled setting. At times, this process can be brutally painful and troublesome. However, whatever feelings are encountered, the most important thing is to "experience the moment" and go with it.

From the course description, we knew that this course would enable us to learn some things about ourselves, some of which we might not want to reveal about ourselves just yet. Nevertheless, there is safety in numbers, as the phrase goes. Mary and Georgia seemed to share this concern more than I did. Throughout my life, I had been the subject of curiosity. Being the only special needs child in a public school, in church, girl scouts, etc., I knew my presence raised a lot of questions.

Among the other students in Group Process was Bob, a married man in his early 40s. Bob relished the idea of being the only man in the group. I guess it did something for his ego. As far as the male perspective he provided, Bob's insight was treasured. I think he was genuinely interested in all of us as human beings; however, he seemed to share a growing curiosity along with Sally regarding my relationships with men.

Because of my disability, my experiences with the opposite sex growing up were limited. Adolescence is a difficult period. Psychologists refer to it as the period of "storm and stress." Peer pressure is tremendous. The typical, raging hormones associated with adolescence often bring out new and awkward feelings that we are not quite sure how to handle. The average adolescent male wants the ideal date: one with a good figure, an outgoing personality, and who is intelligent, to put it in their terms, they're looking for "a real babe." Where I was concerned, boys were kind and considerate and often talked to me like a "sister." Because of my awkward movements, my parents never encouraged me to seek dates and felt I should be content knowing that boys respected me. Because I was mainstreamed from day one, I never had another girl with a disability to share stories.

Probably, one of the few incidents that stands out in my mind was when I was a student at Union County College in Cranford. I had been a member of a service sorority, Gamma Sigma Chi, when I established a friendship with Kyle Barnum and Sue Clay. Shortly after we pledged with the sorority, we realized that it had become a drinking click. Neither one of us was into that scene and dropped out. Eventually, however, we stumbled on to another type of service organization – Christian Fellowship. Although some members were deeply religious, we liked it for the clean atmosphere.

FITTING IN

On one occasion, a group of us ventured on down to the shore to watch the sunrise. Six of us, men and women in number, came equipped with sleeping gear and other paraphernalia to spend the night at Sue's house affectionately known as "the flop house." In separate quarters, we all slept over so that we would be up and ready to roll by 3:30 AM. We rose at the designated hour, quickly got dressed and headed south.

As we sat on the beach watching the sun slowly climb over the horizon, we realized how fortunate we were. I felt especially fortunate to be included among this little group who was giving me an experience I would always treasure. Most people with cerebral palsy seldom, if ever, have the opportunity for such an adventure. Afterwards, we went to a little family owned diner for a big breakfast before returning to the beach for sunning and swimming. Devouring heaps of pancakes, bacon, and plenty of coffee, we headed for the beach. We rented an umbrella and setup our beach chairs and blankets and lathered ourselves with suntan lotion, or at least I thought I did.

While I love walking along the water's edge, I never go in the ocean. If it's a question between my balance and the under toe, the latter always wins. So, sitting on the sidelines and watching the others toss the Frisbee around really does not bother me. As I mentioned earlier, evidently, while my friends were frolicking in the water, I fell asleep under the umbrella and received the worst sunburn I ever had.

No one really noticed it until we were on the way home. "Gee, you look a little flushed," Kyle said. Indeed, I was flushed. Apparently, I had fallen asleep on my side and so one half of my body was bright red and the other creamy white. I guess I resembled a zebra only instead I was red and white. By the time we drove up to my doorstep, I was burning up and quite uncomfortable. Despite the pain and discomfort, I had a wonderful day, which was the start of many bonding experiences to come.

Perhaps, this experience falls somewhere under the heading of group dating. Since none of us were romantically involved, I think this is probably right. While one or two might have been hoping for something more than friendship, most of us were temporarily content with the companionship found in this group.

My first and only date was with George Smith, a man I met while volunteering on the staff of Sharing, a newspaper written for and by the disabled. We heard about Sharing through an article my mother read in our local newspaper. Since I already had developed an interest in journalism by writing for my high school newspaper The RAMPAGE, we decided to give it a try.

Sharing is the brainchild of Dorothy Landvater, a Berkeley Heights resident, whose 19-year-old son had suffered brain damage as the result of a serious car accident. David, now multi-handicapped, required constant supervision. Part of her reason for creating this project was to help her son become better established in the disabled community.

A man in his late 20s, George, was the director of the tele-a-college program that enabled homebound students to attend classes via the telephone. As I recall, George never spoke to me very much, but he seemed to admire me from afar. Somehow he got my phone number and one evening he called and invited me out to dinner and then to see the play Anything Goes at Middlesex County College.

Surprised and filled with mixed emotions, I accepted the invitation. While I wanted to have a dating experience, I was both nervous and very anxious. Even though we were both involved with Sharing, we did not know each other or even whether we had the same interests. The truth is that if I had known George better as a friend I would have been more relaxed.

On a warm evening in May, George stood on the doorstep carrying flowers and looking very dapper dressed in a shirt and jacket. We went to dinner in a local restaurant. Conversation was a bit strained, but stimulating. He discussed his job and I talked about the courses I was taking and my dreams of a career. Of course, we discussed Sharing, and movies, books, etc. as well.

Despite my nervousness, I had enjoyed the evening. However, I just did not click with George. While I thought I liked him, there seemed to be almost an eerie feeling about him. When we reached my house, I politely thanked him and he drove off. As they say, the chemistry was just not there. Because I hardly knew him, I was not sexually attracted to him. Perhaps this was a good thing, and I never heard from him again. Three months later, I was to discover that he was arrested for absconding with some funds from the tele-a-college program. While I was very sorry about that, I was glad that I was not involved with him. Good-bye George.

As far as courses go, Group Process was the one that required the most effort in terms of revealing feelings, insecurities and prejudiced about oneself. This is not a course for those who are easily intimidated by discussing their feelings. Let's face it, people, educated or not, usually have a healthy curiosity about a person or situation that they have never before encountered. Some of my classmates were special education teachers and spent years working with the population. However, few of them had been able to successfully follow these students into adulthood. Meanwhile, many of these mainstream teachers were in the process of accepting certain special needs students into their classrooms and they had mixed feelings about it.

Now, seated in one of the graduate counseling courses, they had somewhat of a role model. Someone with an obvious physical disability to observe, question, and get to know. Here was their golden opportunity. Somehow, however, I feel that people fail to realize that I am just as curious about them as they are about me. I want to know what makes them who they are – their problems and concerns, relationships, interests, career choices, etc. Because of my physical limitations, some of my needs and concerns are more immediate, but basically I share the same personal desires and goals as my peers. I have worked diligently educating myself, honing my skills as a writer, and developing both male and female relationships.

I took this course in the summer and it met for three consecutive weekends. We were a group of twelve women and one man who arranged ourselves in a large circle and the proceeded to exchange names and give a brief background of ourselves. And, then it came – that awkward period of silence. Any counselor new to the profession, will admit that those intense periods of silence, when no one utters a word, are the most difficult to handle. Sometimes, these are periods of internalized thinking or coming to terms with an important self-discovery that has uncovered some deep emotional experience. Nevertheless, these lapses in conversation are truly difficult and as a professional counselor it is critical to learn to cope with them. Eventually, I believe that every counselor develops his own mechanism for waiting it out and getting through these periods. Whether it is mentally counting backwards or counting the tiles in the floor, sooner or later, one develops his own method.

Sitting there and waiting for someone to speak seemed endless. After seeming like an eternity, Sally pierced through the barriers of silence to learn why I chose counseling over journalism. Everyone breathed a sigh of relief. Suddenly, a door had opened and everyone wanted a piece of the action. Arousing their curiosity, the group wanted to know more – where I worked, how I managed, and of course, my living situation.

For some reason, the majority of people seem to think that if one is disabled, she automatically belongs in a profession where she will find acceptance and be able to assist others like herself. Perhaps, to some degree, this is true, however, despite our limitations, I believe we can make valuable contributions in other fields as well. After several years as a columnist writing on issues pertaining to disability, the editors discovered that I could handle other subjects as well, which enhanced my value as a writer.

Initially, with the Group Process class, the attention is focused on the group leader who sets the pace. Since the key component of any group is trust and confidentiality, all members heed to this rule. As the group continues, less attention is focused on the leader and slowly is transferred to the other group members. As the only male in this small harem, Bob appeared cool, calm and collected. An experienced educator, Bob was working toward his degree in Personnel Administration with the notion of eventually becoming vice principal. Bob never failed to give the male perspective on several topics that came up during that weekend course.

Another challenging course was Medical Communities, which was taught by Dr. Ruth Ward. This was a rather unusual course because she taught it from home. She was given special permission by the college to do this because of her unique living situation. As with millions of people today, she was caught in the sandwich generation. She was living alone caring for her 101-year-old bed-ridden mother. To say this was a difficult task is putting it mildly. Dr. Ward herself had some physical limitations caused by age and now she needed to be there for her bed-bound mother. As a class, we had nothing but admiration for this woman and her ability to cope with an extraordinary living situation. By having class in her living room we witnessed firsthand what is was like to take care of an elderly person. To be on call 24/7 took plenty of patience and many sleepless nights. While the setting of the class may have been a little different, I don't think we could have witnessed a better view of real life.

Like most graduate schools a thesis was required for graduation. Writing a major paper like this requires a great deal of research and preparation. Most of all, it requires a topic that you are comfortable with. For a long time, I was interested in researching families who are raising children with cerebral palsy in a positive setting. This topic fascinated me for obvious reasons. When I told my professor about my idea, he said he thought he had a better choice. Instead, he wanted me to interview a number of teachers and see how much information they knew about cerebral palsy. I responded that I knew the answer already. Most teachers do not know a great deal about this condition unless they have a student with it. Therefore, I decided to go with my original idea.

Now I had to research my topic. Because I was on the Board of Directors, I had connections with the Cerebral Palsy Center of Union County. I decided to approach them first and see if they could help me with my research. In order to do this, I had to develop a testing instrument or questionnaire. I did this with the help of a couple of books I found in the college library and my own instincts. Then I was able to find six families who met my criteria. For the other ones, I had to think outside the box. One family I found was that of a coworker of mine who had a sister with CP, and they agreed to be interviewed. After calling around, I finally came up with ten families. I interviewed them and obtained the crux of my research. I received an A on my paper.

While I was in graduate school I made two special friends and I still share a bond with both of them today. Maria Soriano was a special education teacher at the high school level. When I met her she was a student aid but as the years passed and her education increased she earned her special education certification. She is an extremely dedicated teacher often rising at

3:30 a.m. to get a jump-start on her day. Granted most teachers are still turning over in bed at that hour, not Maria! She claimed she was a morning person and that was her routine.

Maria and I met in one of the introductory courses in the program and we quickly established a friendship. Outside of the classroom we got together about every couple of months for an all-day Saturday adventure. We went shopping, went out to lunch, and we also toured college campuses. One of our favorite hangouts was the campus of Princeton University where we once witnessed a wedding at their chapel. In the summer, we would often go down to the beach and spend the day basking in the sun and strolling the boardwalk.

Still living at home, Maria takes care of her mother who is in her 90s and is in retirement. She comes from a very close knit Italian family to whom she is devoted. She has a brother who has been married three times. I sometimes wonder if her brother's track record with marriages has prevented her from taking the plunge. She claims she dates every once in a while but nothing serious. I guess she just isn't interested in a long-term relationship.

The other woman with whom I formed a long-lasting friendship is Helen Maslinkowski. She is an older and a woman of average height and blonde graying hair who was an established high school counselor when I met her. Contrary to me, Helen is a very outspoken, loud, and opinionated person. However, she is kind, caring, and has a good heart. When some people learned we had become friends I think they viewed us as the "odd couple." I liked Helen, but I could only take her in small doses. When I first introduced her to my parents, they were shell-shocked. Helen was not usually the type of person I brought home. However, I think as the years went by they began to really like her.

One of the requirements of my graduate school program was doing an internship in the area of my chosen profession. Since I wanted to be a counselor of the physically disabled or a college career counselor I choose one of those avenues to pursue. Because I had connections with Union County College, I decided to ask them if I could do my internship experience in their Counseling Department. They agreed. So, once a week, I would come in for the afternoon and do some hands on counseling with the students. Most of it was academic in nature, some of it was personal counseling, and other times it was a combination of the two.

At times, a student was taken aback to see someone like me sitting opposite them. However, most students took it in stride, and if they did not understand my speech very well they would ask me to repeat what I just said. Usually I could tell if they could not understand what I said because they had a look of confusion on their face. Noting this, I was happy to repeat myself. I remember one instance where a student came in carrying a paper that they just received back from their professor. Unfortunately the paper had a big red F on top. The student was practically in tears because they did not know the reason for the grade. I asked to see the paper. Right away I could ascertain the problem. According to the student the English professor asked the class to write a paper and be as creative as possible. I explained to the student the creative part came with their ideas. However, they thought that they could get away with not following the rules of grammar and write the whole paper in one straight sentence. I explained that the teacher was looking for creativity in their ideas only and was not asking them to disregard the rules of grammar. The student may not have liked my explanation, but after I showed him a few things he agreed and understood. I asked him to see if his professor would let him redo the paper provided he explained what happened and the miscommunication. I guess he did. A couple weeks later he came back with his paper and this time he had a smile on his face.

Part of the reason for doing an internship was to be able to get feedback on our counseling style and hear suggestions as to how we might improve. Unfortunately, Dr. Cangelosi was the head of the internship program and he was supposed to visit every student in their environment. After a few months, I asked Dr. Cangelosi when he was coming to critique me. He said that he did not visit any of the students and that he did not have any intention of coming. He claimed that there were too many students to visit and that he did not have the time to do it. I was very disappointed and if I had had the nerve I would have gone to his boss and reported this. All of us had spent many hours learning the profession and to not receive any kind of feedback as to what we were doing right or wrong was a disservice to us and to our future clients.

One of the electives I choose to take was a course on the hearing impaired. I choose this course for a number of reasons, one of which was that my mother was losing a great deal of her hearing. In the class we learned about diagnosing a hearing disorder, cochlear implants that were just coming out in those days, and some other interesting things related to hearing impairment. The professor was very knowledgeable, and as he got to know me better, he decided to introduce me to a colleague of his at Robert Johnson Rehab Institute where he also practiced his profession.

11

What a golden opportunity I thought to myself as I dialed the number of Johnson Rehabilitation Institute affiliated with JFK Medical Center in Edison. Finally, I was going to get a story – a rather unique but inspiring one to tell my readers. Thanks to Dr. Terr's introduction, I had an appointment within minutes.

Briefly, I told my editor what little I knew about this extraordinary man whom I was about to meet. He was the only person I knew with cerebral palsy who had a "real" job, and I was greatly impressed to learn that he was a medical doctor who actually treated patients. Occasionally, I read of stories about people with disabilities who were involved in research and worked as professionals behind the scenes, but I never read or heard about individuals who were in the spotlight, let alone who practiced medicine.

Prior to our meeting, I made arrangements with Joe Buscaino, the paper's photographer ,to come and get a shot of Dr. Thomas E. Strax posed behind his desk doing some paperwork. Ideally, I would have preferred a shot of Dr. Strax using his medical expertise to examine a patient. Dr. Strax was a physiatrist and medical director of Robert Johnson Rehab Institute in Edison, NJ. A physiatrist is a doctor of physical medicine and rehabilitation. Physiatrists treat patients with all kinds of disabilities including cerebral palsy. Dr. Strax treated mostly patients with back injuries and those with chronic pain. In addition, he ran a weekly clinic for those with CP.

Finally, at the appointed hour, we were ushered into his much lived-in office. We were greeted warmly by Dr. Strax, a handsome man of average height, with dark hair and a neatly trimmed mustache. His navy, pinstriped suit offset his sparkling blue eyes. With a warm smile and a firm handshake, he made me feel very welcome.

After a brief introduction, Joe proceeded to get some good shots of Dr. Strax. A shutterbug himself, Dr. Strax gave Joe a few pointers as how to get the best shot for the press. Adhering to his advice, Joe got his pictures, politely excused himself and hurried off to his next assignment. Finally, I was alone with this distinguished man of science in his cluttered office. Books and papers were piled on every surface and on his walls hung numerous plaques and citations each with a story of its own.

FITTING IN

Seated opposite Dr. Strax, I explained a bit about myself and the kind of article I thought I wanted to do. I proceeded to show him my tape recorder, which was quite large and heavy. With a little instruction he was soon a pro interviewee and talking into the recorder presented no problem. In fact, he had so much to say that I occasionally thought he might never give back my recorder.

Born in the early 40s, Dr. Strax was raised in a small suburb of Philadelphia. He was the first born of two educated parents. His father, a prominent physician, who specialized in diseases of the breast, and his mother, an aspiring artist were both determined that their son, Thomas, would succeed. Starting with his right to have equal access in the educational system, they fought the administration and finally won their battles. Indeed, Thomas was to be the first child with a disability to be accepted in the Pennsylvania Public School System.

One of the reasons the Board of Education cited for not wanting to have Thomas was because they did not want the responsibility in case he fell. Of course, with an unstable gait, falling and knowing how to fall would always be a part of his life. Diagnosed with athetoid-type cerebral palsy, Dr. Strax displays all of the classic symptoms: involuntary movements of the extremities, awkward gait, impaired speech and occasional drooling, head lag, and impaired fine motor coordination. Yet, despite all of the limitations imposed on him by his disability, he always managed to find a way to work around them. For instance, since walking long distances tired him, he used a scooter to get around the hospital. Like me, he used a straw for drinking and kept a spare one handy in his left breast pocket.

Of course, as a kid, he experienced more than his share of teasing, and while his family empathized with him, his parents insisted he handle his own battles. As every person with a disability knows, to succeed in life a battle must be fought every day. In some cases, the battle begins at birth as the newborn struggles for its first breath, a first word, a first step and it continues through life as they strive to achieve an education, social acceptance, independence, and perhaps even a career.

Coming from a long line of practicing physicians, Dr. Strax entered medicine to continue the family tradition. He earned his medical degree from New York University School of Medicine and completed his residence at the NYU School of Medicine, Institute of Rehabilitation. While his father may have opened a door or two to get his son into school, once there, like everyone else, Dr. Strax had to prove himself. While in medical school, Dr. Strax was confronted by some rather tough professors who challenged not only his right to be there, but also his choice of career. As one professor said, "Your father may have gotten you in here, but you, and you alone, will be the determining factor as to whether you remain." According to Dr. Strax, this particular professor was determined to challenge him every step of the way. In reality, this professor was doing Dr. Strax a favor. By being tough and uncompromising he was preparing this future doctor for some of the many obstacles he would encounter as he practiced medicine. Of course, the patient would be his biggest challenge. While this is true of any physician, Dr. Strax's challenges would be increased because of his disability. Gaining their trust and respect would be of paramount importance especially if one were to accept treatment from him.

He told me, "I remember I once knocked over a five gallon can of sulfate acid in chemistry lab. What a mess! After that near catastrophe, I had a contraption built to hold that container firmly in place."

Like other medical students, Dr. Strax did his three year residency and rotated from specialty to specialty. When it was time for his residency, he was the assistant resident and helped with some of the minor cases. He explained, "With my coordination, surgery was not likely a possibility especially if I wanted to make a living." On his obstetrical rotation, Dr. Strax delivered the babies of clinic patients who did not have the financial means for a private physician. These were uncomplicated, normal deliveries.

For obvious reasons, Dr. Strax chose to specialize in rehabilitation medicine. Aside from treating others like himself, Dr. Strax's expertise lends itself to back injuries as well as chronic pain patients. Just as importantly, Dr. Strax serves as a role model for patients with disabilities as well as their families. As a parent himself, Dr. Strax knew that there is nothing worse than a spoiled child and a spoiled child with a disability is worse yet. All children need structure and discipline. The sooner the child learns to live within certain boundaries, the greater his chances are to be a contributing member of society. Raising two teenagers, Dr. Strax knew first-hand the difficulties associated with child rearing. He knew that even a child with a disability craves all of the same kinds of growth experiences as his able-bodied peers such as dating, driving, career opportunities etc.

After confronting the challenges of medical school, Dr. Strax's first appointment was as a medical director with Moss Rehabilitation Institute in Pennsylvania. Several years later, the Johnson Rehabilitation Institute approached him with an offer he could not refuse.

A few weeks after our interview, I received a call from Dr. Strax thanking me for his article. He was also interested in developing a good working relationship with me and wanted to make another appointment to meet at a mutually convenient time. I was overwhelmed with joy. To think a man of his position wanted to see me so badly that he was willing to meet at my convenience!

We made a date for a couple weeks later. Wearing my

one and only grey suit, I walked into his office armed with a tape recorder and a smile. I did not have any clue as to the topic. Once again, we were seated opposite each other, but this time I was definitely more relaxed. We talked about my job with the paper and the column that I had started in the late 70s. Even though I loved writing my column, I felt frustrated because I was still filing tearsheets. I guess I had a lot of repressed anger because I felt my disability was holding me back from the career I so desperately wanted.

Eventually, we began talking about cerebral palsy and the way my condition affected my coordination and speech. Because he himself was an athetoid and suffered with involuntary movements, Dr. Strax advised me to do as he did and take a mild tranquilizer to relax my muscles and gain better control. He took two milligrams of Valium five days a week. Over the weekend, he gave himself a rest and let the half-life of the drug wear off. Two milligrams of Valium is not even considered a clinical dose. Since I was not on any medication, I decided to give it a try.

He gave me the prescription and I had it filled. On Monday morning, I took my first dose of Valium. Well, was I surprised! One minute I felt like I was floating on air, and the next I thought I would fall asleep at my desk, or worse yet, standing up. I was like a rag doll in slow motion. I could not concentrate and I was drooling terribly – something I never really did.

Obviously, two milligrams was too much for me. Some people are more sensitive to medication than others and I guess I am one of them. Since my father has the same sensitivity to medications, we decided to cut the dose and see what happened. We both knew Dr. Strax was on the right track and once we found the correct dose, Valium might prove to be very beneficial for me. After some experimentation, we found the right dose and once on it, the benefits far surpassed any of our expectations. Both my coordination and speech improved dramatically enabling me to perform better at work as well as at home. With Valium, it was still important that I discontinue its use on the weekends to allow the half-life to wear off.

Introducing me to Valium was probably one of the best things Dr. Strax could have done for me. Not only did the medication improve my chances for advancement in the workplace, but it also helped improve the quality of my interactions with other people. Friends, acquaintances, salespeople all respected me more because they were able to understand me better.

For several months, Dr. Strax and I met on a weekly basis and discussed everything from current events to legislation centering on the Americans with Disabilities Act (ADA); he was one of the key people who was instrumental in developing this law. Indeed, this three-year task was a landmark victory for 36 million disabled Americans. ADA covers all areas including education, housing, employment, the right to proper medical and rehabilitation services, and much more. It is the most comprehensive piece of legislation since the Civil Rights Act to protect against discrimination. As disabled people, neither Dr. Strax nor I were strangers to discrimination. In fact, between the two of us, we had enough stories to write a book or at least a couple of chapters.

On the weekends, Dr. Strax would usually hang out with his kids, especially his daughter, Heller. On occasion, they would go out to dinner. One night they were sitting at the table preparing to give their order when the waiter turned towards Heller and asked, "What will he have?" Dr. Strax quickly interceded and ordered his own meal. Because I have had similar experiences and worse, I could relate to his situation with a few tales of my own.

Those of us who are afflicted with cerebral palsy, especially those of us for whom it causes slurred speech, are often thought of as either mentally retarded or drunk. I remember Dr. Strax telling me about an episode he had with the State Trooper. While driving on the Pennsylvania Highway, Dr. Strax was pulled over. The trooper came to the driver's side and asked him to step out of the car. When Dr. Strax did, the trooper noticed his unusual gait and slurred speech and assumed he was intoxicated. Asking him for his driver's license, the trooper was growing quite impatient. Finally, Dr. Strax handed over his license. Looking it over, the trooper saw the M.D. after his name.

Fortunately, Dr. Strax was not asked to submit himself to the humiliation of the Breathalyzer test. Neither Dr. Strax nor the trooper will ever forget that incident.

Years ago, I wrote an article for the New Jersey Section of the New York Times, titled "Understanding A Misunderstood Minority." I wrote about how all of these common daily experiences, ones which the average person takes for granted, can become so unnecessarily demoralizing for someone with a physical disability. If someone has a problem with either their speech or coordination, the general public automatically assumes the person cannot think or make intelligent decisions for herself.

Aside from finding someone to relate to about my experiences with CP, another advantage of having regular meetings with Dr. Strax was that I had finally found a physician who was an expert about my condition. While I had a kind and trusted internist, he was by no means an authority on cerebral palsy. He gave me annual physicals and tended to other minor ailments, but as far as cerebral palsy was concerned, he had no more insight than his patient.

According to a booklet titled "I'm Worried About the Future…" The Aging of Adults with Cerebral Palsy distributed by the New York State Developmental Disabilities Council at a national conference held at JFK Medical Center, Edison (September, 1993), cerebral palsy is a diagnostic label given to a group of conditions by variations in movement and/or balance which may be accompanied by delayed physical development. "If ambulatory, an individual with cerebral palsy has an awkward and difficult gait and poor balance. Most have abnormal muscle tone with floppy or tight muscles, impaired control and coordination of movements. In addition, one or more of the following problems can occur: involuntary startle-like movements, convulsive seizures, absent or poor speech, visual and hearing impairments and delayed intellectual development." More than 90 percent of individuals with cerebral palsy have a congenital form. That is, the neurological condition was caused by a lack of oxygen before, during, or after birth.

There is general agreement that cerebral palsy is due to a non-progressive lesion or injury in the fetal or infant brain the location and extent of which determines the exact characteristics of the condition in each individual. No two cases of cerebral palsy are exactly alike. Although the lesion is non-progressive the effects on the young and developing brain causes an ever-changing posture and movement disorder that persists throughout the lifespan of the individual.

Cerebral palsy is not inherited. Some rare genetic disorders may be hard to distinguish from cerebral palsy. Rarely, there may be a second sibling with cerebral palsy in the family; there have been very few reports of a parent or parents with cerebral palsy having a child with the condition. Cerebral palsy is a life-long condition. There is yet no way to repair the original lesion in the brain and cerebral palsy is not a disease amenable to treatment and cure. The major goal of management is to maximize the functional abilities of the person with cerebral palsy and to minimize the handicapping effects. Good management involves the earliest possible intervention by physical, occupational and speech therapists.

Dr. Strax told me that at the time (around 1988), it was generally accepted that 2 out of every 1000 individuals have cerebral palsy, which translates in the United States to about 500,000 persons of all ages. About 40 percent are under 20 years of age. A substantial number of individuals are in their 50s and 60s – some are palsy appears to be comparable to that of the general population, except for a small number of institutionalized persons who have more severe and numerous handicaps.

As the months rolled on and Dr. Strax and I continued our weekly meetings, I had the urge to try to become as independent as my mentor. Since I never was really encouraged to learn to cook or become skilled in food preparation, I decided that perhaps a therapist could at least show me the basics. Looking back, I think it was fear that prevented me from doing more in the kitchen. Mostly, I was afraid of either cutting or burning myself. Because of my poor coordination and weak wrists, I could not imagine myself handling pots of boiling water, removing casseroles from the oven or even opening aluminum cans.

After listening to my concerns, Dr. Strax agreed that perhaps it was time for me to work with an occupational therapist and address the issue. With a prescription for cooking lessons, I was about to enter the world of culinary arts.

I remember sitting in the waiting room wondering if this therapist could really teach me how to cook. Only time would tell. Finally, a woman in her mid-forties introduced herself to me as Arlene and said she would give me an evaluation and we would find out if it were possible for me to cook.

Measuring my coordination and motor involvement was really the key. After a simple battery of tests, trial and error, Arlene determined that I could prepare simple, but nutritious meals with the use of the microwave and toaster oven. Unless it was electric, the idea was to keep away from an open flame of a gas stove as much as possible.

The next phase of this combined cooking evaluation/lesson was to prepare a meal. In the process, I would learn some basic techniques as well as to overcome some minor obstacles that would enhance my mastery of the kitchen. Since baked chicken is one of my favorite dishes, to which we added a baked potato, sunshine carrots, a salad, and brownies for dessert. The baked chicken was popped into the toaster oven and everything else was to be cooked via the microwave. With cooking, timing is everything. The brownies were made first since they needed to be cooled before they were frosted.

Especially with today's packaging, opening a box of ingredients can be a trying chore. To help accomplish the task and still keep my sanity, I learned to keep a good pair of lightweight scissors around. A good paring knife can be useful too.

A package of brownies can now be purchased with all the ingredients except water. One merely adds water and mixes the contents into the container and pop into the microwave. To prevent the container or bowl from slipping, I place a rubber mat or terry cloth underneath.

As the brownies were baking, we prepared the chicken. With the paring knife, we cut the wrapping away and laid the drumsticks in the pan. We lightly buttered them and added some pepper and paprika before popping them into the preheated toaster oven. Since it was still too early to cook the vegetables, we prepared the salad and set the table.

With a salad, one can be as creative or simple as possible. We decided to make a simple lettuce salad by pulling off the freshest leaves, rinsing them under cool water and drying them. We put them into a bowl added some croutons and sprinkled some grated cheese and had our salad.

After placing the salad into the refrigerator, it was time to do the vegetables. Not only can a baked potato itself become a meal, but also one is very easy to do in the microwave. After washing the potato, take a sharp knife and cut an "x". This allows the heat to escape and prevents the potato from popping. Unless adequate provisions are made for the excess heat to escape, the potato explodes leaving a scattered mess in the microwave.

Sunshine carrots is a simple dish too. Mix half a cup of orange juice with carrots, follow the directions on the package, cover with a clear plastic, and pop into the microwave. The carrots come out tender and juicy.

Even though the interest is not really there to develop into a gourmet cook, I now know the basics and can prepare a simple meal for myself. While there are a number of special products one can purchase to assist in opening a can or opening a jar, sometimes good old plain common sense works the best. Plus, because we have such a wide variety of prepared prepackaged foods on the market today, a person like myself, has a good chance of preparing simple, but nutritious meals.

Being able to do one's own food preparation is a major step towards independence. Of course, living on one's own, in her own apartment is the ultimate. Since my late teens, I had always envisioned myself living on my own in my own apartment. In my father's eyes, that dream was totally unrealistic. While I do need a certain amount of help, I think probably the biggest obstacle for me to overcome was loneliness.

Like every conscientious parent of an adult child with a disability, my father was concerned about what will happen to me after my parents are gone. He cautioned, "Now, we must be realistic." Because my father suffered periodic bouts of depression, he was an eternal pessimist and always seemed to focus on the negative. Dad, however, preferred to think of himself as a realist.

One of the reasons we moved to a ranch-type house in the Elmora section of Elizabeth was to be closer to The Daily Journal, where I worked at the time, as well as someday to be able to share my home with another woman as roommates. Finding a compatible housemate might not be easy, but the idea was that she would share my home at a reduced rent and, in return, she would help me with the chores I could not do.

Contrary to my father's beliefs, various sources confirmed that this type of arrangement usually works out very well for all parties involved. For a while, my father thought this arrangement might be a real possibility and then "reality" set in. "What woman would want to give up her independence and move in with someone who has special needs?" While it might not be an ideal option, it could be a temporary lifesaver for someone in financial distress who could not afford to live independently. Why, good friends live together all the time. At my father's request, I discussed the feasibility of this arrangement with Dr. Strax who confirmed what I had been told previously either by other professionals or disabled people themselves.

What happens, however, if one does not have a "best" friend with whom to share their quarters? Since I have connections with all of the hospitals in the area due to the nature of my work, Dr. Strax suggested that I contact the personnel offices and explain my situation and the kind of person I was seeking. Because I need such minimal help, he explained, it should not be a problem. However, to protect myself as well as the other person, everything needed to be written out in contract form.

To avoid any misunderstandings or hard feelings, a contract or written document should be made stating the needs of the person with the disability and in what specific areas help is needed. To protect both parties, a trial period should be set to see if the new arrangement is a workable one. Lifestyle and tastes may be totally different and the only way to find out is by actually living together.

Six months later, my father had another brainstorm and changed his mind again. This time, he reversed his previous idea and thought that I should go live with someone else. His argument was that there are so many widows out there who are left with a big house and a limited income. As a result, it's a real struggle to make ends meet and by taking in a boarder like myself, she would stand a better chance of maintaining her house and perhaps gaining some companionship.

What would the advantages of this arrangement be for me? None that I could see. With this arrangement, I would be a travelling nomad with a big wad of cash and no permanency. I would be at her mercy and if for some reason the arrangement did not work out, I could find myself on the street. It would also be dangerous for me to be known as the disabled woman with lots of money. Who knows what could happen? While I am quite independent now and able to go up and down stairs, who's to say I will still be able to do this when I am older?

Another option for my future would be to move into an assisted living residential facility where light housekeeping, meals, activities and transportation are all part of the deal. While I was considering my options, one such location in Cranford opened its doors.

I first saw the advertisement in The Suburban News, a local newspaper for which I then wrote. At first glance, I thought it was an announcement for a nursing home, but the words, "assisted living facility" caught my eye. I wondered what the phrase really meant. Curiosity got the better of me, so I called to find out.

I remember thinking as I dialed the number that perhaps this could be a possible living arrangement for me. An answer to a prayer maybe. A few minutes later, I had the director on the line and explained my situation. As she listened, I could almost hear the wheels turning as she was considering this unusual request.

As always, I was very upfront and honest about my condition and what I thought I would need in the future. Of course, no one has a crystal ball! Even though I had cerebral palsy, I had a master's degree and was a features/medical writer for The Suburban News, a semi-weekly newspaper with a circulation over 100,000. Aside from my financial state, I lived with my parents because I still needed minimal assistance with my activities of daily living. Now, for the big questions: age and cost?

I was impressed by what I heard the establishment was part of a long line of facilities. For a monthly fee, a person 55 or over had a choice of a private or semi-private room, furnished or unfurnished, with three well-balanced meals a day, recreational activities, transportation, plus 24 hours on-call assistance to help with bathing, dressing, etc.

Could this be my answer? Even though they only

accepted seniors, were they willing to make an exception?

    Excited, I could not wait to get home and tell my parents – what would their reaction be? As it turned out my mother had already seen the advertisement but quickly dismissed it thinking it was a nursing home facility. However, rereading the ad, she realized that it was not a nursing home but an assisted living facility. Overhearing the conversation, my father's interest soared. "Well, the only way is to call and find out." And, he did.

    Within minutes, he was introducing himself to the same woman I spoke to, and she was telling him the exact same thing she had told me. Ending the conversation and placing the receiver back in the cradle, he said, "Interesting, very interesting." I could tell that the wheels were already spinning.

    Since the next day was Saturday, we decided to go over and see the place. Purchasing the property of what had once been a motel, the building was converted into a residential facility for seniors. Construction was well underway to transform the building to meet the needs of their future plans.

    Coming through the entrance of the still existing motel, we made our way to the coordinator's office. I think she was as eager to meet us as we were to meet her and to tour the facility. For some reason, when you tell someone you have cerebral palsy, he or she always imagines the worst. By the expression on Peggy's face, I could tell that she was very pleased to see me walk through her door.

An attractive woman in her early 50s, the coordinator delivered a straightforward and professional presentation about what the assisted living facility had to offer. She then showed us into another room, much like a sitting room and showed us detailed floor plans of what they envisioned the finished product to be. Next, came the tour.

We wandered by a single room complete with wall-to-wall carpeting, beautiful maple furniture and an inviting turned down bed with a bathrobe draped over the far corner giving the appearance that the room was already occupied. Furniture was optional. A resident could bring as many personal pieces as she wished or use the furnishings provided. The room for two was equally as beautiful and the suite was as luxurious as ever complete with television, stereo, and a bar-size refrigerator. The price varied with the size of the accommodations.

Glancing at the calendar of events, one could tell this was a "swinging" place. Aside from the usual crafts, sing-a-longs, and bingo, they also hosted day-trips, picnics, and nighttime entertainment. These folks would certainly not be bored, that's for sure. Elegant dining is featured with a choice of three entrees for every meal. There is also a separate dining room for any resident to entertain occasional guests.

Aside from all the amenities, I think the one most reassuring features is the 24-hour personal assistance.

At 39, I certainly did not fit the age requirement. However, rules are made to be broken or bent. Impressed with my insight to make some sort of preparations for my future, Peggy had taken it upon herself to consult the facility directors. After she conferred with them, they decided that they would accept me as a resident if I came in with a parent. Naturally, the rule would be eliminated when I approached the appropriate age of entry. However, Peggy offered me the option of living in the facility for a month to see how I liked it.

I gave the offer some serious thought. The experience of living apart from my parents and on my own would be an invaluable one. Getting a taste of the future and what it might be like would prove beneficial for all of us. Being the youngest kid on the block in a residential facility would have some disadvantages and hopefully I would be prepared to cope with them. For instance, while I might tire of listening to endless stories of the past, I have the comfort of knowing that I could always seek refuge in the quietness of my room. Living with seniors, I knew I would get my share of well-intentioned advice. I would always try to listen with an open mind, but that's all I could promise. I know too, that I might occasionally find myself lonely for people my own age, but by still living in the same community, I would be able to see and visit all my friends.

My folks and I agreed that the facility would be a viable option provided I was still working. By working, I would be gone most of the day. So, I definitely would not feel trapped in a place designed to accommodate the elderly. While some nights I might enjoy a lively game of Scrabble or some other form of entertainment, I just may want to hang out in my room. Whatever the case, the choice would be mine.

Fortunately, the Suburban News and the assisted living facility were only about a mile apart so the coordinator assured me that transportation to and from work would not present too much of a problem. If this arrangement proved otherwise, I had the option of calling Union County ParaTransit System, a countywide transportation service for the elderly and disabled populations, or a cab. Since meals were included in the monthly fee, I would be entitled to a boxed lunch five days a week.

An assisted living facility is only one of the many choices I had to explore. My living arrangement would depend on my specific circumstances at the time. Indeed, it was comforting to know that I was not alone in my pursuit of an alternative living arrangement. There are hundreds of thousands of people with a limitation of some kind who are confronted with this awesome decision every year. I would venture to say that the majority of people with disabilities have a supportive family member within the area who will oversee their care.

Since my brother and his family lived in another state and I would be the one uprooted, depending on my family members for care would be an unwise move for me. I needed the reassurance of being well established and connected in the community where I had been nurtured and supported throughout the years. Almost everyone I ever broached the subject with wholeheartedly agreed that moving would be detrimental to my career and to my emotional health.

People over 65 now comprise a large segment of the population. This is a well-known fact. However, what people may not know is that our disabled population is rapidly growing also. Because of the high technology associated with modern medicine, many babies who otherwise would have died years ago are surviving today. Newborns weighing less than two pounds at birth manage to survive. Unfortunately, oftentimes, these children grow up with developmental delays as a result of their low birth weight.

So, as the age of the population continues to increase and the numbers of those with special needs rises, the need for residential facilities will expand. In fact, it would not surprise me if a residential "quarters" would be designed for the working physically challenged. Hopefully, I will see this occur in my lifetime.

Seven years have passed and Dr. Strax and I still continue to see each other on a semi-regular basis. As both of our careers have expanded, time is even more precious. Serving as medical director for two rehabilitation facilities as well as on several boards that require a lot of traveling, Dr. Strax is an exceptionally busy man. Despite his hectic schedule, he always finds a little time for me. As always, he takes special pride in me for every time I win an award, he wins the joy of knowing that his efforts have contributed to my success as well.

Our paths would have probably never crossed if it were not for Drew Cangelosi who took my cold to heart and decided that it was time to become acquainted with a specialist in the field of rehabilitation so that I could learn to function to the maximum of my ability in spite of my disability.

12

As the oldest newspaper in Union County, The Daily Journal had a circulation of more than 100,000 readers. The offices of The Daily Journal were located in the heart of Elizabeth and its building was a one story structure with few windows and several cubicles. The Editorial section was housed in the middle of the building with the Advertising, Business, and Circulation departments located on the border of the building. Even though I was connected with the business office I sat in the Editorial department with the other reporters.

In the late 80s, newspapers were beginning to become a dying industry, especially the daily papers. With the advent of computer technology, people were able to get their news online and therefore were no longer interested in buying a newspaper.

Of course, I am speaking of the younger generation. As for the older generation, they were the ones who were keeping newspapers in existence.

As for me, there I was still sitting pulling tearsheets. By this time, however, I was writing two columns. One column, "Being Independent," was designed to appeal and disseminate information to the physically disabled. I believed that what one didn't know could hurt them. I started this column when I was working for the state. Now, I was also writing a second column titled "Today's Health," which discussed topics new to the medical community. It was the brainchild of one of the new editors, who happened to be a woman. She wondered why I was sitting in the editorial department with the ability to write columns and still pulling tearsheets. This made no sense to her nor did it to me. Even though she was there only a short time, Isabel Spencer was able to convince her superiors that I could do more.

Isabel, an inquisitive chatterbox, would always find time to talk to me and ask questions. I soon began to notice that her questions became more probing. One day, she flat out asked me why I wasn't doing more writing. I responded, "no one has given me much of a chance." Her response was "Well, I'm going to give you the opportunity." Then she talked to the publisher and the business manager to get their consent. They wholeheartedly gave it. I sometimes wonder if they were hesitant to promote me in case it did not work out. However, sometimes you just have to take the bull by the horns and go with it. Now I had my chance!

In addition to having two columns, I was now going to be a medical features writer. With this came more responsibility and a larger paycheck. For several years, I had been working 25 hours a week, just 5 hours short of full time. With my new promotion I would have full time status with health benefits included. Prior to this time, I was paying privately for health insurance, which ate a big chunk of my paycheck. However, everyone agreed this was something I could not do without. One complicated health incident could have wiped out my whole bank account. Now I was going to be covered and no longer needed to worry about it.

Within a few days, I was sitting in Isabel's office trying to figure out how I was going to handle all of this. My first thought was that I needed to explain about my disability to all twenty hospitals. So, I wrote a letter about myself explaining that because of my physical limitations, I would need to use a tape recorder and that people would need to listen closely because of my speech impediment. I presented my first draft to Isabel and after a few minor corrections we sent it out.

Now that I was going to become an official member of the editorial staff I needed to attend their weekly planning meeting. This is where we all sat around the round table and discussed our stories for the week. Some weeks we did a lot of brainstorming to come up with new and creative ideas for how to present material. With feature writing, there is a lot of leeway, and usually there is time to interview multiple sources. Features are considered a staple of the newspaper to be used when hard news runs dry.

About three days later, I received my first phone call and response. It was Doug Harris, the PR Director from Elizabeth General Medical Center. He was very pleasant and he was eager to help me in any way including transporting me to and from the hospital. Doug told me he would put me on their mailing list and if I saw anything that I would consider newsworthy and needed an article, to just give him a call. More press releases started coming and I began to choose topics according to their newsworthiness.

The first topic I covered was about the new MRI machine. Being a new invention no one knew much about it. But, as time went on, people began to realize that this MRI machine would eventually replace the need for exploratory surgery. I read in a book about the inventor of the MRI machine that he used himself as a guinea pig to test for the accuracy of the images that the machine produced.

On the scheduled day of my interview, Doug picked me up and dropped me off in the lobby while he went to park the car.

Doug was a tall, thin, rather handsome guy with red hair and a gentle but upbeat personality. We met up in the radiologist's office. He was very prepared for the interview. I had my handy dandy tape recorder and my questions with me and we began my first real assignment. I think Doug had explained my circumstances beforehand because no one seemed surprised or ill-at-ease. Within minutes, I had my interview and I was on my way back to the office. The next day, Doug called me again with more ideas for articles he wanted me to cover. I must have impressed him and the hospital because I was always over there covering some story.

As soon as other hospitals saw my articles about Elizabeth General Medical Center, they began to contact me with their ideas. One of the other medical facilities was Overlook Hospital in Summit, which is about twenty minutes away. Their PR person was interested in pursuing an article about a new concept in Labor and Delivery called the birthing chair. If a woman chose to deliver via this method, she would sit in a special chair for both labor and delivery. The thought behind this was that gravity would be working with her instead of against her. Unfortunately this method only lasted a couple of years before women began to seek other options.

One of the other options for women was called the underwater birth. Featured on national television, this underwater method was being offered by some other major hospitals.

Delivering underwater was thought to be less painful and much easier on the mother. Being a new concept the medical personnel had much to say about it. While it brought relief to the mother, some physicians thought it might be detrimental to the baby.

Some doctors argued that if the baby was not brought to the surface quickly enough it might get too much water in its lungs. This article was very controversial. I interviewed several doctors and wrote about their differing opinions that made for a fascinating read.

Around the same time, Lyme disease was in the headlines due to the increased instances of the illness. It was first diagnosed in Lyme, Connecticut, hence its name. This was brought about by the deer tick, which is smaller than a pencil point, but if not pulled out of the skin properly, it can cause a bull's-eye rash and several other symptoms. In fact, this disease can manifest itself in achy joints and can even lead to rheumatoid arthritis. Medical personnel were trying diligently to educate the public about the various signs of Lyme disease and encouraged them to avoid places where deer ticks may be.

Not only did I write an article about Lyme disease, but I managed to find a local person who had contracted it and interview her. She was very forthcoming in telling her story and wanted to caution people about the warning signs.

By this time, I had befriended two part-time feature

writers. Jane Gould and Carlotta Swarden who introduced me to the idea and possibility of writing features for the New York Times. She had been doing it for a while and seemed to think I could write for them as well. While I was writing for the Daily Journal, the New York Times was not a competitor. So, with Carlotta's approval, she advised me to call Robert Richards the editor of the New Jersey section of the Times.

So, the next day I did. I had planned to leave a message, but instead I spoke to Robert Richards personally. I explained that I wrote for the Daily Journal and was looking for other avenues in which to publish feature stories. He listened rather intently and told me to send him two copies of my best writing and to call back in two weeks. I called back and he gave me the go ahead. Now I had to figure out what to write. I chose to write an article about myself and the many misconceptions people have about my disability because of my speech. The article was accepted and about three months later "Understanding a Misunderstood Minority" came out in the New Jersey section of the Times, I was so proud. My friends, family, and fellow staff were amazed. I even received a bouquet of flowers from a friend from church who happened to be an author as well. A year later, I sent in another article about the Yard School of Art in Montclair, New Jersey who taught mouth painting to quadriplegics. This article was also well received and earned a lot of attention.

I was still writing medical feature articles on various topics for the Daily Journal. In those days, everyone was afraid of the big C (cancer). Many people saw it as a death sentence and, in those days, it often was; however, thanks to modern medicine if certain cancers are caught early, they no longer have to be. People also had many misconceptions about the disease and its treatment. In many instances, it was because they did not understand all the medical jargon and that was scary to them.

So, I decided to write a series about cancer, what it was, what treatment options were available such as radiation and chemotherapy. These treatments were two of the mainstays of cancer and some of the statistics. Elizabeth General Hospital had an established oncology department. When I told Doug about my intentions, he set up a series of interviews with two of the leading physicians in their department. I also visited two other hospitals in the area just to get some varying opinions. When I finished the series, the articles concerned the early detection of cancer and the treatment options available. For instance, women are advised to do monthly breast exams to detect new lumps that were not there previously.

I explained cancer and what it was in layman's terms. I also explained what chemotherapy was and its side effects. I did the same thing with radiology. By the time I was finished, I had a seven part series on the subject. Since my friend Jane Gould's husband was a radiologist, I had asked him to proofread the series for accuracy, and he was very pleased to do so.

Writing a series takes a lot of planning and preparation. Not only was I dealing with my own material, but I also had to think about pictures and the best way to illustrate what I was trying to say. I had several meetings with Isabel and the photographer to talk about different ideas for illustration. We had photos, charts, and diagrams. This process was a lot of work, but it was well worth it. It ran for seven days straight and I received a lot of positive feedback.

Little did I realize Isabel was setting me up to enter a national health-writing contest. She had to write letters of recommendation and submit my series. Since it was a national contest she had serious doubts that I would win. Lo and behold, she received word that I was one of the 32 people chosen to come to the School of Specialized Journalism in Maryland for 10 days to study cancer and AIDS research.

Since I had surprised everyone by winning, now the company North Jersey Newspapers had to come up with the money to send me and they did. Because of my unique situation, I also had to have someone accompany me to the conference. I chose my mother.

FITTING IN

The date was August 23, 1989, and that date I will never forget. I was sitting at my desk typing out one of my stories when the phone rang. It was my mother telling me that I had just become an Aunt. My niece Kaitlin Mary had just been born weighing 6 pounds, 10 ounces and had red hair. Then, about five minutes later Isabel came out of the office to announce that I had just won a national fellowship to study cancer research. What a proud moment! I couldn't figure what event made me the happiest. It was a defining moment for me.

To mark the event of my niece's birth, my mother came down with shingles, a painful disease that can take months to

recover from ill effects. So, for several days, we could not even see the baby. Rick and Kathy were living in Connecticut then. For weeks my mother fought pain from the shingles and relied on painkillers to get her through days and long dark nights. However, this did not hold her back from accompanying me to the conference. She was one tough cookie and was going to be my companion no matter what!

Since her stroke, my mother continued to make steady progress and by this time she was driving again. Driving was a big step toward independence for both of us. To say the least, driving with one arm is challenging. However, she returned to Kessler Institute of Rehabilitation to take some driving lessons. This was at the recommendation of her physician. Of course, she needed to be tested first for her reaction time, etc. Her teacher was an amputee himself and drove using only one hand, so he was a wonderful role model for her.

Kessler Institute is in the heart of East Orange and off of a busy main street. So, teaching took place up on the roof of the building. That was scary enough, but it worked, and within a matter of a couple of weeks, she was once again driving with my father. It took several weeks to build her confidence. One of the features that Kessler recommended was a spinner or a Necker's knob to be attached to the steering wheel. This allowed her to make turns with ease.

So, with a packed car containing our suitcases and other items we might need, we were off to Maryland. It was a five-hour drive from our house. We left a day ahead to give us ample time to make this journey. Some of our friends thought we were taking a big gamble, but by this time we had our minds made up. My mother had gained a lot of confidence in her driving ability and nothing was going to stand in her way.

When we got to the campus, Howard Bray, a man in his 50s who was in charge of this conference, greeted us warmly. He escorted us to our room, gave us the necessary materials, and we were on our way. We were to meet in the dining room for our first meal together.

Meeting my colleagues from all across the country was an experience I will never forget. There were about 18 women and only 5 men. For some reason, the men decided to stick with my mother and myself. I think they felt safer and less vulnerable. The classes met for six hours a day. Most of them were on campus and some of them were in the leading hospitals such as Bethesda Naval Hospital in Maryland. We heard some of the leading oncologists speak on their latest cancer research as well as infectious disease specialists on the AIDS epidemic. It was fascinating. We received numerous handouts as well as other literature that we could use to quote from in our articles.

As far as amenities were concerned, the meals were plentiful. Chicken seemed to be a favorite as we were served chicken 13 times in 10 days. By that time, some of us were beginning to cluck and grow feathers. I guess chicken must be a mainstay to serve when there is a large crowd. One night all of us got together and went out to a local Italian restaurant to enjoy some different cuisine.

Back at the office, I walked in and found a copy of Playboy Magazine on my desk. Thinking it was someone else's, I didn't pay much attention to it. Several minutes later, I met the publisher in the lunchroom. He asked me what I thought of that issue of Playboy Magazine. I said I had assumed it was for someone else. As it turns, out the publisher had put it there because on the cover there was a picture of a disabled woman in her wheelchair. He thought that would be a great story for my column.

So I called Playboy in New York City and had an over the phone interview. I asked to speak with the cover girl. I waited for several minutes and finally she came on the line. I explained that I was a news reporter for The Daily Journal and I had some questions I wanted to ask her. She was very kind and answered all my questions however, she sounded rather tired because she had been getting calls all day about the article. I guess agreeing to pose she just did not know what to expect. After the interview I spoke with another woman who asked me some rather odd questions. For instance, she wanted to know my weight, my height and my eye color. I asked her what her purpose was. She said since this issue appeared they received a lot of phone calls of disabled women wanting to pose. She thought I was one of them. I explained that I was a reporter only calling to get a story and I had no intentions of anything else. When I told my publisher about the incident, he just laughed.

As I began writing medical features, I soon started to get calls from other sources. One day a dentist called and told me about his traveling practices. He said he was the only dentist who got in bed with his patients. Piquing my curiosity, I asked him to please explain himself. With the elderly and the disabled population increasing, often times it's difficult for them to get proper dental care. These homebound patients often suffer in silence because they cannot physically get to a dentist. So he brought dentistry to them. We made a date and he brought his mobile dentistry to my office. On the appointed day, he pulled up in our parking lot. He had a fully equipped van where people in wheelchairs could roll right in. However, sometimes in more severe cases the patient is bedbound. So as part of his job, he would need to literally crawl in bed with his patients to treat them. Some dentists may find this above and beyond the call of duty. For some patients who otherwise wouldn't be able to have dental care, this service was a Godsend.

Writing these kinds of stories brought me joy. I had the satisfaction of knowing I was truly helping people. I was informing them of various technologies and treatments available to better their lives.

On another occasion I found a brochure from a pharmaceutical company on my desk announcing a contest that was sponsored by the New Jersey Health Products Council at the New Jersey Press Association annual meeting. Since I had just finished writing an article about a new treatment for wound care, I thought I would enter. To qualify for this contest, I had to submit an article about a new treatment, and this was the one. Oftentimes people who are diabetic have many problems when trying to heal a cut or sore. It can take weeks or months to properly heal. However with a new treatment called Procuren the chances are much greater. The limb can be saved and the risk of amputation is reduced.

So, I entered the contest. Several weeks later, I received word that I had won. With this prestigious award came two plaques and a check for one thousand dollars. I was very excited and so were my coworkers. When I brought the check home, my parents looked at it twice. My father then said, "She did it again!" One plaque hung in the lobby of the Daily Journal and the other plaque I brought home.

Subscriptions to the paper were decreasing and advertising was becoming harder and harder to acquire. Eventually, the Daily Journal shut down in 1992. It had been around for over 100 years. That was a very sad day. Fortunately, I was one of the people they decided to keep and they transferred me to one of their sister newspapers, the Suburban News, a weekly publication.

Prior to the shutdown of the Daily Journal, I had been meeting with the feature writer for the Suburban News Mike

Helrigel. Mike was thin man, high strung, and a smoker; he was married with one child and a baby on the way. As a journalist, he liked my style and seemed to think they could use my health features in their paper as well. We were all grateful that I was not to be let go but just transferred to a sister paper only five miles from home.

13

Saying goodbye is never easy. In the editorial department, we had become like a family. If someone needed help moving, we were there. If there was a health crisis within a family someone was always willing to lend a hand. We celebrated birthdays together, had holiday parties, and we even had a baby shower. We were a close bunch.

While we had to bring these good times to a close, we knew we would never forget each other. I was delighted to be invited to Frank Scandale's evening wedding. He was the one who hosted his annual backyard birthday party. By this time Bill Murray was the father of triplets, two girls and a boy. Unfortunately the boy didn't survive and I cried along with everyone else.

Now it was time to move on. I was pleased to join the staff at the Suburban News. This was a small weekly paper with many editions circulating which covered many towns in the surrounding community. Owned by North Jersey Newspapers, most of the staff were older and very family oriented.

I was now a part of their editorial staff. Because of the high volume of press releases they used, most of the staff was part time. Now that I was joining the ranks, I would have full time status because not only would I be writing featured articles, but also I would be writing a health section that would be in many of their papers.

The first day of any new job is the hardest, and this was no exception. The receptionist Annette greeted me warmly. She showed me to my cubicle and desk. Because the editorial department was so small, I would be sitting with the sales people. It didn't matter because I knew many of them since they had been with me at The Daily Journal.

Later that morning I was introduced to Ellen Fox the editor of the Suburban News and her small staff. Ellen was a tall woman in her late 30's and somewhat aloof. Her staff consisted of four middle-aged women who were part time and mainly just typed press releases into the computer.

Laurie, a woman in her late 40's was one after my own heart. I say this in jest because she loved books and chocolate, preferably M&M's. I also met Fran Harris who was in her mid-70's and very friendly. She worked about four hours a day and then her husband Bob would come pick her up and they would go out to lunch. Fran loved working; it gave her a great sense of accomplishment and a little extra spending money. Even though the Harris' were an older couple they had a compelling zest for life. As the parents of four adult children they were very involved in the community, especially with their church.

While I was still at The Daily Journal, I became involved in the New Jersey Press Women's Association. This is a statewide group of professional journalists who come together on a monthly basis to network and fellowship. Introduced to this Association by Carlotta Swarden, I met some wonderful women. One of them named Ann lived about six blocks from us in Elizabeth and she was more than willing to transport me to the Press Women luncheons. We dined at some very fine restaurants throughout the state. In addition to dinning, we heard some very interesting speakers. I found this group to be inspiring and very supportive. Some of the women were authors of new publications.

At first, the women were a little surprised by my presence. They had never had a woman with a disability as part of their group. However, as time went by and they learned of my background and awards, they were very impressed.

Every year New Jersey Press Women sponsored a writing contest and I always submitted several of my articles. For a small fee these articles were critiqued and returned to the writer. This was a great way to receive feedback on my writing. I received several first and second place certificates.

Even though Ellen was the editor-in-chief, I mostly worked with Mike H. on the new health section we were creating. After several discussions, we decided to write a main health feature as well as several columns to make it a well-rounded section. For instance, there was a pediatric column discussing different children's diseases. I also had a column focusing on dentistry. There was also a column focusing on senior health as well as men's health and women's health. Periodically, I would change these columns around depending on current news topics. Features articles were always on a current topic with multiple sources.

Because I was asked to write a health section, I worked under Mike Helrigel who was the special sections editor. We got along great and it was a good thing. Shortly after we started working together his wife went into premature labor and delivered a baby girl with multiple heart problems. They named her Morgan and she fought against all odds to live. She was hospitalized numerous times and when she was home she needed to be carefully monitored. Both Mike and Sharron were very devoted parents and spent countless days and nights watching over their daughter at the hospital and when she was home. It was a 24/7 precarious time. In addition to tending to their daughter's needs, they also had a 4-year-old son, Matt to raise.

Due to Mike's extenuating circumstances, I was often left on my own to do the section. This was a great responsibility that I never imagined I would have. Oftentimes, Mike would call me from the hospital and give me an update on the baby's condition and ask how I was doing on the section. If I asked him about something, he would often say do what you feel is best. When he was in the office he was often tired and distracted. Of course, who wouldn't be given his present situation? It was a difficult time for both of us but for very different reasons.

Despite the ill health of his child, life, as well responsibilities of his job went on. Fortunately, I was able to work independently and did not have to bother Mike very often. Most of the time he came in to the office at odd hours and work on the section and then leave to get back at the hospital. I knew he had been there even though I didn't physically see him.

The staff was very understanding, and the publisher made every accommodation possible to relieve Mike of unnecessary pressure at the work place. Noting all of the work that suddenly thrust on me, my father thought it was time that I get a little monetary compensation. So, he went to the publisher and pointed out that I was doing more than twice the amount of work but still getting the same salary. The publisher said he did not realize this and made the necessary correction. My next paycheck reflected all of the work that I was now doing. I think that was the first time I had ever gotten my father involved in a work-related situation.

Mike was forced to be at work less and less. Morgan was dying a slow death. She was now over a year old and wanting to walk. While her little legs wanted to accommodate her, her heart would not cooperate. Every time she tried to walk, her parents would need to find a way to prevent her from even trying. The exertion was just too much for her weakened heart.

We were all asked to pray, as this was the beginning of the end. Then one day we received the call that Morgan had passed away. Even though we all knew it was coming, it was a bitter pill to swallow. A few days later many of us were standing at the gravesite watching the small casket being lowered to the ground. It was one of the saddest days, and I will always remember it. Many years have passed since Morgan's death, but I still remember it as if it was yesterday.

By then we had left St. Luke's Episcopal Church and joined First Presbyterian Church in Roselle. There were many reasons why we did this, but at the time we thought it was a good move especially since I was well acquainted with Max, the pastor, from years ago. He was the pastor at First Presbyterian Church where I went to vacation bible school as a child. That was also the first church in the world to have electricity.

After Morgan's death, I called Max for a little counsel since her death was difficult to understand. One of the main reasons we left St Luke's was that I felt the majority of the congregation still saw me as a child instead of the adult I had become. Even though I had served on a committee I was still seen as an adult child. So my parents and I felt it was time to move on.

For some reason, it often is difficult to find acceptance in a church. I think this can be due to a number of reasons the primary one being that most members of a congregation only see each other for one hour a week and do not have a real picture of each individual's abilities. Even though many claimed they read my articles on a regular basis, I don't think they thought of me as someone who could contribute to the lifeline of the congregation. Max, however, saw me in a different light.

Several months after we joined the church, I was asked to become a deacon and was, therefore on the board of deacons. In the Presbyterian structure, the deacon served the people otherwise known as the congregation. For instance, if someone was hospitalized or incapacitated the deacons would visit them or bring them food or whatever else they needed. The deacons also made decisions regarding the health and state of the congregation.

At one time I was even the president of the deacons. As no one else volunteered, I offered my services and leadership. As a leader I was the stern one, but I got the job done. I think people were pleasantly surprised.

Eventually Mike found his way back to the office and I was no longer holding down the fort. No doubt, the loss of his daughter was indeed very stressful and it took Mike quite a while to recover. However, thankfully he had his job to come back to and that seemed to push him to continue not to mention his young son. Meanwhile, I became closer to Fran Harris in the editorial department. After several weeks, I realized that the Harris's would probably be good companions for my parents. So, we set up a date and invited them to our home. That started a new friendship and helped my parents to see what it was really like at the Suburban News. My parents had always been private people and had few friends. Some of these friends had drifted when my mother had her stroke because they could not accept the new Gwen. Of course, Fran and Bob did not know my mother before the stroke so it was much easier for them to accept her. We often got together over the weekend had picnics, celebrated Christmas together, and we were even invited to Fran's 80th birthday celebration at her church.

Among the new friends I made at the Suburban News was a salesperson named Tim Shock. He was a tall, handsome man who always had something to say. He had just returned to the workforce after being a Mr. Mom for three years with his young sons. His wife was a corporate executive in New York. Because she was the main breadwinner, he chose to stay home with the children. Prior to fatherhood, he had written a couple of books. He was very proud of that and he always promised to bring them in to show me but somehow that never happened, and eventually, for reasons unknown, he was fired. I guess he was a better writer than he was a salesperson.

Choosing topics of interest for my readers was always a chore. For instance, one month I decided to talk about heart disease and some of the new treatments to manage it. For this I interviewed a number of cardiologists as well as physical therapists who worked closely with heart patients to regain their health. I remember going to one hospital and talking with a patient who pulled up his shirt to show me his "new zipper." Cardio fitness is very important and patients were encouraged to exercise as much as possible in order to avoid a recurrence.

Sometimes when writing a story another story presents itself. While I was gathering information for my series on the heart, I came in contact with a man who really had a family dilemma. He was a driver for St. Elizabeth Hospital and he would drive me to the hospital to conduct interviews. He drove a station wagon and I commented on some of the things he had in the back of it. For instance, he had a carton of pampers, a small box filled with toys, a suitcase and several bags filled with miscellaneous things. Kiddingly, I asked him if he was moving. He hesitated before replying. Finally, he said that he and his family were sleeping in the park at night because they were homeless. He had a young wife and four little kids ages 9 months, 2 years, 3 years and 4 ½. I asked him what happened. It seems that they were evicted from their apartment and their family refused to get involved. Since it was October, the nights were really starting to get cold, and I was concerned about the small children becoming ill. He said his wife worked part-time but because of the small children she was needed at home.

That night I laid awake thinking about this family and their desperate situation. Being the kind of Christian I am I just couldn't ignore it. So the next day I called my PR contact at St. Elizabeth's, which was run by the Sisters of Charity. I told her that one of their employees really needed their help. I elaborated on the situation and I encouraged her to please see to it that this family received some sort of assistance ASAP. She assured me that she would look into and would get back to me. A few days later she called me and told me that she made arrangements for the family to temporarily stay in their convent. In the convent, they would have food, shelter, and protection from the inclement weather.

I make it a policy to never interfere in other people's business, but this time I felt it was necessary. This young man with his wife and children did not know what to do. I think he was embarrassed and he did not want his coworkers to think he could not provide for his family. However, every now and then, we all need a helping hand.

In addition to the list of hospitals I was already covering, I acquired some others. By this time, I added Staten Island University Hospital, a teaching hospital with multiple specialties one of which was pediatric urology to my list. I offered to give the urologist an over-the-phone interview but he insisted that I come to the office. As I did when I worked with the Daily Journal, I explained my situation and some of the accommodations that I would need. He said that was no problem and that he would send a car to pick me up. The day arrived for the interview and to my surprise as well as everyone else's there came up the driveway an extended white limousine. Carrying my bag and my recorder, I was helped into the limousine and felt like a queen. Once inside, I noticed its many features including a wet bar. This was the trip of a lifetime.

Reaching the doctor's office, I met this very kind man who was about to educate me about ambiguous genitalia, meaning not being able to tell the sex of the baby. To determine the sex of the baby, extensive testing including genetic mapping was involved. Because I had not even heard of this, I found it to be very surprising and interesting. People who are born with disorders such as Down syndrome have an extra 21st chromosome, likewise, children born with an extra 23rd chromosome present with ambiguous genitalia. The doctor went on to explain how they do a lot of hormone testing to try to figure out the sex of the baby. Once the sex is determined, sometimes extensive surgery is needed to create either a penis or vagina.

Several months earlier, I had interviewed a genetic specialist and she explained her role in helping parents to determine what kinds of abnormalities their child could have as a result of delayed parenthood. For example if a mother is over 35, the parents are at increased risk of having a child with a genetic abnormality. She went over what each chromosome represented and determined. Sometimes, after parents learn of what they may be facing, some parents may choose not to conceive or abort and go about other methods of having a child. Not all parents are able to accept a less than perfect child. She also counseled parents after a child is born and diagnosed with a genetic abnormality concerning what to expect in the future.

I received a press release from Visiting Nurse Services explaining that they had just opened a daycare for medical-needs children. These children had multiple problems and needed oxygen tubes, feeding tubes, and other kinds of equipment that the average daycare would be unable to assist with. More and more nurses were visiting homes where babies who otherwise would not have survived now lived. Some of these babies had seizures, heart problems that required them to be on pacemakers, sucking difficulties, and other serious needs. Each child received around the clock nursing care and there was a physician always on call. To help address these ongoing needs in the community

Visiting Nurse Services opened this medical-needs daycare, which also helped to educate parents on the medical needs of the child.

Since mental health month was approaching, I decided to do a series on some of the more common issues related to mental

health such as depression, bipolar disorder, and undiagnosed schizophrenia. Children with ongoing behavior problems sometimes have an undiagnosed mental disorder. Some adults who are homeless and who wander the streets looking for food and other resources often have an undiagnosed mental problem.

Oftentimes, these people are forced on the street because they do not know how to access the proper care that they need. Some families do not know how to manage or to help their loved one with mental illness. Mental illnesses have a lot of stigmas, but if properly managed, people who have them can have a full life.

I contacted the medical director of Fair Oaks Hospital in Summit, New Jersey, which was a facility that specialized in mental disorders. The medical director was very accommodating and he offered to have me come and tour the hospital to give me some ideas of new treatments available for various mental disorders. So, I went into Fair Oaks and learned more about schizophrenia and bipolar disorder, especially how it affects people in their late teens and early 20s. I guess he must have liked me because he offered to get a group of psychiatrists together so we could all go out to lunch.

A couple weeks later, I was dining in a very elegant restaurant with seven psychiatrists. I brought my handy dandy tape recorder with me and proceeded to do some interviews. I think our topic was schizophrenia. I learned about and shared some of the newest treatments with my readers. We also talked about some other mental disorders that are not well known but still relevant in today's society. For instance, especially among young women, eating disorders such as anorexia and bulimia are not unusual and yet they tend not to be discussed. Unfortunately, there is so much pressure these days to conform and some people just cannot handle it and they have mental health issues. If these are left untreated, sometimes they can lead to debilitation. It is a very sad commentary on our society because many of us do not understand or recognize mental health issues as a sickness. I received some very helpful information that I was able to develop into a series. Each psychiatrist had his own area of specialization and some of them even worked with kids as early as 3 years old who were acting out and in some sort of mental distress.

As I was writing more and more of these health articles, it became apparent to my publisher that somehow I needed to have my own office. Because several people came over from The Daily Journal, the office was already crowded. We decided to create a makeshift office by converting one of the storage closets into an office. I had a lot of fun decorating my own space. I even bought posters. This way when I had people come in for interviews we would have some privacy. I remember one surgeon came in to show me a new form of a hip replacement, a ball and socket. He was a rather large man with a booming voice, and so it was in everyone's best interest that I had my own personal office. On other occasions, I had former patients come in and tell me their stories. Some of them wanted to remain anonymous.

About six months later, I received a letter in the mail telling me that I had won Union County Commission on the

Status of Woman Award for outstanding journalism. This honor came as a complete surprise to me because I did not even know I had been nominated. It appeared that I was nominated by a former co-worker Angela Harrington whom I had worked with at The Daily Journal.

This honor was bestowed on women in several different categories; education, business, medicine, entrepreneur, civil service, marketing, sales and journalism. This award was to be presented at a banquet dinner held in our honor. We had the option of inviting our coworkers and family to join us on this special night. Because my brother's family lives out of state and my sister-in-law had just given birth to my nephew, Christian Richard who was born at 7 lbs. 11oz, my brother and sister in-law were unable to attend. However, I decided to invite two of my former professors Paul Evans and his wife Mary Ellen, and Drew Cangelosi and his wife, Kate. A few of my coworkers were invited to come as well, but did not appear because of inclement weather. As a special surprise my fourth grade teacher, Joy Wanat, came. I was very surprised and touched to see her after so many years. She had read the article in the newspaper about the award and felt she had to be there. We renewed our relationship that night and made it a point to get together at least once a year thereafter.

Despite the weather, the room was packed. We had a delicious dinner of either chicken or beef and it there was cake for desert. As each winner was called to the podium, we each were asked to say a few words and to receive a small clock with our name engraved on it. Because my father asked me not to make a speech, I just accepted my award with many thanks. For some reason my father did not like seeing me speak in front of large groups of people. So to accommodate his wishes I declined to give a speech. I was sorry that no one from work appeared to share in this occasion, but there were letters of congratulations from the president and the publisher of the company. Not having a representative from The Suburban News was disappointing and not well received by Union County Commission on the Status of Women.

14

After working at the Suburban News and experiencing some tension and conflict, the president of the company asked me to relocate to the Herald News, a daily newspaper that was owned by North Jersey Newspaper Company. Even though it was 22 miles away, I decided to take the job.

The question remained, 'how would I get there?' My father offered to drive me and this lasted a few months. However, this was a long commute and he was getting older. Fortunately, New Jersey transit came out with the Access Link program. Provided that a person lived within a mile of a bus stop, this program provided curb-to-curb service for anyone with a physical disability. It was a Godsend and came just at the right time.

Because of the distance involved, I had to be ready by 7:05 a.m. for the bus to come and pick me up. So, this meant getting up at 5:45 a.m. every day. Sometimes, depending on traffic, or if the same bus had to pick up someone else, I would arrive home anywhere from 4:30 to 6:00 at night. It was a very long day. Since there were so many hours involved in commuting, the company agreed to have me work at home two days a week. This came under the heading of a reasonable accommodation. Back in the late 90s, this was considered a new thing. People were beginning to discover that employees were more productive, less tired, and better able to handle their workload and their families if they worked from home part-time.

My primary editor was Jim Emilo, a tall man in his mid-40s, divorced, and who was very set in his ways. Several months prior, I had already met Jim because he had asked me to write a weekly real estate review for the Sunday edition of the Herald News. This was not my favorite thing since I had no experience in real estate nor did I get a chance to personally visit the houses I was reviewing. However, I did speak to each realtor and they did send me a description of each home. For some reason, Jim wanted me to change all the wording around to make it my own piece. I found this very difficult because I had not seen the homes myself.

Some of these homes ranged in price from $80,000 to a million dollars. The houses were all shapes and sizes. I remember featuring a million dollar home that had 7 bedrooms and 5 full bathrooms with whispering toilets. The staff laughed about that one for days. Usually the homes featured fireplaces, Jacuzzis,

Olympic sized pools, etc. I hope I was able to properly describe these homes even though I never personally visited them.

I sat in the editorial department just outside of the president's office. I guess because of the situation that occurred at the Suburban News, he wasn't taking any chances that someone would ignore the standards set by the American's with Disabilities Act. I liked sitting just outside of Rich Vezza's office as he had been one of my first editors and by this time, I knew his whole family. I was also sitting with a small staff of the Dateline Journal headed by their editor Albina Sportelli, who I instantly liked.

Even though I still wrote for Mike in the Health Section, I now was working on several other projects. Since I was still writing health features, I had to become acquainted with the hospitals up in the Passaic County area. So, as I had done in the past, I wrote a letter to all the PR heads at the hospitals explaining my needs and what I would need from them. This turned out to be a much easier transition than I thought it would be. They too supplied transportation and I was able to get around on my beat.

One of my favorite features I recall was about an 18-year-old girl who was born weighing less than a pound who was now the valedictorian of her high school class. The PR department at St. Joseph's Hospital made arrangements for me to interview her and her mother right outside the NICU. She was a very outgoing young lady who had big plans. Her mother described her birth as she arrived three months early. She said it was touch and go for a long time, but thanks to the wonderful care that she received from the staff at St. Joseph's Hospital, she is what she is today. The doctors described how far they have come in treating premature infants. Back 30 years ago, a baby of this size would otherwise have died, but nowadays, thanks to early intervention and more medical advancements the majority of these infants survive. Some of them do have developmental delays but many of them become successful individuals.

I soon began to realize that working at home had its advantages. My parents were getting older and they needed more and more help. So, I was able to work around their schedule as well as my own. By this time, we had sold our split-level home in Roselle and moved to a ranch-style home in the Elmora Heights section of Elizabeth. Moving was a monumental task. After living in a home for 30 years we had collected a lot of junk. My mother was a packrat and saved every newspaper for whatever reason, I still do not know. So, we had much to sort out and get rid of. This task took several months. Because we did not have any family around us, the bulk of this project was left to my father.

After searching for several months and contacting some real estate agents, we found a three-bedroom ranch that was perfect for us. Across the street were a couple of stores, which were also close to a bus stop. The owner of the house was also a realtor, so she knew how to sell a home.

While we wanted a smaller home, we did not want to leave the area. We were well established with our church, my job and my mother's volunteer work at Rahway Hospital. Meanwhile we had joined The First Presbyterian Church in Roselle, NJ. My mother and I had known Max and his congregation for several years. Within a year after joining the church, I was made a deacon along with my father. Two years later, I became the president of the deacons. In the Presbyterian Church the deacons are responsible for serving the people. While some people were hesitant to have me as the head of the deacons, they really did not have much of a choice, as I was the only one who volunteered.

According to The Book of Order, the Presbyterian Church has three levels of government: The Session rules over the policy of the church, the Deacons take care of the people of the church, and the Trustees take care of the property of the church. I served two terms as a deacon performing many tasks for individuals in the congregation including visiting the sick and shut-in, helping the food banks, and ministering to the lonely, etc.

At the beginning, it wasn't easy to work from home.

There were a lot of distractions. However, as time went on, I began to discipline myself and to get on a better schedule. Some of the doctors that I interviewed preferred to have conversations in the evening especially if they were surgeons and had a hectic day at the hospital. So sometimes as late as 9:30 at night, I would be conducting an interview.

Of course, like most people, I will never forget September 11, 2001. It was a typical Tuesday, and one of my days to work from home. On that day, I was scheduled to have my annual mammogram. When I left to go to the Radiology Center, kids were going to school and parents were going to work. However, during my brief visit to have my mammogram, the whole country was changed. While I was waiting for the results, a technician came in to say that one of the towers of the World Trade Center had been hit. We all felt bad. However, several minutes later when she came in to announce that the other tower had been hit as well, we knew something was dramatically wrong. We as a nation were under attack.

Everyone was in shock. Leaving the center it was like a ghost town. No one was outside. People who were usually very talkative were now quiet and fearful. As soon as we got in the car, we turned on the radio to hear what was going on. We did not like what we heard and could not wait to get home. Driving the five miles to our home, it was a very strange feeling. Somehow we knew that what happened had changed the world forever. Once we were home, we turned on the TV and saw all of the chaos. Buildings were on fire and people were jumping out of them. Sirens were blasting. Parents were panicking. Many parents were jumping into cars to get to the school to get their children. Everyone just wanted to be with their loved ones.

Even though I was working from home, I called Albina and said, "What can I do?" Even though I was not scheduled to go into the office the next day, I had called St. Joseph's Hospital and they arranged for me to interview an emergency medicine physician who gave up his time to go to New York City to help the thousands who were wounded. I called him and he described what he had been going through. He said he was going from floor to floor in the building looking for wounded. He was low on supplies but he figured just by his presence people would know that help was coming. He had a cell phone and was able to call for backup help.

By Tuesday evening, a special ship that had been converted into a hospital pulled into the Hudson River and docked at the harbor. Victims were pulled out and rushed onboard to get medical attention. There were so many of them and the smell of burning bodies was a lingering odor that will always stay with me. Living just 18 miles away from New York City, I could still see the big clouds of black smoke. The smell and the stench will always remain with me. It was a very frightening time.

A nurse that I interviewed described a scene that she witnessed of a newly pressed shirt hanging in a tree. She said she did not know how the shirt got there, but it was amazing to see that despite all the chaos there it just hung in the tree. She went on to say that not all of those injured were adults but children were victims as well. In one of the twin towers there was a daycare, and, unfortunately, there were no survivors.

That night, I received a call from my girlfriend Carol explaining to me that our mutual friend Colleen Frasier was gone. She suffered from a vitamin D deficiency that stunted her growth. She was less than 4 feet tall and walked using a cane. When I first met her she was working for the Office of the Disabled in Elizabeth. Now two years later Colleen was working for United Cerebral Palsy. On 9/11, Colleen was on her way to a national conference on cerebral palsy for her job. She had been on board the flight that went down in Pennsylvania. It was on its way to Washington D.C. and the passengers were able to avert the plane from reaching the capitol. The hijackers & the passengers were killed when the plane blew up in a field in Pennsylvania. There were no survivors. Unfortunately, I was unable to attend her funeral.

While I was not a designated hard-news reporter, because of the magnitude of what happened, I was called on to interview and write a story from a medical angle covering the news. It was a horrific story and it needed to be covered by as many angles as possible. We were writing for days. Each day more and more information came forth.

I remember talking to my brother Rick a few days later and he was concerned about my young nephew Christian. He was 8 at the time and suddenly he refused to go outside. Rick asked him one day why he didn't want to go to his friend's house. He replied because he did not want a plane to fall from the sky and kill him. Of course, at his tender age he had no idea how far New York City was. He just saw what was replayed on television over and over again. Of course he was frightened. Many youngsters fell into the same category because they couldn't distinguish fact from fiction. Time passed, and life went on, but the memory of that day and the many tragic weeks and months that followed stay with me.

15

In April 2011, I had started to work with Albina on the education section of the Dateline Journal. Spring was in the air and it was time to think about graduation. As is customary, the valedictorian and the salutatorian are interviewed for features that run in a special graduation section. At this time, I was able to visit the high school and interview each student involved. As I toured the high school, I soon began to get ideas of other feature stories to do in the future.

When I was growing up school nurses were the ones who administered eye exams, measured one's weight and height every year, handed out Band-Aids for cuts and bruises etc. Nowadays, a school nurse is called upon to do much more. For instance, she monitors students with diabetes, those with epilepsy and asthma, plus a host of other serious illnesses. Some schools, depending on the size of the student population, have more than one nurse. In writing this story I was amazed at how much the role of the school nurse has increased.

As an education reporter, I also covered stories about students with special needs. Much has changed since I was in school. Depending on the disability many students had aides to assist them in the classroom, to accompany them to the bathroom, and to also be with them outside. The law involving section 504 is very specific about having a child with a disability in the classroom. School aides are hired to help meet their special needs and to allow the teacher to focus on the entire class. When I was attending school there was none of this. A student was either put into special education or had to find a way to function with his able bodied peers. Of course exceptions were made, such as physical education was not required and most students with disabilities received physical therapy instead.

As with most students who wanted to attend college, they strived to achieve some sort of scholarship to offset the cost of tuition. In addition to merit scholarships that are offered for scholastic achievements and/or athletic ability, there are so many other scholarships available that many people do not even know about. For instance, I remember one scholarship that offered $1,000 for anyone with blue eyes and blonde hair. While this may seem like a joke, I guarantee that it wasn't. Another scholarship calls for anyone who spoke more than two languages fluently.

Scholarships are offered through churches, businesses and government funding, organizations such as the boy scouts and the girl scouts, the Kiwanis club, the American Legion etc. It is important to check with the student's counselor as well as the library. There are several scholarships that are left untouched

because most people do not know about them. Scholarships can be found in many places, such as the internet or simply by speaking with your student advisor if looking to attend college.

A student of Clifton schools was invited to participate in the National Scripps Spelling Bee held in Washington D.C. She was a seventh grader of American Indian descent. She had been involved in many of the spelling bees held in her school as well as statewide. This young lady finished in second place at the National Scripps Spelling Bee in Washington D.C. and she received a $10,000.00 scholarship to be put towards college. Her parents, her school, and the residents of Clifton were very proud. When she returned to Clifton, we sat down for a one-on-one interview. I was amazed that she was able to spell words that I never even knew existed. She was one up on me!

As a long-time fan of Jeopardy with Alex Trebek I was pleased to learn that a Clifton resident was chosen to be on the program. He had gone through the preliminary screenings and now he was going to be a contestant on the show. Of course, all of Clifton was enthusiastically rooting for him. He did very well and he was on the show for three days. When he came back, I interviewed him. He said it was a dream of a lifetime being on the show and meeting Alex Trebek. However, the most difficult part was getting the clicker to come in on time. He said, "There were several questions I could have answered, but darn it that clicker just wouldn't come in when I needed it to." That was very frustrating. Being on Jeopardy was one of several things he had on his bucket list.

The Dateline Journal was moved to Clifton, New Jersey. It was decided that in order to adequately cover a town or city the staff of the Dateline Journal needed to be in the heart of it. We moved to a professional building on the center of Main Street and shared the space with a dentist, an eye doctor, and a lawyer.

Clifton is a large metropolitan city representing 37 different nationalities. It had at least 15 houses of worship and a well-rounded educational program. Clifton has always ranked high in education and was one of the first school districts to offer special education. Clifton also has one of the largest special education programs in its part of the state. The city has always ranked high in education with at least 80% of their graduates going on to either college or a trade school.

When we first decided to move, we were in the midst of acquiring a Spanish speaking staff to help us develop an edition of the Dateline Journal specifically for the Spanish speaking community. Thinking that this was a wise move to increase circulation, it turned out to be a fiasco. The Spanish speaking community was getting its news from other sources and was not interested in having a local paper in their language.

However, I did make a friend, a lovely lady in her mid-40s raising a teenage son and living with her mother. She had some great ideas for stories and she did not hesitate to share them with me. I think her name was Fran. She was a wonderful baker and we appreciated her kindness but not the extra pounds that all of her goodies contributed. Fran had her staff, which consisted of a feature writer, an advertising executive and an editor.

The new headquarters of the Dateline Journal were not that far from the Harold News so I did not have to change my bus route. I just had to ride a little bit farther. Being housed in a professional building had some advantages. Since I was the first to arrive in the mornings at the Dateline Journal office, some of the staff in the other offices would keep a lookout for me. This was especially helpful during the winter months when some of the sidewalks were quite slippery and I needed an extra hand or when the bus was late and it was getting darker earlier.

When my family and I moved to a smaller house, we thought that would solve most of our problems. And for a while it did. Unfortunately my parents and I were aging. My parents were now in their late 70s early 80s and they needed more help than I could provide. At the age of 80, my mother was advised by her physician to give up driving. In addition to her physical problems caused by her stroke she now had macular degeneration, which weakened her eyesight. While she had the wet kind, it still was serious. Her having to relinquish a big part of her independence meant more responsibility for my father. His health was also deteriorating due to a number of mini strokes he suffered over the years. While he was still driving, dad was not considered a safe driver.

One day during the fall, he was struck by a hit and run driver about a block away from home. Even though spectators called 911, he managed to get himself up and drive himself home. He came in and lay down on the couch. That was probably the worst mistake he ever made. At 4am I was awakened by him calling me and asking me to call 911. Dad could not move. Apparently from the fall, all his muscles had stiffened and he was more seriously injured than he previously thought.

Calling 911 was a new experience for me but one I could handle. Once I was on the phone with them they told me to put the porch light on and to stay on the line until help arrived. Approximately 3 to 5 minutes later the ambulance pulled up. While they were preparing him for transport, I woke up my mom. She was immediately alert and came to the living room and saw Dad's condition. Dad suggested that he go to the hospital alone and then we would follow in the morning.

Dad was in the emergency room for several hours since his condition was not life threatening. When we arrived at about 7:30 a.m. he had been diagnosed with three fractured ribs. While his injury was painful, it wasn't life threatening. Dad was discharged later the same day. Meanwhile, I had to decide whether I felt comfortable enough with the present situation to travel 22 miles to work.

Needless to say I was perplexed as to what to do. So I called my boss Jim Emilio and explained the situation. He was very understanding and told me to just focus on my parents and not worry about my job. I stayed home about 3 weeks. Because of the stress and strain of the situation on me, I developed some problems that affected my coordination. My father's accident took a greater toll on me than I thought. He recuperated rather quickly and I needed some medical intervention. Too much stress causes my CP to go haywire and that is just what happened. Unfortunately, we didn't have the support that we needed and the stress just took over my body.

For several nights, I had some insomnia, but was more than that because I could not seem to get my arms calm enough to allow me to sleep. Finally, we contacted my internist who suggested I see a neurologist. The neurologist performed some simple tests and decided that all I really needed was a prescription for a sleeping pill and to relax. Of course, relaxing is easier said than done but somehow since I saw my father improving, I think my nerves calmed down. Eventually, I was able to get back on a regular sleep schedule and return to work.

Unfortunately, the neighbors were hesitant to get involved and so was the church congregation. It wasn't as though they did not want to help; these people just did not know how to help. Max, our minister at the time, came to see me and he was quite overcome. He had known me for a number of years and never saw me in that condition. I guess he wished he could offer more help, but at that time, the congregation was getting smaller and smaller. He said that several years ago, when women were at home, the church had a service where they provided meals and aid to anyone who needed it. But, nowadays, they just did not have the manpower to provide the service. I did have a cousin in the area, but she claimed that she was unable to help. As I look back on the situation, I guess this was the first of many wake up calls we needed to convince us that we needed to relocate closer to my brother who was living in Ohio.

Meanwhile, the Dateline Journal eventually wanted to expand its religion pages. It had been covering churches as far as having a directory of service times and events, but it did not have any features about up and coming programs, holidays and the like.

One of the first pieces I did was about the shortage of students in seminary. After I called Drew University in Madison, I learned that the enrollment was about 50% men and 50% women. The increase in female enrollment was due to the fact that more and more women were being accepted and even encouraged to enter the ministry. I found this fascinating and I even wrote an article about this very subject. A woman can be a wife, a mother, and a minister and still lead a congregation. Some women are just as effective at leading a congregation as a man. In fact, in the Methodist Church, there was a husband and wife co-pastoring and they seemed to think that it was a great way to serve the congregation.

While this was a rather unusual duo, the husband and wife team worked for this congregation. Aside from their professional duties, they were the parents of six children. Prior to entering the ministry, the woman had been a teacher and her husband was a malpractice attorney. One day when he visited me, he asked me about my disability. He was particularly interested in how it occurred and whether or not my parents sought counsel. I told him that my parents were so thankful that my mind was not damaged and that I was able to make a life for myself that they did not sue either the doctor or the hospital. Of course, nowadays parents are encouraged to sue primarily because medical expenses are so high.

The Journal did some interesting stories concerning the Methodist church and the church in general. While many people had a clear view of their particular religion, they did not have much knowledge of individual denominations. It is very healthy to have some idea of how others worship because essentially, we are all worshiping the same God.

Speaking of second career ministry, I also interviewed a Catholic priest who had been a Physician's Assistant. He says he was glad he had been out in the secular world because it gave him a better understanding of what the average person experienced. As a Physician's Assistant, he dealt with people from all walks of life and their problems, which better prepared him for the priesthood. He remembers giving a sermon one Sunday when a man from his congregation passed out. He was able to administer CPR and did a few other things to save the man's life. If he had not that prior training, the man might have died. Plus, since the congregation knew about his medical background, many of them felt more comfortable talking to him about their personal issues.

Around this same time, one of my colleagues from the New Jersey Press Women's Association wrote a biography about women who enter a convent. Most of us think a woman who desires to become a nun does so at a very young age, however, nowadays there are some women who enter the convent at a much later age, usually as a widow or as someone who has never married. These women bring a new dimension to the sisterhood. On Sundays some of these women are visited by their children or grandchildren from previous marriages. This is a side of serving God that most women do not even consider. However, if they are no longer interested in marriage and they want to serve God in a more devout and intimate way, the sisterhood is often a good match. Women who enter the order later in life usually make a more rounded nun because they have had some life experience normally only had by lay people.

As part of the series of articles I did on religion, I also met Eric R. Ziegler who was the pastor of St. John's Evangelical Lutheran Church. Prior to entering the ministry, he held a number of positions including ones in banking and teaching. As a kid, he always liked going to church so it seemed quite natural that one day he chose to study ministry. He always had a lot to say no matter what the topic. He was always willing to be interviewed and, as a result, received a lot of publicity for his church. As a pastor of a small congregation, he was always looking to increase its size. As most churches do, his church hosted a number of support groups and conducted other activities for the community. He would often talk about the special Cub Scout troop for boys with special needs that met in his church. These special needs ranged from autism to cerebral palsy to downs syndrome. Of course the scouting activities were brought to a level that everyone could handle and the boys took great pride in earning their badges. Through the months that I worked for the Dateline Journal, Eric Ziegler took a special interest in me and even invited me to his home for dinner and to meet his lovely wife. He took great pride in Joan and always bragged that he could not have picked a better pastor's wife.

After I recuperated slowly from my little episode after my father's accident, I returned to work and everyone was so glad to see me. In the 24 years that I had been with the company, I had never taken off more than three days for a cold. Even though I was back on the job, I was still concerned about my parents and their failing health. My girlfriend, Betty Jo, suggested that we try Meals on Wheels because that would cut down on the marketing and the cooking. After doing some research, I discovered that every county has their own rules and regulations concerning qualifications. For instance, in Union County where we lived, we could get Meals on Wheels for my parents and not for me.

According to their rules, the recipients of these meals had to be homebound and since I was still working, I did not qualify to receive them. I explained to them that because of my coordination, I could not cook, but they were not able to make an exception. So we tried Meals on Wheels for about two weeks and realized that our father still had to cook something for me. I suppose I could have had TV dinners but with the amount of salt in them, my hypertension would have gone sky high, and so we were back to square one.

At Betty Jo's suggestion, we also tried getting help through the Easter Seals. Even though the Easter Seals is a well-known organization and offers a lot of different kinds of support, when it comes to providing home health aides, they do not interview them in person. This is a big disadvantage, and I will explain why. A woman from the Easter Seals called and said that she was sending a woman over to be interviewed. Not having had an in-person interview, they had no idea who they were sending. That night, when the doorbell rang, I answered it and there was a woman of the evening standing in my doorway. She had a tight miniskirt and a blouse that revealed all, 6-inch heels and jewelry like you would not believe. She told us that she would be available to work during the day only as she also had several night jobs. Within minutes after she left, I called Easter Seals and told them about the prostitute that they sent over. They were speechless and apologized several times and claimed it would never, ever happen again. Two days later, they sent over a lovely lady in her mid 50s, who took a real liking to us. Eventually she even went on vacation with us, which happened to be the last vacation we took as a family.

With my father's accident and my nerves being impaired followed by the latest incident with Easter Seals, my brother, Rick, decided that we need to do something drastic. We needed to move to Ohio to be closer to him and to be able to get the help that we needed. My friend Betty Jo was very much against this. She did not want me to give up my career, my church contacts, and my friends. However, I really did not have much of a choice. With my parents' deteriorating health, we could not see us living in New Jersey without any family support. It was time to move.

Max had retired, remarried, and he and his new bride moved to Pennsylvania. So, at the same time that my family was making a major decision about our next move, the church was going through a tremendous transition. Max had been there for 29 years and now we were seeking a new pastor. I had served on the Board of Sessions and even extended my term because they could not find people willing to serve. This period of transition was difficult on everyone including Max.

No one likes change, but life is full of it. As much as we tried and wanted to stay in the area, we knew it was a losing battle. Even though my friend Betty Jo was opposed to our moving, she finally relented, and we decided to move to Ohio.

Before I left, I was notified that I would receive two more awards from the New Jersey Press Association for two pieces I had written. The awards banquet was held in another county in the state and two of my coworkers agreed to transport me as they were also receiving awards. It was a wonderful evening. I saw many people that I had worked with in past years even some from the Daily Journal who were now working for different papers within the company. That was a wonderful night and a memory I will always cherish.

Even though I had the career any disabled person would envy, I still had to put my parents and myself, including our health and safety, as top priorities. I remember when I told my editor Albina that I was giving notice and leaving. She was very concerned and sorry. I did not like having to resign or retire, but I had to do something. Even my friend Dr. Strax was very surprised, but I think he realized that I was in over my head where my parents were concerned. So, I gave three weeks' notice. As much as the company wanted me to stay, I couldn't. They had hired me as a long shot and as someone to satisfy the ADA law, but they could not have gotten a better person.

On my last day, the staff of the Dateline Journal gave me a beautiful plaque and a lovely cake to commemorate my retirement and service. For that I will be ever grateful. Before I left, Albina had asked me if I would like to be a phone correspondent. So, while the door was closed, a window will always remain open.

16

Saying goodbye is never easy. As a family we were well established in our surroundings. However, as my parents aged and with my disability, we just didn't seem to be able to access the help that we so desperately needed.

We had moved to our small ranch in Elizabeth thinking that I would be able to manage by myself and still have a career. However, that was not realistic. The winter of 2003 was a particularly harsh one and we endured several feet of snow. It was very difficult shoveling, but getting around was another matter altogether. I worked from home for several days because of the inclement in weather. The mounds of snow were just unbelievable, and while I was able to get out to the bus with my father's help, I had a hard time getting around the mounds of snow to get to the building. I was afraid that I would be stranded trying to get into the building because I arrived earlier than my colleagues.

As much as we hated to admit it, we had to move. My brother was on board. Every time we saw my brother and his family, Rick noticed subtle changes in my father and my other signifying that they really needed more help. My father had endured several TIAs (mini strokes), and my mother was aging, which was compounded by the severity of her major stroke back in 1979 and the macular degeneration she was experiencing. Life was becoming more difficult for her. Even though she was still volunteering, playing bridge, and was fairly active in the community, we witnessed changes in her over time.

Prior to our decision to move, every time we went out to Ohio, we started to look around at retirement places in addition to assisted living arrangements. The problem was that most places would take my parents, but they would not take me. Claiming that I was too young, most of these places were set up for seniors and did not want to admit anyone under 55. However, we found two that were willing to make an exception. Both of these retirement communities were located in Stow, Ohio. Rick had sent us tapes of each of these places so that we could see what they had to offer. That Thanksgiving when we went to be with the family, we visited both. While we were impressed with each, we were most interested in one which offered different levels of care that could accommodate us over time as our needs changed.

Moving was a major undertaking. We had lived in our ranch for 18 years and accumulated a lot of junk. We were moving into a two-bedroom efficiency apartment and needed to downsize. This was not easy. My mother is somewhat of a packrat and she wanted to keep everything, which was just impossible. Finally, when my brother came out to take us to Ohio, he had to secretly dispose of many of our treasures or what we thought were necessities that, in reality, we could do without.

Downsizing was difficult but with the help of the Harris family, friends that I made at the Suburban News, we were able to hold a garage sale. We sold a lot of furniture, pictures, and nick knacks, and that was a big help. However, there was still much more to dispose of and slowly but surely, my brother was able consolidate and help us to get rid of as much as possible.

I retired on August 8, and we left for Ohio on August 13, 2003. My brother flew out and drove us in our car to our new home. It took two days to get there because we stopped and saw some sights along the way. We knew that this would be our last trip together as a family, so we were taking our time. Once we arrived in Ohio, we stopped at our two-bedroom apartment to try to visualize how we would set it up once our furniture arrived.

The two independent living managers greeted us warmly. We were very impressed by our apartment. It already had curtains and it felt like we belonged there. Granted, it wasn't home, but it was the next best thing. Our furniture arrived two days later, and, in the meantime, we stayed with Rick and Kathy and the kids. It was great to get re-acquainted with the kids – they had grown so much and they were into all kinds of things.

Once our apartment was set up with our furniture, it began to look like a mini-version of home. Since my father was still driving, one of the first things I did was visit the library where I got a library card got acquainted with the librarian. I found out that they made regular visits to our senior living community, so I would always be able to get books. In addition, the facility had their own personal library. About a week after we arrived, a new friend by the name of Phyllis, gave me a book about 9/11, and that was an icebreaker. I was able to tell her about my career and how I covered some aspects of that horrible tragedy. I think this made her realize that despite my handicap, I really had a lot on the ball. Outspoken Phyllis spread the word that I had been a journalist. People were curious and we were accepted.

I was not there more than a month when Nancy and Phyllis asked me to do something for them. One of the residents, Anna Mae, who was in her early 80s, needed to have a D and C and they did not have the staff to accompany her to the hospital.

So, they asked me if I would do the honor. They said since I had been a medical reporter and that since I cared for my mother, I should have no problem doing this little task. My mother thought it was rather unusual to ask someone who had just arrived on the scene, but I was willing to help out. On the morning of the surgery, I accompanied Anna Mae to the Outpatient Surgery Center. I stayed with her until they took her up for surgery and then I went downstairs and had a Coke. They said she would be in recovery in about 30 minutes. I stayed in the waiting room. Finally, a doctor came out and asked me if I was Nancy. I said "yes" and he said Anna Mae was doing fine and she could go home in about two hours. I asked him if I could see her and he took me to the recovery room. Eventually, the nurses helped her get dressed and we were on our way home. Needless to say, we were both pooped but for different reasons.

My parents and I loved our little apartment and we decorated very nicely. It was a two bedroom, and I liked the fact that I had my own walk-in closet and bathroom. In fact, I had more space to myself than I previously had at home. Not having to worry about cooking and preparing meals was a major weight off of my father. The facility served delicious food and if you happened not to like something, you could always get their second choice. Usually after dinner, a group of us would congregate either in the lobby or out on the porch. This was usually a time when a good discussion would ensue. While there were a number of activities, Friday night was a movie night and I was asked to be in charge of the movies. As I look back, I think they were taking extra steps to make sure I felt needed and involved.

Sunday was approaching and I wanted to attend church. Even though we had worship services every Wednesday, I wanted to find a church where I could make some friends my own age. I remembered passing by Stow Presbyterian Church and noting that they do not have any steps so there would be no problem for us. So Sunday came, and for some reason, I attended service by myself. My father dropped me off and said he would be back in an hour. So, I walked in and a man who introduced himself as David pleasantly greeted me. I introduced myself and he showed me a seat. Little did I know that this man was the Pastor. He was very welcoming and seemed to have no problem relating to me. Several years later he visited my mother in the hospital and told her that when he was in college, he was a caregiver to a young man with CP. My walk and the way that I stood were similar to his college friend. I also met a few other members of the congregation and felt an instant connection. The next week I brought my mother and she was very appreciative of the kindness shown to me. At that point, my father was not interested in church, but my mother and I attended regularly together.

Several weeks later, I called David and asked him if there

were any women's groups I could join. He told me about the Simple Spirits that met on Tuesday nights and to call Edith if I wanted to go. So, Edith picked me up and off I went. I met such a wonderful, caring group of women, many of whom are still my friends today. We met in the church library and sat around a rather large table. I met Donne, Peggy, Patrice, Jean, Edith, and a few others who would pop in once in a while. These women became my friends and whenever I needed anything they were there.

My friend Edith was married to a philosophy professor and had three children, actually three separate families. Her children were 18, 10 and a baby just one-month old. She was a psychologist and had a few clients while she was busy with motherhood. She was a devout Christian and her father was the associate pastor of our church. Peggy is married to a Vietnam Veteran who was a medic. He suffered from PTSD. Their son had some issues with the police and did some time in prison. At the time I met Peggy, her son was a handful to say the least. However, today he is a respected member of the community. Patrice was a working mom and raising her daughter Jasmine. She too was a devout Christian and led numerous Bible studies. When I met Jean, she was recently divorced after an 18 year marriage. Since there were no children, and she loved kids so much, she decided to foster. She fostered a few children before deciding to adopt a little girl named Melody. She brought

Melody to church when she was four days old and introduced her as the child who was born in her heart. Donne and her husband tried for many years to have children but never succeeded. Donne was a wonderful homemaker, wife and friend and she hosted the Simple Spirits annual Christmas party at her home.

I was so happy to have a group of women that I could relate to. They were my salvation because they gave me the friendship and the stimulation I needed especially since I was living with people that were so much older than myself. For my 50th birthday, The Simple Spirits and I went out to celebrate my special day with a luncheon. I remember it was snowing and I thought we needed to postpone, but we braved the elements and we had a wonderful time. I think that was the first time I have ever been with a group of women in which I was the center of attention. I also learned that Peggy's birthday was March 4th and so now we celebrate our birthdays together.

While the living facility we settled in may not have been the ideal place for a woman of 48, they certainly tried. Eventually as I got to know people, I was able to form a Scrabble group and we met each Monday at 1 o'clock in the library. My group consisted of a former history professor, a teacher, a nurse, and myself a journalist. It was a tough group, but it kept the mind sharp.

Adjusting was not as difficult as I thought it would be. I

felt accepted. Eventually I was asked to write for their monthly newsletter. I would ask residents for their ideas and their feedback. Each month I would feature one resident and tell his or her life story. So I was kept busy. I also was asked by David to write for the church newsletter. I learned very fast not to tell all at once because it can become overwhelming.

As the months rolled by, we got into a little routine. Since my father was the first one up in the morning, he went down to the dining room to get our continental breakfast. My dad soon developed a group of friends that he chatted with. By the time 8:30 rolled around he was back with our breakfast. So mom and I ate in our room and listened to the gossip of the day. On Friday's it was our day to have the apartment cleaned. Cindy, our housekeeper, would come do the major cleaning. She was very kind and chatty. Usually at night there was some sort of entertainment going on after dinner. Depending upon the activity, my mother and I usually joined in. On the other hand, my father just liked to lay in bed and read.

While I was adjusting rather well, I still missed my friends in New Jersey, and I decided to fly back and visit with them. Since my brother was close by, I knew my parents would be taken care of and therefore I had piece of mind. So, I called my Godmother, Aunt Charlotte, and asked if I could come and stay with her for a week. She was rather hesitant, but then encouraged me to come. When I told David of my plans, he contacted his brother Jim who was a travel agent and asked him to book me on a flight to New Jersey. Since Aunt Charlotte was in her late 70s, I asked my friend Joy and her husband to pick me up from the airport and drive me to Aunt Charlotte's apartment. Once I arrived at Aunt Charlotte's she claimed that she had little food and wanted me to go grocery shopping with her. I guess I did not realize that I was imposing. I bought my own groceries. I knew that she was on a fixed income, so I didn't mind.

Prior to arriving in New Jersey, I made plans to get together with several friends and they agreed to pick me up from Aunt Charlotte's place. I saw my friend Maria and I also went to see Betty and Ed Gill who were both in their wheelchairs and living on their own. It was great to see everyone and the week flew by. I also had time to stop and see Eric and Joan Ziegler who I met while I was working for the Dateline Journal. Eric was the Lutheran minister who never quite left my side. So, it was a successful trip in giving me time to relax.

Several months later, my father decided to start using a walker to help himself to get around. He complained his legs were getting weaker and that he needed something to hold on to. While he had started going to a doctor on a regular basis, he never really shared his diagnosis. We knew he had coronary artery disease and that it was now affecting his heart. For so long we had been concerned about my mother's health, we should have been equally vigilant about my father's condition. Even though my father had several TIA's and was able to get disability at the age of 57, we were never told the whole story.

Because my father was the first one up in the morning, his routine was to sit on the patio and have a cigarette or two. Dad had been smoking since the age of 13 and now all that nicotine and smoke was drastically impacting his health. One morning I heard a thud on the patio. My father had fallen and broken his hip. He was calling for me to call the rescue squad. That fall was the beginning of a domino effect and nothing was the same afterwards.

Within minutes the rescue squad came and they transported him to Akron General Hospital where they performed surgery and gave him a new hip. Considering his other medical problems, the doctors decided to give him a spinal rather than general anesthesia. After three days, he was transferred to the nursing home in our community, where he spent some time recovering. Because of his age and his other health conditions, recovery was a very slow process. Since he was getting rather antsy, I suggested that perhaps he should be transferred to Edwin Shaw Rehabilitation Hospital for a more intense rehab. To our delight, he was soon walking with a walker and making steady progress and we assumed all was well. However, we stopped by to visit him a few days before my brother's birthday and he was complaining about chest pain. No one liked the sound of that.

That night my brother received an emergency phone call stating that my father had to be transferred back Akron General Hospital. He had suffered a heart attack. Since the damage was extensive they were going to do a triple bypass. However it was very risky. My father died two days later in the cardio intensive care unit. I think the doctors realized that significant damage had been done and time was not on his side. Walter R. Jaekle passed at 2:02 p.m. on November 9th 2005. While we were not expecting him to die, we knew that the odds were against him.

Because he was not a church member and it would not have been fair for us to ask Pastor David to do the funeral, we asked his brother the Reverend Charles R. Jaekle to officiate. He gave a lovely service and a meaningful homily. We were thankful that his brother and his sister were both able to be there. I think I had mentally prepared myself for my father's death. However, when it came to be a reality, it was devastating. And, now I had the daily responsibility of my mother on my shoulders.

The day of the funeral, Kay, the manager, came to assist us with dressing, grooming etc. She took over the role of overseeing our care. We really appreciated it, and as soon as things settled down, we looked into hiring a home health aide for an hour a day- just to get us going in the morning. Within 2 days, we had one who came everyday on a regular basis. She was a big help. As the days went by, mom and I fell into a little routine. Even though we missed my father, we were able to function quite well on our own.

After my father's death, my mother had changed somewhat - she was no longer as outgoing as she had been. I don't know whether or not she was depressed or simply worried about how we would be able manage. At that time, she did not have any close friends to confide in and there is only so much you can tell your daughter. Now, as a widow, she was facing life from a different perspective.

Looking back, I realize how lonely and frightened she must have been. However, she did have the comfort of having Rick close by. I know when I got together with my little Scrabble group on Mondays, I felt somewhat guilty. I asked her to join us but she said she didn't want to disrupt the game. Finally, she managed to get a group together for bridge, a game that she loved dearly. I think part of the problem was they were afraid to get too close because of her disabilities. Even though every resident had some sort of health issue, I guess they felt hers was a little more noticeable. Her mind, however, was fairly sharp.

We were managing quite well. I now did the laundry, which was right across the hall from our apartment and very convenient. Between Cindy and I and the staff, we had things pretty well handled. I think my mother adjusted to her new life as a widow rather well.

Several months later, a friend had just dropped me off

from my Tuesday night Bible study. After talking with Lisa a few minutes my mother went into her bedroom. Lisa had left and my mother came out and she tripped and fell hitting her head on the cement floor. I ran and got my neighbor Louise who came and tried to rouse her. We called 911 and they came and took her to the ER. My brother met them at the hospital. Finally the doctor told him that her head injuries were extensive and that nothing could be done. They transferred her to hospice in Fairlawn, where they made her comfortable until she passed. Peggy and Wally, who is our assistant pastor, stopped by to say goodbye to mom. The hospice nurses were wonderful, very compassionate and understanding. They told me that I had to give my mother my blessing so that she would die in peace. Saying goodbye to my mother was the hardest thing I ever had to do. My father and mother died within 11 months of each other. She passed on October 23rd at 9:02 p.m. My brother was with her.

    I stayed with my brother that night. I woke up several times because I still could not believe that my mother had passed away. I returned to the apartment the next morning. By now everyone knew about my mother's death and stopped by to give their condolences. Later that day, Pastor David came to help plan her funeral. I had chosen the hymn For All Thy Saints. This hymn was one of my favorites and I believe it was also one of my mom's favorites as well. I asked David to choose the scripture and together we wrote the homily based on what I told him about mom's life. Meanwhile, my brother was contacting family and friends, and making other funeral arrangements. There is so much to do when a loved one passes that it's incredible. Between choosing caskets, funeral homes, preachers, obtaining death certificates, bank statements, which is a very time consuming process that was placed on my brother's shoulders.

When I arrived at the funeral home, I was pleasantly surprised to see a beautiful bouquet of flowers from Max and Meredith, our previous pastor and his wife, who were from our church in Roselle. I was also grateful to see my former Professor Paul Evans and his wife Mary Ellen there to support me. So many people from my church came as well as some of my brother's friends.

Now that both of my parents had passed away, it was time for me to move into a one-bedroom apartment. Fortunately, Kay had found one a few doors down from where I was living. Peggy helped us to dispose of my mother's clothing and other belongings. My brother sorted through some other miscellaneous items and took home those that were of sentimental value to us. Going through pictures and other trinkets brought back plenty of memories. We were surprised that mom had saved so much of our childhoods; even old report cards were kept.

FITTING IN

My new apartment was beautiful. It already had a newer sofa with curtains to match. Apparently, the lady who lived there previously had great taste. After my furniture was all moved in, I could not have been happier. To me it was a dream come true, for I had always wanted my very own apartment. In the back of my mind, I always knew that, someday I would be living alone. Now that I had the opportunity to live in a controlled environment, I could live on my own with the right help. I had my own schedule. I even entertained my Bible study group as well as the Stephen Ministers whom I later joined.

Shortly after my mother's death I was asked to become a Stephen Minister and to serve the congregation in that capacity. I'd studied nine months to finally become ordained. Since becoming a Stephen Minister, I have counseled three people and hopefully helped them to understand and to support them in times of need. Many people simply need someone to listen and pray with during hard times.

Although I lived alone, I was not alone. I adjusted to living alone rather quickly. Being a part of a senior community, I had the option of being alone when I wanted to be or joining in whatever activity was going on at that particular time. I guess in a sense I had the best of both worlds. Every day, I would call Rick and Kathy just to check in. I would also call Peggy and chat with her for a few moments. Sometimes she would come and stay the night with me. I enjoyed this and it gave her a break from her husband and his alcoholism. Peggy was truly my right hand woman.

Living on my own had its advantages and disadvantages. Once a week, I took the center's bus over to the Acme to pick up a few essentials, such as my chocolate. I am a chocoholic at heart and I love a few pieces every day. I also picked up some personal items as well as anything that attracted my fancy. Once I was back, someone carried my packages to my apartment for me and I would put them away. At Christmas time, we all took the bus to see the holiday decorations at night. We also went to E.J. Thomas Hall for some delightful concerts. We went to plays in the park, etcetera. There was always something to do. However, as time went on, I had to pull back from these excursions because my walking was just getting so poor. For example, I needed to hold on to the wall or pieces of furniture when I walked around the apartment. That had never happened before. At first, I thought it might have been a delayed reaction to my mother's death. With CP sometimes an emotional trauma can cause a physical trauma too. Perhaps my body was just tired from all the stress of moving, my parents' deaths, and adjusting to a new life alone.

I was not the only one who noticed these subtle changes in my balance. My family noticed them, the managers at the senior living facility, and even some of my church family noticed that there was something different about me, though they could not quite pinpoint what it was. It was pointless for me to go to a doctor because they had not known me in the past and therefore had nothing to which to compare my changing condition.

I was beginning to get scared, so I talked to my brother and we decided to get a lifeline emergency alert button for me to wear around the apartment. Several times this came in handy. I

fell once in the bathroom; I fell a few times in my bedroom; and I even fell in the living room. I am not sure, I think I just tripped and could not get my balance, so I pressed the button and help arrived in the form of one of the managers coming to see what the problem was. Oftentimes, I just needed a helping hand to get up. This went on for several weeks. After communicating their concerns to my brother, it was decided that I would move to assisted living, at least until they could figure out what was going on with my body. I hated giving up my lovely little apartment, but I had no choice. I needed more help than independent living could provide.

Assisted living provided each resident with a large room and a private bathroom. We were able to bring some of my furniture, books, etcetera, but the rest of my belongings had to go into storage. In their dining room, I ate with three men, all widowers. That in and of itself was interesting. The men were very cordial and they tried to be helpful. When my meal was served, my meat was cut for me, the roll buttered, and any other kind of help I needed was readily available. Walking down to the dining room was a chore. I was hanging on to walls even though I had an aide walking with me. It was getting to the point where I needed a wheelchair. Unless one was able to maneuver the wheelchair independently, one was forced to move to the nursing level of care. Assisted living had five levels of care, and within a matter of weeks I was unable to fit into any of those levels.

At this point, my family was getting even more concerned. One morning, my brother took me to the ER to see what they could do for me. Not having any real knowledge of CP, they were as baffled as my brother. Finally, my brother talked the ER doctor into admitting me for a few days until they could come up with some kind of game plan. The doctor agreed and I was admitted to Akron City Hospital where I had some intense physical therapy and I started to walk again. However, this did not last long. Finally, I was admitted to Edwin Shaw for what the doctor called a "tune up."

Meanwhile, my very concerned friend, Peggy, was checking out some things on her own. With the help of the internet, Peggy was able to find a physical therapist who specialized in pediatric CP. Not only that, she lived within our own backyard. Peggy could not believe that this woman, Marcia Stamer, lived five blocks from her and this was the first time she had ever heard of her. Now, I believe this was God's divine intervention. Peggy contacted Marcia through the internet and explained my symptoms and what people were noticing. Right away Marcia knew what was happening and she told Peggy that it was imperative that I get some help. According to Marcia, the spinal cord was being compressed due to athetoid movements from the type of cerebral palsy that I have. Athetoid movements are ones that are involuntary, and my movements are mostly neck extension which overtime has caused spinal cord compression.

Marcia recommended that I have an MRI, and so my brother's friend who is a doctor ordered the MRI. By this time, I had been transferred to the nursing section of the assisted living community. We were awaiting a diagnosis. On the day of my MRI, I was given 10 mg of Valium and transported by ambulance to the MRI center. Rick met me there and I was so groggy that I do not even remember seeing him. They did the MRI and as soon as the pictures were developed, he took them to his friend who was able to pinpoint the exact cause of my problem. He referred us to neurosurgeon who scheduled me for surgery to decompress the C4 & C5 vertebrae on the spinal cord. Surgery was scheduled for September 8th.

Over the three months I waited for this surgery, I became more anxious and nervous. When contemplating surgery, one always imagines the worst, and I had too much time on my hands to think; I tried to make the best of it.

I was still writing to my favorite professor, Paul Evans and his wife Mary Ellen who decided to pay me a personal visit from New Jersey. Since Mary Ellen is from Ohio, they came to visit her sister, and, on the way, they stopped off and visited me. It was quite a shock for them to see me sitting in a wheelchair after I had been so active. Since there was a Wendy's close by we decided to take a short walk and go over and have a treat. Not a very nourishing one, but it satisfied the palate. We talked about family and friends and a lot of things. Towards the end, Paul asked me about my upcoming surgery, and I said, "well I am nervous about it, but if it is going to alleviate the problem, then I am all for it. Who knows, maybe I will be able to walk again? However, even if I am not able to walk, at least I had that ability for 53 years." Neither one of them said anything more about it. I guess there was nothing to say and they did not want to pursue it and risk upsetting me.

On the morning of my surgery, Pastor David and Wally met us in the lobby and before I went into pre-op. We all had a word of prayer together. I was very touched to have both Pastors by my side. I think Rick and Kathy were both grateful that the church showed so much concern for me.

After the surgery, while I was in recovery, the doctor asked my brother to come in and see what he thought about the way I was acting. Apparently, my head was in a funny position and they thought maybe I had a stroke, but upon closer observation, the positioning was due to the cervical collar around my neck. I was not in a lot of pain, and if I had pain, a couple of Extra-Strength Tylenol took care of it.

A few hours later, I was transferred to the step-down unit. As far as I understood, there were no rooms available because someone had overbooked. The step-down unit was great. It was one nurse to two patients, so I had private care. Because of my neck being in this collar, I was afraid to move, so I had to be handfed. The nurses were very kind to me and they kept a close watch. However, perhaps they were too kind because they neglected to get me up the next day and the day after that when I was supposed to return to the nursing home, and I had developed a slight case of pneumonia. For several days afterwards, I received breathing treatments three times a day from a respiratory therapist. As soon as that cleared up, I was transferred to a regular room where I spent one night before returning to the nursing home.

If I had not had this surgery when I did, I would have lost a lot more of my function. However, if I were able to have surgery on C4 & C5 sooner, I would not have lost as much function. After the surgery, I had physical therapy at the nursing home as well as Marcia coming in at night. She helped the nursing team to understand my limitations and gave them some insight as to how to best help me. I was hoping that I would regain some of my function that I had previously lost. However, Marcia explained that physical therapy would enable me to keep what function I still had and enable me to do as much as I can but from a wheelchair. For instance, the nursing home had a sit to stand machine, which would help me to be upright and bear weight through my legs, which was helpful. The sit to stand would also be helpful in transferring me from the chair to the bed to the commode. Then when it came time for a shower, I would sit in a shower chair, which is basically a wheelchair that can get wet.

Physical therapy sessions lasted only about six weeks. After that time, a patient was sent to restorative therapy where they would help me maintain the progress I had made in physical therapy. Kathy and Jill were my restorative therapy aids. Every day one of them would help me walk up and down the hall. This was in lieu of physical therapy. In the mornings we would meet as a group, myself and several other residents, and toss a big ball around amongst ourselves to give us range of motion exercise. I found this very helpful because I was maintaining my progress and still getting together with the other residents. After the group was over, Kathy and Jill worked with the residents and had one-on-one therapy time.

Meanwhile, I was getting adjusted to living in a nursing home. During my three-year stent I had four different roommates.

My first roommate was Lillian. She was a very quiet woman in her 80s, and if I had not been able to see, I would not have known she was in the room. She sat in her chair and that was about it. When her family came to see her, I found out that she had a twin brother who would pop in once in a while. Other than that, she was a loner.

My next roommate was Matilda. Everyone called her Tillie. She was well over 400 pounds and every time they needed to get her out of bed, the staff would use the Hoyer lift and about four staff members to assist her. Needless to say, it was a major undertaking. Tillie loved to eat and even though she was supposed to be on a 1200 calorie diet, her family would sneak her food. She ate bags of potato chips. She also loved peanut butter cups and cookies. Don't get me wrong, I love my sweets too. However, she was not very disciplined and instead of eating one or two, she would eat the whole bag. Tillie loved to color and she had beautiful adult coloring books. One of her favorite coloring books was of stained glass windows and she colored one for me as a gift on my birthday. She had been a widow for over 30 years and was the mother of five children, two of which lived in the area. I remember the Saturday that she went to her grandson's wedding. That was a big day for her for a number of reasons. Number one, it was her grandson. Number two; she had not been outside of the nursing home in two years. And, number three; it really gave her something to look forward to. It took three aides to get her ready for the big day and she was so looking forward to it. One of the male aids who was rather handsome promised to be her escort and he came through. So, they went off and had a wonderful time.

 Joan was my third roommate and she was only there for a temporary stay due to a broken ankle. As a former nurse, she made for a very needy patient. The staff wanted her to sit with her leg up and keep off of it. However, she always found a reason why she had to get up and many times a staff member would walk by and find her standing up. As often as they tried to get her to stay off of her ankle, she was determined to be independent. Many times, she would make me nervous because she was so unsteady on her ankle that it was a miracle she didn't break them both. Her son who was in his 40s and divorced was about to remarry. However, he was a very devoted son, and he would come every day and read the paper.

My last roommate was Virginia. Virginia was very ill and she was on hospice. Her children were very devoted to her and some of them even came to spend the night. Her family was very appreciative that I was her roommate and that I would get her help if she needed it because she could not remember how to work the call button. Her daughters would come by every day and visit with her. As time went on, I got to know each member of the family and I felt like the "adopted" daughter. For my birthday, they gave me a beautiful skirt and blouse from Macy's. I was very touched as well as surprised. I asked how they knew my size. One daughter commented that she pretended to put something away in my closet and when she did she peeked at the size on my clothes. They said it was the least they could do because they knew their mother was in good hands under my watchful eye.

Adjusting to the nursing home was a major undertaking. By this time, I had downsized so much that most of my "stuff" was put in storage and I had very little. I guess the biggest problem was getting used to the constant noise. Most of the residents had hearing problems, so they would talk very loudly. Some were incontinent, so as hard as and as much as they tried to keep the nursing home clean there was always a lingering odor of urine. Thankfully, I had none of those issues. My biggest problem was that if I needed to use a commode and my roommate or I had company, I would hold it. I was not comfortable relieving myself with just a curtain around the bed. Of course, holding your urine is not a wise thing to do because it can lead to a bladder infection or a urinary tract infection. Fortunately, I never had either of those. However, I was not about to take the chance of someone seeing me on the commode.

Some of the aides were very kind and I really felt a kinship with them. Perhaps the aide I most admired was Rachel. She was a role model for everyone with a disability. Not only was she married and the mother of four children, she only had one hand. Apparently, when she was younger, she was holding a firecracker and when it exploded, it took her hand. Rachel had months and months of physical therapy and she learned how to do most things one-handed. She was great with the patients and they all loved her, including me. Her friend Crista was another aide who was very hardworking and tried her best to please. There were other aides such as Mercy and Diana who worked under the supervision of Ken on the night shift. When I first came to the nursing home, I had a lot of difficulties with sleeping and I would constantly call them at night, needing nothing more than reassurance.

For some reason, nighttime was my worst time. There were times when an aide would bring me to the T.V. room so that I could watch television for a while until I finally fell asleep.

Finally, after talking with my brother, he and I decided to get me a prescription for a mild sedative. That really did the trick. With a good night's sleep, I was like a different person.

Another issue I had difficulty adjusting to was the fact that Medicare only allowed for two showers per week. I always felt unclean. Even though I was sponge bathed every day, I still felt unclean. I remember once I was going on a Saturday church retreat and I desperately felt I needed a shower. Fortunately, I had made friends with Ken, the nighttime nurse supervisor and he approved it.

When I first entered the nursing home, they told me that I would be there about three weeks. Well, that three weeks turned out to be three years. I think, they tell everyone who is cognizant that it is only a temporary measure. Days turned into weeks, weeks turned into months, and months turned into years.

Thanks to Peggy and Wally, I was able to get to church almost every Sunday. I also had a Stephen Minister by the name of Mary Butcher, who personally came to see me every week; she started me on my Precious Moments collection. In addition to Mary, I had a secret cookie baker who would sneak homemade chocolate chip cookies. Unfortunately, most of the time when she came, I was napping. I would wake up and find a bag of homemade chocolate chip cookies on my stomach and wonder what was going on. I eventually found out who my secret baker was and I will be forever grateful for Betty Weber. She is now in her 90s and still sits behind me in church.

Living in the nursing home has its ups and downs. I think the holidays were probably the worst times. Even though everyone put their best foot forward to try to make these times special, it just wasn't home. We had some special entertainment including church choirs, but it just was not the same. Every family, every person, has their own special traditions and being a part of a large group takes away some of the autonomy. One is just not able to freely celebrate with their individual traditions. As far as Christmas shopping was concerned, I was thankful that I still maintained my gift catalogs and that I was able to buy presents with my credit card. That was a big help. I did not like to be on the receiving end without being able to give.

As time went on, I began to really wonder whether or not I belonged in the nursing home. It seemed that most long-term residents were there to stay because they could not cognitively function and the nursing home provided security. As a matter of fact, some of the nurses who got to know me would ask me why I was there. I never knew how to answer that question. If I asked my family, they would say because they didn't have any other place to put me. Obviously, I could not live by myself because I needed 24/7 care. I was not a special needs person because I had obtained a master's degree and worked for 24 years in private industry. So, where did I fit in? That was the million-dollar question, and no one seemed to have a definitive answer.

While Ohio seems to have an abundance of group homes for the cognitively impaired, we have yet to find anything for the physically impaired but cognitively intact. We have explored Summit County Department of Developmentally Disabled and they do not seem to have anything for those with just physical disabilities. This has been a goal of mine, to find someplace where the physically disabled can live and pursue their own interests and not be grouped with the mentally disabled; the needs of each group are simply too different.

Peggy and I checked places out. After all, "where there's a will, there's a way." So, we checked out a few assisted living places, but I need more care than they could provide. Then we heard about group homes. However, group homes were typically for those with cognitive impairment or hearing impairments. We thought we would check one out anyway. They seemed to have it all together, or so we thought.

17

I continued to ask myself, "Where do I fit in?" One might say I outgrew the nursing home in terms of needing nursing care. However, I would always need some type of physical assistance especially since I am confined to a wheelchair. So Peggy and I explored other options.

We were driving around one day and we came upon a sign for a facility that we thought looked promising. Peggy called and discovered it was a group home for MRDD (mentally retarded developmentally disabled) clients. While I didn't fit that description, I was developmentally disabled in terms of having a physical disability, and I could not live on my own. So, we set up an appointment with the director and several of their staff. We sat around a large table and they explained to us what their policies were and how they worked. We learned what they could provide and how I would be taken care of. While I had some doubts, after I thought about it, I decided to give it a try. After all, I was tired of the nursing home scene.

We discussed this with my brother who was very surprised that I would even consider a group home since I did not fit their typical client description. Despite these misgivings, I decided to take a tour of one and see how it played out. So, one evening, my brother, Kathy, and I visited a group home. We walked in and found a beautifully decorated living room with an open kitchen with easy access. The bathrooms were large and spacious to accommodate a wheelchair and the showers were also wheelchair accessible. There were four rather small bedrooms, however, they could easily accommodate a bed, dresser, night table and TV stand, and perhaps even a bookshelf or two.

While touring through the home, I met a young woman with Down's Syndrome who was sitting at the kitchen table coloring. Her name was Theresa. She was the artist of the group. Theresa's talent was in drawing and coloring. Shortly after I moved in, she drew me a picture of our house and she put everyone in their own window. She even drew grass, the flowers, and the sun around the house. She said this was our house now and she really made me feel at home. That small gesture of friendship stayed with me throughout my 15 months in the group home.

On the downside, Theresa would have deliberate bathroom accidents, especially on Saturdays when she felt she was not getting enough attention. This would incense the staff and cause more verbal abuse for the rest of us. Then I met Judy, who was in her early 60s, and seemed very glad to meet me. She told me that I would have the room across from her and asked me if I liked Dr. Seuss. Next, there was Leigh Anne who had athetoid CP and some cognitive impairments. She came from a family of 13 children and she was the youngest so every weekend, one of the older sisters would pick her up and take her home for a few days. Leigh Anne really was in seventh heaven as the weekend rolled around. All three women attended Day Centers. Their level of function determined which Day Center they would attend.

The group home organization was founded by a woman who had a severely disabled son. She was very concerned about his future and what would happen to him once she passed away. She realized that they were not the only family in this predicament, and so, she started these homes in hopes of giving people with developmental disabilities a place to live and grow and to give their families peace of mind that their loved ones would be well taken care of. This was her brainchild and she turned it into a reality.

After meeting some of the staff and touring the home where I would be living, I decided to give it a try. Because I was mainstreamed from day one, I never had much contact with those who had developmental disabilities. So, this was a new ballgame for me. I was not too educated about what kinds of attention and care was required of the developmentally disabled, but I was willing to learn. So, I moved in.

Prior to moving in, the house manager, Dana, told me that I could have my room painted any color I wanted. So, with Peggy's help, I chose a very lovely peach color. By the time I moved in, it was painted and I loved it. It was a small room, but my furniture fit very nicely. Across the hall from me was Judy.

It took a while to adjust to the new routine. We all ate in the kitchen that had one big table. The meals were delicious and most of what they served, I really liked. There were a few dishes here and there that I did not really care for, but I think that was to be expected and I was satisfied with a sandwich.

As I got to know the staff, I was very impressed with some of their qualities. I remember Michelle. She was single and dating a man with two teenage kids. She had a lot of issues to resolve about mothering teenage children, but she recognized them and was willing to work at it. Michelle was very good to me and she and I had no problems whatsoever. Then there was Irene, who was a wonderful and devoted aid. She had raised four boys and now was a grandmother of 14 kids and counting. One of Irene's favorite past times was shopping in thrift stores and she would find me bargains. Quite often she would come in with a skirt or a blouse that she had found for $2, and they would fit so I would keep them. My family wondered how my wardrobe kept growing. I explained that Irene was a good shopper.

Then there was Francine who was the home supervisor and did all of the grocery shopping. She had rheumatoid arthritis and was a phlebotomist by day and a home health aide by night. In addition, she was raising two teens. Often, by the time she got to her second job, which was taking care of us, she was tired and cranky. I know she was in chronic pain and if she really did not need the money, she would not have been there. She was short-tempered with everyone, including me.

Then there was Nicola, a 21-year-old woman who also did not have much patience. I do not think being an aide was the right fit for her. If she did not get her way, she was always screaming at one of us. I remember one night, my brother brought me home and there was some sort of disagreement between two aides and no one realized we had come in. Upon witnessing our presence, they were embarrassed and ashamed. After my family had left, Nicola came up to me and yelled in my ear how dare I come back and not give them prior notice. I told her that I lived there and I did not realized why prior notice was required. She again proceeded to yell in my ear and this time she woke up my neighbor Judy. Not long after this incident, she was let go. She just did not have the patience for the job.

There was an aide named Theresa who was on the night staff. She was very kind. Once when I was sick with a terrible cold, Theresa made me a non-alcoholic hot toddy and that really opened up my chest and made me feel better. I later learned that Theresa was a collector of dolls. One night, she brought about 30 dolls of various sizes and shapes in to show the girls. They were ecstatic and this act of kindness brought all of us closer together.

As I became more acquainted with my roommates, I learned more and more about them. For example, Judy suffered from seizures, and every once in a while, she would have one. The staff would be either watching TV or doing something in the kitchen and did not realize that Judy needed help. As time went on, I began to recognize when the seizure was coming on and yelled for the aide. It turned out they did not like my interference and told me to mind my own business. I stated that they were not watching Judy as closely as they should. They were still incensed and they did not like me getting involved.

Every Saturday Judy's two sisters would come and take her to McDonalds. As time went by, I got to know them and told them about her seizures. Her sisters were very thankful that I told them because apparently the staff had not said anything to them and she needed to be checked out. They were more and more grateful that I was there to keep an eye on Judy. Not having a male figure in her life, Judy liked my brother. Every time he came over, she would hand him a Dr. Seuss book and ask him to read to her, and if he wasn't in a rush, he was happy to comply. Judy was everyone's favorite. She loved Dr. Seuss, Mickey Mouse, and Lucille Ball. For Halloween, she dressed up as Lucy.

Part of the group's services was that all the clients got to go wherever they wanted one Saturday a month. I remember I chose Wal-Mart and I was able to get everything I needed including a sandwich at Subway. Another time, I went to the Dollar Store, and I was able to stock up on some things. One time, the staff decided to take everyone out to the Golden Corral. Since it was a surprise, they didn't tell us until the last minute. Unfortunately, it didn't work out very well. Two clients had diarrhea on the way back and they just could not handle all the excitement. Probably part of the problem was that it came as a surprise and some people do not handle surprises very well. Unfortunately, we never went out as a group again.

Living in a group home, one is required to either go to a day center or some type of sheltered workshop or some other activity where they can be supervised and engage in something productive throughout the day. They had their own day center and I started to attend it. I met quite a number of people. These people were faced with all kinds of challenges. Some of them, in addition to their developmental limitations, had some type of physical challenge. Some clients were in their 70s and 80s and others were in their 20s. That was a large variety of people who needed to have their needs met. The clients were a mixed bag in terms of personality needs and physical needs. However, I was impressed by the amount of caring and dedication that they received from the aides and the supervisor.

Never having been with a group of cognitively impaired individuals I really did not know what to expect. However, I was very taken with their warmth, curiosity, and interest. I met Lenore, who was in her 50s, and also had CP. She lived in a group home and always had something on her mind. Her constant companion, Patty, was a woman in her 60s, with little to say, and she relied mostly on Lenore to do her talking for her. In addition, there was this little old man, Howie, in his 80s, who loved to watch me sleep. On Friday afternoons, John would put me in a recliner and we all watched a movie together. However, for some reason, I always managed to fall asleep and Howie would report that back to John and when I would wake up he would let John know about that too. Then there was Sam, who was in his 60s and always looking forward to a trip. Sam was not happy unless he was on the go. These were some of the folk who made the day center fun.

The supervisor was a middle-aged man by the name of John who seemed to have everyone's needs down pat. He knew who could take a little teasing and who liked which activities and who among the women liked to flirt with him. There were two older women, Helen and Charlotte, who especially liked John and would try to corner him the kitchen. While it was funny to watch, it was a handful for John. He graciously handled it. It didn't take long for John to figure out that I needed more intellectual stimulation than most of the other clients. He soon discovered that we had something in common, our love for Scrabble. Come the end of the day, when things would start winding down, John and I would get out the Scrabble board and have a go at it. Sometimes, it took us several days to finish one game but this was our little thing that we did together. Perhaps some of the women thought there was a romance going on, but we were just friends having a good time.

The more we talked over the Scrabble board, the more we realized how much John and I had in common. For instance, we were both Protestants, we both had Master's Degrees in the same field of counseling, and we both loved Scrabble.

Later, I learned that John's sister, Becky, also had some mental challenges, but that she was very successful working in a structured environment. Becky lived with their mother who was now in her 70s. Even though they had tried a group home for Becky, it didn't work out. Because Becky was high functioning, she did not require an aide all the time and could be left alone for hours. However, one day her mother went to visit her and discovered that no one had been there for the past eight hours, so she pulled Becky from the group home and she has been living with her mother ever since. I think John realizes that Becky will probably be his responsibility when something happens to his mom.

As time went by and I began to feel more comfortable at the day center, I asked if I could have my physical therapist, Marcia, come weekly for some therapy. John authorized it. Prior to that, Marcia had been coming to my group home but that didn't seem to be working out very well. Some of the aides, especially one, did not seem to like having Marcia's presence and her knowledge in the house. One night, she and an aide got into an argument and Marcia never felt comfortable coming back. Sometime later, that aide was let go, and so, Marcia was very comfortable at the day center and so was I. If John had the time, he and Marcia would walk me around the day center. With John on one side and Marcia on the other, I could walk quite a few feet. The exercise was good at keeping me moving. However, for some reason the aides wanted John to toilet me claiming that I was getting too heavy for the three of them to help. Neither John nor I liked that idea, and, eventually, I left.

I was having some issues with the group home as well and my brother did not always like the tension. Even though we had a beautiful living room, most of us were told to stay in our rooms because the staff wanted to be in the living room. I remember many a Saturday with all four of us in our rooms with all four TVs going and no interaction of any kind. Unless someone had a member of their family visiting them, there was no socialization. Many of the aides were kind of taken aback that I had my friends Peggy, May, Jean, and others visiting me on a regular basis. I remember one night, I had my Pastor David and his wife come to spend some time with me and I was told that I was under no circumstances allowed to have them in any room in the house except my bedroom. I thought that was a little bit much and it was not long after that when I decided to look for a new home.

As I got to know people at the day center and to realize the amount of activity and stimulation that went on in their group home I realized that something was definitely wrong with this one. John came over one evening to give me some counseling books from his personal library and he asked, "Why is everyone in their rooms?"

I replied, "This is the way it is in this house."

He said, "Well, it doesn't have to be."

Shortly after that, I told them that I was not happy there and that I was moving. I did not know where I was moving to, but I was definitely getting out of this environment. Someone associated with the organization recommended that I try a smaller agency that was based out of Akron. This was a small group home run by two retired nurses. Neither I nor my brother liked that fact that it was in Akron quite a ways from Hudson where my brother lived. However, despite the distance, I thought I should look into it.

One day after I got home from the day center, one of my aides took me to see the place and to meet the owners. It was quite a distance but the house was rather large and two stories. I was shown where my room would be and then they told me that their other client would be living upstairs. Somehow, I was not impressed with the setup. They severed me chicken salad and crackers and some pop. According to my staff at my group home, this was to be my supper.

When I got back to my home thinking that there must be some miscommunication somewhere, I asked for something to eat. The staff said no, that I already had my supper. I explained to them that I had just been served chicken salad with crackers and that that did not constitute a meal. They argued with me and I said "I am calling my brother because I cannot take this anymore." Whatever my brother said to them, they finally made me a sandwich and gave me something to drink.

After that experience, I knew I had to get out of there. By this time, my brother was in full agreement. No one should have to beg for food. So, my next move was to call Todd Weaver, my SSA, and explain to him what happened and that I needed to be relocated ASAP.

18

A couple weeks after the horrible dinner incident, I met with Todd Weaver. He had been my SSA for a few years now and we knew each other pretty well. He was filled in as to what had transpired and he agreed that that this group home was not a good fit for me. John was also concerned about what happened and he felt that perhaps if I had been in a different group home I might have really enjoyed it. However, at that point, I was not willing to take the chance.

Within about a month, Todd had put my profile on the system portal so that other group homes could see that I was searching and he had the owner of one interested in meeting me. It was a smaller company that was started several years ago. The organization consisted of five group homes. Most of the clients were men, but over the years a few women were been placed in smaller more homey settings with one aide to one client. So, it was one-on-one care.

After hearing more about the organization from Todd, we decided to go over and investigate. Rick, Kathy, and I, met Richard, who was the assistant director, on a Saturday morning. The house was vacant, so we had free access to every room. I was impressed with the size of the bedroom and that I would have a sitting room as well. The sitting room was an area where I could entertain as well. Unlike in my previous living arrangement, I would have plenty of privacy and not disturb any of the other clients. I really liked the set up. The only concern I had was the size of the bathroom, because I was not sure if I could get my wheelchair through the door. However, I had a shower chair on order so that taking a shower would not be a problem.

Seeing the layout of the house and meeting Richard, I was impressed. For instance, Richard said that if I wanted to go out to dinner, all I would need to do was to tell my aide. If I wanted to go shopping, all I would need to do was again tell my aide. So, he made it seem like a perfect utopia. Of course, I realized that he was trying to sell me on the idea and that anything I wanted he would agree to. Whether or not this would come to fruition would be another story. However, it could not be any worse than what I experienced at the group home. So, I decided to give it a try.

Shortly after relocating, I decided to have a small gathering of family and friends so they could see my new home. Actually this was Dawn O'Brien's, one of my aides at the time, idea. We asked Richard and his partner for their permission. Both of them agreed to the gathering and several guests supplied the food. I think the owner saw this as a way to advertise his business and in a way it was. Many people came from the church, and in no time I had a house full. A few of my aides were there and everyone seemed to get along quite well. Contrary to

how I felt at the group home, I was encouraged to have my friends come and visit in my new home.

According to Richard, I was to have a housemate and they were waiting for her to move in. Bonnie was in her early 20s and lived with her very over protective grandparents. She was diagnosed with autism, cerebral palsy and cognitive delays.

Unfortunately, Bonnie was not able to talk, so she was unable to express any of her wants or needs. She was tall, attractive, and had long, dark hair, which her grandmother refused to have cut. Therefore, anyone who cared for Bonnie would also have to work with her hairstyle. Bonnie was expected to move in by July, but, due to her grandmother's hesitation, she did not come until early September. This meant that I had a few months with the house all to myself.

Even though Bonnie was unable to verbally communicate, she was able to make some of her needs known. She knew a little sign language and at night when she was tired and wanting to go to bed, she would get up, go to her room and bring her pillow to us. That was a sign that she wanted to go to bed.

I soon learned that Bonnie did not walk until she was 12 years old. She had a few surgeries on her legs and feet and that helped her gain balance and confidence. As part of her physical therapy, Bonnie took horseback riding lessons at Pegasus Farm Equestrian Center. It is on a beautiful campus with an indoor arena for the winter months. Through the years, Bonnie has won many ribbons for her ability to ride horses. Horseback riding really puts a smile on her face and she loves it. In addition to horseback riding, Bonnie loves to eat as well as to listen to her music. Her music consists of mostly children's tunes and nursery rhymes. Anytime she got upset, music is the one thing that would always calm her.

Moving out of my former group home was a very awkward situation. I do not think my housemates realized I was moving until they saw the van and men taking my belongings out of the house. My housemates were instructed to stay in their rooms and to not speak with me. We thought this was rather strange but we followed their orders and really did not say goodbye to any of them. To this day, I regret this decision. I was not moving because of them, I was moving because of the abuse I was getting from the staff. Once my stuff was packed up in boxes, we pulled away and tried to never look back. However, four years later, I still think about leaving these three girls and wonder how they are doing.

Back at my new home I was adjusting to my new life. After a few months I decided to leave the day center that I was still attending. This gave me a clean break. Meanwhile, my SSA, Todd Weaver, decided that I try a day center, which was run by another group home agency.

Upon investigating, I found it was bigger and had much more to offer. Instead of a one-room day center, we had several classrooms including an art room, a regular classroom and a lunchroom. In addition, every day was a bit different. Classes were offered that covered a multitude of topics such as sign language, facts about animals, arts and crafts, current events, the sound of music, which was a course on different genres of music, cooking, learning to budget, social skills, and many others that pertained to everyday life such as nutrition, exercise, etcetera. We partnered with Akron University School of Nursing and every Thursday four or five student nurses would come and do a presentation on a particular topic. This was something that everyone enjoyed. Last year, we even had acting lessons taught by a woman who specialized in teaching people with autism about the theater. She brought in her dog, Hamlet, and he was a big hit with the clients. Hamlet was a quiet dog and once he found a spot to lie down, he did not disturb anyone. Several clients participated in the acting class. As a special treat, I asked my former pastor, David Weyrick, to come and give a performance with his puppets. He has been a puppeteer for the past 30 years and now since his retirement, he has been doing this for several school systems and churches.

In addition to classes, the director and her staff made arrangements for us to purchase chickens. The chicks came when they were less than 24 hours old and had to remain in the incubator for several weeks. As they grew, we built a chicken coop and when the chicks became old enough they began to lay eggs. We sold them for $3.00 a dozen and the profits from this venture went to their upkeep and care.

In compliance with the new laws regarding the developmentally disabled, we are trying to place as many clients in sheltered employment as possible. If they are not capable of employment or if they are of retirement age, they are being placed in volunteer positions. I guess the goal is to have everyone regardless of their ability to be as productive and independent as possible.

Of course, my aides were very sweet and patient because they knew that I had come from somewhat of an abusive atmosphere. The first aide I met was young Jenny who was only 20 and this was one of her first jobs. She had never been an aide before and really did not know what to expect. I had never worked with a 20-year-old before, so I did not know what to expect from her either. While it took us a few weeks to get to know each other, we made a great team. Since she drove and did not mind taking me places, Saturdays were our day to explore the area around us. We also ate out quite a bit and Jenny loved that as well. Jenny and her boyfriend were living together in an on-campus housing site. She brought me to see their apartment and to meet her boyfriend and then together, all three of us toured the campus. It was a wonderful day and I really loved being on a college campus again.

In addition to Jenny the aide, I also had Dawn who was my aide in the mornings and got me up and ready to go to the day center. She was a lovely woman in her 40s with three growing children and a husband at home. While she was waiting for her youngest to grow up a bit more, she decided to take this job. Dawn was a refreshing breath of fresh air. She was very attractive and she was a social worker. In fact, she worked for several years at Akron Children's Hospital. She would often tell me stories about some of her cases. Some of them were happy and some of them were tearjerkers. However, right now, she was working as a part-time gym teacher and part-time aide to pay for her children's tuition at St. Vincent-St. Mary's. I was very fond of Dawn and we still get together at least once a year for dinner.

Jenny the aide was with me a little over a year until she discovered she was pregnant and could not do the lifting any longer. After Jenny left I had Millie. She was a lovely Christian woman in her late 30s. She loved accompanying me to church every Sunday and Peggy did not mind having one extra person with us. Sometimes, all three of us went out to lunch together. Millie would have loved to have been able to go places with me but, unfortunately, I was not able to get in her car. However, we did find other things to do. We love playing Scrabble and doing some extra things around the house. However, Millie did miss her own church, The Chapel, and she was eager to get back. She wanted to participate in one of their mission trips and in order to do that she had to attend regularly. Eventually, Millie left and Tabitha came along.

Tabitha was a single mother and working as a secretary. Raising a teenage daughter, she needed some extra cash, so she decided that she would try working with me on the weekends.

Tabitha was very round and lifting me was a chore, but she did manage. Once she discovered that she could get me in her car, we were off. Being a Christian and raised in the Methodist church, Tabitha was all for attending service with me every Sunday. Eventually, Tabitha made a set of friends at my church and we went out to lunch with them frequently. On occasion, Tabitha would bring her daughter with her for the day and we would drive her home at night. Not having her mother around on the weekends caused some friction between them. Even though I think Tiffany realized her mother had to work, she rebelled a few times. Tabitha tried to compromise by having her daughter come here with her. Depending on the day and her daughter's mood, sometimes that arrangement worked and other times it did not. Tabitha and I still became very good friends.

Julie was a long-time friend of another aide and she decided to apply for an aide position when Bonnie entered the picture. Married and the mother of three growing children, she needed to work to help support the family. Julie took care of Bonnie and her friend, Maureen, was an aide of mine.

Thanks to Julie, I met Polly. Polly was a single gal in her late 30s and always seemed to have some aches and pains. After many trips to the doctors, Polly was diagnosed with multiple health issues. Some days were better than other days. The summer was her best time of the year. Polly was a wonderful aide. Despite all of her aches and pains, she was still able to get me up into her SUV and we would go places especially on Saturdays. We went to craft fairs, restaurants, movies and Hudson's Concerts in the Park in the summer. Sometimes, her boyfriend, Jack, would accompany us. He was a very kind man and very pleasant to have around the house. Some Saturday nights, he would bring us pizza and we would sit around the kitchen table and talk. In addition to working many hours, Polly was also helping to raise a very active 4-year-old, Matt, who took up a lot of her energy.

Karen was mostly a nighttime aide. When I first arrived, she was in charge of the household, which included shopping, cleaning, upkeep, etcetera. I remember an aide called off one night and Karen had to come in under much duress because it was her birthday and she had a house full of company. For some reason, she decided to take out her frustration on me. She said that I had to stay in my room, eat in my room and that I would not get a shower that night. She was just going to put me to bed and that was it. Well, I did not like her attitude, and I thought she was handling me rather harshly for no apparent reason, so I called my brother. He called the owner and they both came over. The owner took Karen outside and I spoke to Rick in my room. Both men tried to figure out what was going on. It turned out that Karen was just angry that she had to interrupt her birthday celebration to come to work to take care of me. Even though she was spoken to and reprimanded, she still did not want to take care of me. After they left, she put me to bed and said, "I better not hear from you tonight." The next morning, Dawn, my aide, asked why I had not been properly bathed. I told her what happened, and she reported Karen for neglect. Needless to say, Karen no longer worked in this house.

Maureen was a one-of-a-kind aide. She was friends with Julie. In the beginning, we got along fine but then as time went on, she always demanded her own way. For instance, I would try to tell her that she was transferring me incorrectly and that her way could cause injury either to her or to both of us. She insisted on doing it her way or no way. I even had Marcia, my physical therapist, try to teach her a few tricks to help both of us. Marcia tried to teach her different and safer ways of doing things, but she insisted on her own way. Finally, she and her friend Julie, who was taking care of Bonnie, decided to trade patients. I was so glad because what Maureen did not realize was she was hurting my back. Maureen was a very fast worker and liked to do things as quickly as possible. She was not fond of giving me a shower, so I would get the fastest shower possible. I complained that I did not feel clean and she said, "That's too bad." Maureen was close to Richard and they decided that I would only get a shower every other day. This was mid-August, the hottest month of the year. I said something to my brother and he spoke to Richard about it. Within that week, she was back to giving me a shower on a daily basis. Of course, she was annoyed with me, but I didn't care.

Several months later Maureen became in charge of the house because Karen left. With Maureen being in charge of the grocery shopping each week, she would get a certain amount to spend. According to Maureen, I was allowed to pick two items of food that I wanted. So, I chose chocolate ice cream and apples. She reminded me that Bonnie got her say too. How could Bonnie voice her wants when Bonnie couldn't even speak? So, Maureen came back from the store with the groceries and I asked her about the ice cream. She said that Acme did not have chocolate ice cream. This seemed rather odd to me since Acme had about 10 brands of ice cream and I brought that to her attention. She walked out of the room in a huff.

Time passed and Maureen's disposition and attitude toward me was worsening. I did not know what to do about it. My other aides, like Polly, began to question Maureen's intentions and at times, Polly and Maureen would argue in front of both Bonnie and me. Everyone realizes that no one is going to get along with each other all of the time. However, if aides have an altercation with each other, it should be taken out of earshot of the clients.

One day, I had just finished getting prepared to go to the day center and tension was rising. Maureen and Polly were going at it full force. I finally said to Polly, let's go sit outside and wait for the bus. While sitting on my ramp, Polly called the owner and explained what was going on. He said he would be right over. He came and asked me if I was alright and I was just a bit shaken up. As soon as I boarded the bus, the owner, Polly and Maureen talked and tried to settle their dispute.

Since I was not there, I don't know what transpired. However, Maureen was terminated from this house and the owner tried to place her in another home but that did not workout. The situation was thoroughly investigated and eventually Maureen was terminated fully. I remember my social worker making an unexpected visit and noting that there was not enough food in the house. Polly and I took over the groceries for a few weeks until new staff was brought in.

A few months after I came to the new house, I met Tanya and she was a wonderful aide too. On Saturdays we would go all over the place. She would often try to incorporate her errands into our little schedule. I remember one Saturday in particular; she and her husband took me to the Akron Zoo. We had a ball. I enjoyed Tanya's company and she enjoyed mine. One thing I really liked about Tanya is that she would sit me on the regular toilet and I really appreciated it. Most aides were fearful of sitting me on the toilet because they didn't have the experience working in tight spaces.

Linda was an aide with plenty of experience with cerebral

palsy. She had once worked for the Hattie Larlham Agency. In addition to doing the basics, she was very much into arts and crafts. I enjoyed watching her making her various creations and she enjoyed making various pieces for me.

Within a few weeks we had several new staff members including KeKe, who was a refreshing change. We now had food and a home without tension. KeKe took over the shopping, and that led to us having some great meals. Meanwhile, the situation with Bonnie and Maureen as her primary caregiver was investigated and Bonnie's grandmother decided to remove her from the house and eventually place her elsewhere. I chose to remain here and since I am able to speak up for myself I have been very happy. I do miss Bonnie, and I hope that she is doing well.

Fortunately, I have had plenty of wonderful aides. However every once in a while I have one who for various reasons does not work out. Let me give you a few examples.

One day I had an aide, Al who was almost 400 pounds. She was not aware the amount of lifting involved in the job, and because of her size she became short of breath. Just wheeling me from the bedroom to the kitchen was a monumental task. I remember she brought me into the bathroom and she had to walk in sideways so that both of us could fit.

Another aide by the name of Fran who was an older

woman was someone Richard had known from the Hattie Larlham Agency. He felt that she would be a wonderful caregiver for me. However she was in her 60s and did not have the upper body strength to transfer me from the bed to the commode. So she could not get my underpants down before she put me on the commode and therefore cut them off. Of course, she was sincerely trying, and I was embarrassed. I think at that point we both knew that this was not going to work out. I had another aide who did not realize she was pregnant and soon as she was aware of it she left.

Aides come in all shapes and sizes and with all kinds of backgrounds and baggage but with the best of intentions. Not every aide is for everyone. To have a successful match, one needs to have a variety of skills ranging from cooking to cleaning to lifting to driving to sharing common interests. Aides are a unique breed and serve a variety of clients. As our population continues to grow older, more and more aides are needed by families to help take care of their loved ones.

Even though I left my former group home, I still received a call from John around the holidays that he wanted to come over and talk to me. Apparently, he missed me and our Scrabble games, and so even though I was no longer a client, I still was his friend.

Since Maureen had a background as an activities director,

our home hosted the annual Christmas party including a visit from Santa Clause who was played by Richard. It was an event filled with food, fun, and merrymaking. This was the one single party where everyone was invited including clients, aides, and a few family members as well. In addition, Bonnie and I had our own Christmas feast and we each invited our family and friends. Bonnie would have her grandparents and I would have my friends Peggy, Marcia, and Brenda. It was a great meal filled with plenty of holiday favorites.

Four years later, I am still living here with a new set of aides. At this time, I still do not have a housemate. Only time will tell. Even though I would like a housemate that I would have more in common with, I do not mind living alone. Through my life, I have met many people who have become my mentors. I appreciate their thoughts and positive encouragement throughout my journey and I hope that my life has blessed them as well as their lives have blessed me. I hope I have influenced them and perhaps changed their attitudes as to what can be done if someone truly wants to fit in today's society.

These last few years have truly been a learning experience from many perspectives, including coping with the loss of my parents and adjusting to my new and more involved physical limitations. I am glad I do not have any permanent scars from it. I do not know what the future holds for me, but I know I can cope with it as long as I find a way to fit in.

# SAMPLES OF NANCY'S ARTICLES

Journal writer, editor honored

The Daily Journal's medical writer Nancy Jaekle and City Editor Frank Scandale have been selected to attend journalism conferences designed to further their knowledge in their respective fields.

Jaekle was awarded a fellowship by the Knight Center for Specialized Journalism to study the topic "Covering Cancer." Earlier this year, Jaekle wrote an eight-part series explaining cancer in layman's terms.

She will spend two weeks in Washington, D.C., beginning Oct. 9. The course moves from basic medical science to cancer treatment to public policy issues.

Jaekle's career began in 1979 with a letter to the editor asking that a column addressing the needs of the physically disabled be reinstated. Soon after, Jaekle was asked if she would like to write the column. "Being Independent" was the result.

Last May, Jaekle became The Daily Journal's medical writer. She now writes medical news features on current issues.

Scandale was invited to the Poynter Institute for Media Studies in St. Petersburg, Fla. He will attend a conference entitled "Coaching Writers: The Human Side of Editing" between Nov. 28 and Dec. 1.

The conference is designed to not only teach editors to help writers, but how to help editors help writers.

"Winning these prestigous fellowships is a fine testimony to the consistent work done by both Nancy and Frank," said Daily Journal Editor Isabel Spencer. "I know attending the seminars will enhance their work and, along with it, the newspaper our readers receive every day."

From The Daily Journal Wednesday, August 30, 1989

Understanding A Misunderstood Minority

By NANCY A. JAEKLE

"ISN'T it nice that she knows her name and address," A salesperson in a store in Westfield made that comment to a woman as she and her daughter waited to be helped.

Because of the daughter's slurred speech and awkward gait, it was assumed — automatically — that her mind also did not function very well. When their turn came, the woman asked her daughter, a graduate student who has cerebral palsy, to give the necessary information for the charge account.

This is but one example of the kinds of things that members of "the misunderstood minority" go through. Because of the daughter's physical handicap, she is often treated as a parental juvenile; even the salesperson chose to deal with her as though she were a child.

The physically handicapped are America's largest minority group, comprising, according to recent statistics, 18 percent of the population. Included in this percentage are people with orthopedic problems, the wheelchaired, the deaf, the blind, amputees, those with congenital impairments and an increasing number of elderly people.

Sociologically speaking, a minority is a social group whose members experience, at the hands of another dominant group, prejudice, discrimination, segregation, persecution or a combination of these things.

Members of the minority group share special mental or physical characteristics that the dominant group holds in low esteem. Often, the shared traits form the basis of an esprit de corps, a sense of belonging to a group apart.

To quote from the sociological tract of Wagley and Harris:

"In addition to whatever special traits they share, their sense of isolation, of common suffering and of a common burden makes most minorities self-conscious groups apart from all others in their society."

Thus, the physically handicapped are "the misunderstood minority."

For generations past, the physically handicapped have met with rejection and pity from the vast majority. For some reason, people are inclined to feel that, if the body is less than perfect, so is the mind — and over the personality. The cliché, "A sound mind in a sound body," can have negative implications as well: "Twisted body, warped mind, distorted personality."

In most cases, this is untrue. I recall Broadway's "The Elephant Man" and how this deformed man won the hearts of many with his intelligence and charm.

These misunderstood social reactions stem from a lack of understanding of the consequences and limitations of a disability. The handicapping character of the physical defect is thought to permeate the total personality and behavior of the individual, and thus he can be both classified and identified by this one discernible trait.

It is not unusual for people to associate maladjusted behavior with a physical handicap. In most instances, this association is false.

Studies have indicated that 35 to 45 percent of the disabled are as adjusted as the average nonhandicapped person. Moreover, the kinds of maladjusted behavior exhibited by physically handicapped people are not peculiar to them; they are the same as those of "normal" people.

The problems of adjustment and acceptance of the physically disabled is as much a problem of the able-bodied majority as it is of the handicapped minority.

"Isn't it nice that she knows her name and address."

Those words reveal an attitude of pity.

The salesperson chose to make a generalization based on hearsay and gut feeling. She made a prejudgment without bothering to verify its merits. Her perception of the handicapped, her beliefs about the minority and the common traits she attributes to its members led her to assume that the young woman was of low intelligence. Contact with the daughter evoked fear, pity, hate, anger, contempt and sympathy, and, although the salesperson probably felt a combination of all these emotions, she responded from fear and sympathy.

Salespeople are not the only ones who display negative feelings. Surprisingly, the medical community, even more than others, has repeatedly been accused of belittling behavior.

Studies indicate that doctors, nurses and workers in rehabilitation centers and hospitals view the handicapped as having much lower status, as incompetent and as in need of help. And that if you help someone, you look down on him.

For the most part, I find some physicians guilty of this. They tend to categorize people according to social visibility, grouping individuals into pigeonholes and responding to them in terms of this classification rather than in terms of their uniqueness.

Take cerebral palsy as an example. Unfortunately, most physicians do not know a great deal about it. Confronted with someone having the condition, most physicians usually stereotype the person.

Stereotyping — pinning a label on someone — is an outgrowth of prejudice. The label that one wears is an indication of how one is to be treated by society, especially for the misunderstood minority.

For example, those with speech impediments are usually labeled "slow" or even "retarded." People in wheelchairs are frequently talked down to, and the blind are almost always stereotyped as vending-machine operators or street-corner beggars.

The tag on the label is "Helpless Victim."

Much has been done to try to eradicate the negative image associated with the misunderstood minority. Recently, the theater has tried to portray the physically handicapped in a more humane light. I speak of two plays in particular, "Whose Life Is It, Anyway?" and "Children of a Lesser God."

"Whose Life Is It" focused on the feelings of someone newly handicapped by an event beyond her control. As a bedridden quadriplegic, she feels that her life is over. Her profession as a sculptor not only had been her craft, but also her first love, and now that has been taken from her. Nonetheless, she is still a person, with needs and desires.

"Children of a Lesser God" shows an entirely different situation. From birth, Sarah has been deaf, a member of the misunderstood minority. She is taken from a sheltered environment and must learn to live in a world where speech is the source of communication. She wants desperately to be part of the hearing world, but feels left out. Unfortunately, she will always be one of a minority within a minority.

Eventually, Sarah is accepted by both worlds, and one leaves the theater with a sense of admiration for this determined woman.

Audiences at these plays come to realize and recognize the handicapped as people first and then as those with physical limitations.

Each of us is born with inabilities as well as abilities. It is the gift of our abilities that we must focus on. ■

Nancy A. Jaekle lives in Roselle.

From The New York Times Sunday, December 20, 1981

FITTING IN

Journal reporter wins state award

The Daily Journal

ELIZABETH — Nancy Jaekle, medical writer for The Daily Journal for nearly 1½ years and columnist for 11 years, has won a first-place award and $1,000 in the 19th Annual Science Medical Writing contest sponsored by the New Jersey Press Association.

"I entered it without telling anyone," Jaekle admitted yesterday. "I like to tell people afterward about it."

Jaekle, who lives in the Elmora section of Elizabeth, won the award for a story she wrote in February about a treatment at St. Mary's Wound Care Center, Orange, that prevents amputations for patients with non-healing wounds due to poor blood circulation.

"I was so excited that one of my co-workers had to read (the notification letter) to me," said Jaekle, who has cerebral palsy. "At first, I thought (the association) was asking me for membership."

"I proved myself," she said. Editor David M. Levine agreed with Jaekle's assessment.

"We are extremely pleased for Nancy," he said. "The award brings a great deal of credibility to the work she has done for the newspaper over the years."

The 35-year-old Jaekle has a bachelor's degree in English and sociology and a master's degree in counseling, all from Kean College in Union.

Last year, Jaekle won a two-week fellowship with University of Maryland's School of Special and Writing because of an eight-part series she wrote about cancer.

NANCY JAEKLE
Columnist 11 years

From The Daily Journal

NANCY A. JAEKLE

THE DAILY JOURNAL, WEDNESDAY, FEBRUARY 7, 1990

Treatment prevents amputations

Wound Care Center in Orange cures open wounds with Procuren

Today's Health

By Nancy Jaekle

Many patients with non-healing wounds due to poor blood circulation can now be cured without amputations thanks to a new wound treatment called Procuren.

Procuren is the name for growth factors, which are isolated from each patient's own blood and then applied to the wound.

"The substance encourages the growth of cells, making them divide and fill in the wound with healthy tissue," said Dr. Robert H. Rock, medical director of St. Mary's Wound Care Center in Orange.

"So far, more than 2,000 people across the country have been successfully treated with Procuren with virtually no side effects," said Rock.

The most frequently cited causes for amputations include gangrene, infection and non-healing ulcers. Other causes include diabetes, or decreased pulses, osteomyelitis and systemic anxiety, according to Dr. David Knighton, assistant professor of surgery at the University of Minnesota.

The Wound Care Center is in Orange, one of only 15 in the country, treats patients with diabetic skin ulcers, ulcers caused by poor blood circulation, pressure sores and a number of other conditions affecting an estimated 5 million people.

"These chronic, long-term open wounds or sores are usually found on the legs or buttocks," said Rock. "These wounds may be more common in blacks due to a higher rate of diabetes or high blood pressure."

Prior to the development of Procuren, the treatment traditionally involved keeping the wound infection-free with antiseptics and antibiotics.

"For wounds that failed to heal, amputation usually was the only option," said Delores Eggleston, clinical coordinator. "A person must deal with the underlying problems that caused the wound in the first place such as diabetes, poor circulation and infection."

Eggleston said the center offers the team approach utilizing other health care professionals who can deal with the overall health status of the patients and the care of the wound.

Knighton was one of the first scientists to recognize that pieces of human blood called platelets produce growth factors to heal wounds.

"Isolating five wound healing factors is a tremendous achievement because they are present in very small amounts and are difficult to extract from platelets," Knighton said.

For wound healing factors to be medically useful, a practical process was needed for extracting very large quantities from platelets, he said.

"Use the growth factors in the serum ingredients in a solution that is applied daily to the patient's wound to promote the growth of new capillaries, bone and skin tissue needed to heal wounds — especially those in which blood circulation is reduced," said Knighton.

In one study, 49 patients with a total of 95 wounds were treated after having received conventional treatment for an average of 158 weeks without healing. Forty-five patients, including four who required vascular reconstruction surgery, healed completely when treated with Wound Care Center protocol and platelet derived wound healing formula, said Rock.

"I would estimate that approximately 40 percent of my patients have some form of diabetes. An elevated blood sugar can create problems in the movement of the white blood cells, which inhibits the white blood cells from acting normally," said Dr. Mary Herald, endocrinologist at Overlook Eco gical in Summit.

"Procuren is very exciting. I think that if we can prevent problems such as a small ulcer on the toe, for example, from spreading and growing by applying a substance made from one's own blood it is a breakthrough and the public needs to know.

"Being that Procuren is made from a substance in the patient's own blood, there is no chance for an allergic reaction, which is another important advantage."

A former patient at the Wound Care Center, Charles Jordan of East Brunswick had his left foot saved by Procuren.

"About two years ago, my doctor informed me that I had poor circulation in my right leg. I found it very difficult to walk and was advised to have by-pass surgery.

"Unfortunately, Jordan's surgery was not completely successful and he had to have one toe removed.

"The healing process took forever and gangrene set in. Eventually, I had to have another toe removed, which compounded the situation making the open wound larger," said Jordan.

"After another amputation, I was hospitalized 47 days due to complications. At that time, I was told I could do nothing more."

An angiogram showed that Jordan had no arteries in his left leg. "Fortunately, a very good friend told me about a wound care center and the use of Procuren," said Jordan.

Jordan decided to try this new treatment. "I had this ugly open wound on my left foot, which would not heal. So I though I would give Procuren a try. As an outpatient, a nurse would apply Procuren to my wound every night. After 14 weeks, the wound was completely healed.

"I returned from my bed to the wheelchair and back again. Last September, I gave up the wheelchair, started walking and now I am driving. In fact, I have even resumed my hospital volunteer duties."

From The Daily Journal Wednesday, January 20, 1990

464

FITTING IN

TODAY'S HEALTH

Same-day surgery a new option

Depending on the illness and the type of medical treatment required, a lengthy hospitalization stay may no longer be necessary. In fact, for some patients same-day surgery may be a viable option.

NANCY JAEKLE

Within the past few years, same-day surgery has become increasingly popular with the medical community as well as patients who need to undergo minor surgical procedures or tests that require a stay of 24 hours or less.

To date, some of the kinds of surgeries performed on an outpatient basis are: wisdom teeth surgery, removal of small moles or growths, biopsies, breast masses, endoscopy, cataract surgery, hernias, cystoscopies, and the removal of fluid from the thoracic cavity.

"It became obvious as time went on that we, as a profession, began to question whether the amount of time and attention we were focusing on these kinds of things really necessitated prolonged stay in the hospital," said Dr. Bruce Chodosh of John F. Kennedy Hospital, Edison.

"Insurance companies and payors were insisting on tighter utilization. The government, namely Medicare, stated that anything that might be performed on a same-day basis should be done," he said. "This has lead to the attractiveness of doing surgery in the same-day clinic."

With same-day surgery, a patient receives the prescribed treatment or surgery while enjoying the comfort and convenience of recovering at home. At the same time, they have the confidence of knowing that they can use the full-hospital facilities if needed.

If you and your doctor are contemplating same-day surgery, "It ought to be surgery that is planned and needs to be discussed with physician," Chodush said. "The kind of procedure being done should be understood (by the patient.) The pre-operative preparations should be understood."

One question to be considered, for example, is "How far in advance should I go to the hospital?" Appropriate consultation with family doctor to discuss the risks involved is recommended.

"How will this procedure benefit me? What will be the outcome if I refuse to have this procedure? Laboratory assessment? Anesthesia risk?"

It is very important for patients to adhere to specific instructions as how to prepare for surgery. "If instructions are not followed, surgery may have to be postponed at the last minute," advises Chodosh.

"Before a patient is admitted for same-day surgery, it is important to make arrangements to and from the hospital, to pick up any special items that might be needed such as a urinal, walker, etc. In the case of an older individual or one who lives alone, it might be advisable to come in the night before. Remember too, the hospital can provide resources such as a home health aide, visiting nurse etc.," said the doctor.

Aside from the convenience and cost effectiveness of same-day surgery, it is located in a pleasant environment, free from the hospital stigma and infectious diseases.

Birth of Christ inspires composers to pen songs

BY NANCY JAEKLE
staff writer

In most Christian congregations, as is customary during the Advent season, worshippers gather around the Advent wreath. Each week, a candle is lit and a prayer is offered in spiritual preparation for the birth of Christ.

So how did the birth of Christ and candles lead to the tradition of singing Christmas carols?

During the 12th century, St. Francis of Assisi formally introduced Christmas carols to church services. As a patron of the arts, he inspired poets and composers of the day to deliver Christmas music.

The lighter, joyous Christmas songs were introduced many years later in Renaissance Italy, around the time of Leonardo da Vinci and Michelangelo in the 1400s.

When Johannes Gutenberg started his printing presses in 1454, copies of carols could easily be distributed.

"Many of the carols today are not quoted directly from the Bible and they are fairly new," said Rev. Eric Ziegler, pastor of St. John's Evangelical Lutheran Church in Clifton. "The custom of carol singing dates back to the 19th century."

"It was not until Protestants had to flee Europe under pressure from the Catholic Church that Christmas carols made their way to this country," Ziegler said.

In 1750, John Francis Wade, a professional copyrist, included an original Christmas poem titled, "Adeste Fideles" compiled for the English Roman Catholic College at Lisbon, Portugal. Thirty-five years later, a copy of the hymn was spread throughout the world.

"Of course, everyone's favorite is "Silent Night," Ziegler said. "It is ingrained in people's minds that it is the quintessential Christmas carol. Every album, tape or Christmas special all have someone singing 'Silent Night.' However, the story behind it is rather special."

Written in 1818 by Joseph Mohr, an Austrian assistant priest, the song is now sung in more than 180 languages. "Mohr was told the day before Christmas that the church organ was broken and would not be repaired in time for Christmas Day. So, he sat down to write three stanzas that could be sung by the choir to guitar music," he said. "Musically, it is very simple - only three or four chords."

Another favorite hymn is "Away in the Manger." This quiet little Christmas song is often called "Luther's Cradle Hymn," and is considered by many authorities to have been written by him sometime during the early 16th century.

One of the greatest of the Moravian hymn writers, James Montgomery, penned the

See Songs... Page D2

Jingle Bells

Dashing through the snow
In a one-horse open sleigh,
O'r the fields we go,
Laughing all the way;
Bells on bobtails ring,
making spirits bright,
What fun it is to ride and sing
A sleighing song tonight.
Oh jingle bells, jingle bells,
jingle all the way,
O what fun it is to ride
In a one-horse open sleigh

From The Daily Journal

NANCY A. JAEKLE

THE DAILY JOURNAL, SATURDAY MAY 27, 1989

Community Closeup

Traumatic head injuries in children

Today's Health

By Nancy Jaekle

Jenny is an 11 year old who was hit by a drunk driver while riding her bike home from a friend's house after school. She was propelled 60 feet into a field and suffered a broken leg, multiple contusions and lacerations and a traumatic brain injury.

Each year in this country as many as one million young people sustain brain injuries from motor vehicle accidents, falls, sports and physical abuse.

Approximately 165,000 of these youngsters will be hospitalized, with 16,000 to 20,000 suffering moderate to severe symptoms. Statistically, brain injured people are in the 16 to 24-year-old range, but the frequency rate is nearly as high for youngsters under 16 years of age, especially in the transitional middle grades years of early adolescence.

While many rehabilitation programs in the last five years have concentrated on the adult brain injured population, children and youth have received less focused study. To help educators and other health professionals gain a better understanding, Children's Specialized Hospital in Mountainside featured a one day seminar on traumatic brain injury and the problems associated with the re-entry into the school system and the community.

Even in children are fortunate enough to receive intense therapy in a rehabilitation hospital, many of these children will experience transition problems when they return to school. Too often the school system lacks an understanding of traumatic brain injury and the rehabilitation hospital does not know how to access special education services for the child.

Many traumatically brain injured youngsters return to home and school with only minimal support services and little, if any, information on head injury for their families and educators.

One of the things that most difficult for families as well as teachers to understand is the personality changed exhibited by the child. A child who was once quiet and mellow, may now have sudden emotional outbursts often without any seemingly justified cause. In essence, the child may be frustrated with himself for any number of reasons. Some of these might include: attention deficit, personality change and the attitude of others. For example, his classmates may shun him because they do not understand these changes in behavior.

Successful transition of a traumatically brain injured child into the educational system should involve the following four steps:

■ Involvement of the school, based special education team in the rehabilitation setting.
■ Inservice training for all school based staff who will have contact with the child.
■ Short and long term program planning.
■ Continued follow-up of the child by the rehabilitation facility.

As soon as possible the rehabilitation hospital should contact the child's school and let the school know the child has just acute care and is now receiving intense rehabilitation in their facility. Both the school and the hospital often assume that the parents will keep the school informed of the child's progress. However, with all of the major stresses and strains since the accident, parents often forget to keep the school notified. Thus, the rehabilitation hospital usually needs to accept this responsibility.

Besides knowing who to contact, rehabilitation professionals need to understand the parameters of Public Law 94-142. The law requires that a free and appropriate education be provided for all children regardless of the degree or nature of the handicap.

While Jenny was in the hospital, the special educator and school nurse visited her and the hospital therapists. The special educator began to plan for transition and educational programming services while the school nurse set up three training sessions with Jenny's teachers to help them understand the effects of traumatic brain injury. Select staff were given brochures, articles and videotapes on injury.

When Jenny returned to school on a half-day basis, not only her teachers familiar with cognitive, psycho-social motor problem common to brain injury, but the special educational plan in place. The teacher set up a "buddy system" to be sure Jenny had one of her friends always with her. Her seat was moved to lessen classroom distractions and special reading study guides were developed to assist her with her academic work.

I use Jenny as an example of what a innovative school system can do to help the transition of the traumatic brain injured student.

Our columnist, who is locally challenged herself, writes from first-hand experience.

Engagements

From The Daily Journal Saturday, May 27, 1989

INDEX OF IMAGES

Professor Paul Evans A.K.A. "Uncle Paul" with Sailboat given by Nancy (2008) (pg. iv)

Baby Nancy 1955 or 56 (pg. 17)

Nancy, Age 3, Sitting on Grandmother's Stoop in Cranford, New Jersey (1959) (pg. 27)

Nancy and Rick (1960) (pg. 33)

Family Photo Taken on Steps of New Home (1960) (pg. 38)

Christmas 1961 with Grandfather, Father, and Mother (pg. 58)

Nancy and Friend Swimming (pg. 100)

Nancy, Age 11 and brother Rick, Age 8 Standing on Dock Ready to Sail Away in Florida (pg.199)

Grandmother, Rick, and Nancy (pg.219)

Nancy and Family at Nancy's Kean University Graduation (1978) (pg. 249)

Nancy with Mom and Dad (pg. 339)

Kaitlin, Age 2, Playing with Legos in a Box (pg. 353)

Nancy as "Woman of the Year" for her Journalistic Talent (1992) (pg. 372)

Journalist Nancy Hard at Work (2002) (pg. 388)

Rick and Nancy (pg. 419)

Family and Friends Celebrate Nancy's 60th Birthday (pg. 446)

Made in the USA
Columbia, SC
08 September 2019